LOC TALES
The True Story of a California Gangsta'

Eric Nichols

Copyright © 2016 Eric Nichols
All rights reserved.
ISBN-13: 978-1540590404
ISBN-10: 1540590402

[thewritersroom] 123RF.com

This book is dedicated to the memory of my beloved brother Derrick DeShawn Nichols, to my father Curtis E. Nichols Jr., to my grandparents Curtis E. Nichols Sr., Olivia Nichols, and Leola Burton, and to my dear friends Tracy (Tray Dogg) Thomas, and Charles (Chuck) Roberts.

I miss them so much, and can only hope I've made them proud.

ACKNOWLEDGEMENT

I'd like to give all due praise and thanks to God for blessing me with the many talents and people He has placed in my life to help make this book a reality.

A special thanks to my editor, Chantay E. Brown, from The Writers Room, who, with her relentless questioning, inquisitive nature, work ethic, and experience as an acclaimed author, has helped make one of my dreams come true.
Thank you, My friend.

This book wouldn't exist without the encouragement I received from the many prisoners who read every single page I wrote and pushed me to "hurry up" and write more pages because they wanted to find out what's going to happen next.
Thank you all for keeping me motivated.

To those mentioned in my book who are embarrassed or ashamed of what you did with me or in my presence, Thank Y'all! I learned a lot from y'all! Don't hate me, Hate the game. I was just a player in it. I couldn't share everything because some things have no statue of limitations. Oh, and I keep paperwork and keep in touch with those who will gladly confirm my story.

A shout-out to my cousin, Rasheeda Murray, who is also one of my favorite authors and biggest supporters. Thanks for your inspiration and for believing in me from the beginning.

A very special thanks to my mother, Linda, for all your love, support, advice, strong suggestions, and assistance. I love you Ma.

To my family, who are too many to mention, Thank you. I love you all and appreciate your encouraging words and well wishes.

Without God I am nothing and nobody. I will forever acknowledge You in all that I do. And I will always trust and believe in You. Thank You for your goodness and mercy. Your son, Eric.

PROLOGUE

Bakersfield, California- 1983

At twelve years old, there was nothin' more liberating than the wind in my face as I sped down Union Avenues' underpass on my free spin dirt-bike, riding pass KFC, DerWienerschnitzel, Hunt's Pool Hall, and underneath the giant neon "Bakersfield" sign that stretched across one side of the street to the other. It served as a bridge made for walking from one part of The Bakersfield Inn, to the part located across the street. But it also served as a bridge separating territories of the Eastside and Westside parts of town.

    I bunny hoped my way through traffic, popped a wheelie down 4th street pass the pimps and ho's that lined up along 4th street from Union Avenue to "V" street. Most of the ho's were hella ugly. Half of them were my schoolmate's momma, auntie, or sista. And all of them were on drugs.

    I would lay my bike down on the inside of Queen Sheeba Market, next to the pinball and gum-ball machines. Queen Sheeba Market was the store that a lot of the black teenagers living on the Westside would hangout at. They usually played video games and would take turns selling drugs to the pimps, ho's, and dope-fiends in the area.

    I had been selling weed up there for nearly two months before anyone really noticed that I was selling it. I tried to be discreet because I didn't want my parents to find out because my momma would've broke my back. My daddy, he didn't live with us at the time, but he would've put his foot in my ass too. Not because I was selling weed, but because the weed I was selling had come from the 8 ft. weed plants that I'd stolen from my daddy's backyard.

    I knew there was money in the "Weed Business" because one day at California Park, I saw my older cousin Roy sell a matchbox full of weed to some guy. I couldn't believe it! Someone had actually paid $10 for the green leafy stuff that had come from the 8 ft. trees in my daddy's backyard. And from that day forward, all I could do was smile every time I'd hear my momma or anyone else say, "Money don't grow on trees."

I wasn't in a gang yet, but I was around Gangbangers all the time while I sold weed. There were mostly Warlord Bloods and a group of teens who referred to themselves as "Westside Hustlers." I knew a lot of people from both sides of town because my momma, Linda, lived in a shack on 11th and "K" street on the Westside when I was a toddler. And my daddy, Curtis Jr., lived in a duplex that he owned on E. 9th street, on the Eastside. Since my parents had the off again/ on again type of relationship, I was able to experience life on both sides of town and develop lasting friendships.

My momma was only 15 years old when she brought me into this world, and my daddy had just turned 20. His parents, Curtis Sr. & Olivia, whom I call Grandma and Poppy, lived on E. 9th street as well in one of the many homes they had built while raising five children. My daddy is the oldest, followed by Sylvia (Aunt Sivi), Alfred (Uncle Al), Katherine (Aunt Elaine), and Glenn (Uncle Gleek).

My daddy was a highly recommended carpenter in the 70's. He was "The First Kid on The Block" type of guy. The first to get a new car, the first to get his own apartment, and the first to own a tailor made suit in his neighborhood. He was a "square." But all the dope dealers, players, and professional athletes would party at his place. So, he went from "Square" to a "Square Gone Bad" and drug and alcohol abuse eventually became his downfall.

As far as the rest of the family, Uncle Al played professional baseball for the Cincinnati Reds in the early 1980's, and Uncle Gleek played basketball really good, but he didn't end up in the NBA for whatever reasons. Aunt Elaine worked at a bank (Great Western Savings), and I never did know where Aunt Sivi worked. But, it was Aunt Sivi who made sure I made it to church and to my baseball games on time. She and my momma's brother, James (Uncle Pee-Wee) got married and had a son they names James Jr. (J.J), who is my "Double First Cousin." Aunt Sivi would buy me and my little brother Derrick whatever she bought her son J.J. whenever we were all together. I'll never forget the Egg McMuffins and orange juice from McDonalds every Sunday on our way to Mt. Zion Missionary Baptist church.

My Uncle Pee-Wee was always in and out of prison. Every time he would get out, we would beg to spend the night at his place because he'd let us get away with things that other parents wouldn't.

My momma's mother, Leola (Grandma Le), lived in Portland, Oregon, and so did my momma's sista Aunt Gail. I don't remember my momma's oldest brother, Uncle Teddy, because he got killed when I was a baby. But I heard he was really tough.

I never met my momma's father either. His name is George and I used to want to meet him and would often imagine what it would be like to have a relationship with him. I even dreamed of him doing special "Grandpa Stuff" with me and my brother Derrick. That is, until I found out he ignored and denied my momma. He had hid the fact that she was his daughter and failed to acknowledge her in the presence of his new wife. The sorry-ass nigga didn't even look momma in her eyes. Let alone hold her, or kiss her like a father should. My momma was crushed. And so was I once I heard the story. At this point in my life, I could care less if I ever meet him or not. It's not like I miss him. You can't miss what you never had. I believe the experience made momma stronger, although I know initially she was hurt. Every time I think about momma giving birth to me at 15 years old, I still shake my head in amazement, because I honestly don't ever remember a teenager raising me. She was always a "Grown Woman" to me. I wouldn't think of allowing a 15 year old to raise one of my kids. Hell, I wouldn't feel comfortable allowing a 15 year old to babysit any of mines.

Momma's oldest sista, Alma Jean (Aunt Alma) lived in the back duplex next door to my daddy. She is like a mother to my momma. She's the "Head" of my momma's family and has an incredible sense of humor. She's strong and beautiful, with a sexy mole between her eyebrows. Aunt Alma was very popular. Always hosting dominoes and card parties, while raising her two kids (Roy and Renee) by herself. Her kids were 9 and 10 years older than me.

My momma only had two kids herself, me and Derrick. She would dress us alike all the time and most people would refer to us as Eric and Derrick, like we were one in the same. I was 1 year 9 months older than my brother, but he didn't act like it. When I would take the nerf football or bully my way into a game, he would be the only one to stand up to me. We argued all the time like most siblings, but I wouldn't let nobody mistreat him, and he wasn't gonna let anybody mistreat me. I was the wild, aggressive, risk-taker; always doing things I had no business doing. He was the laid back, easy-going type who was afraid of momma's asswhoopin. Only two things scared me back then: Roller coaster rides at Six Flags Magic Mountain, and seeing someone throw up. Yuck!

Being the oldest child meant I got stuff first; like my B.B. Gun, my Baseball glove, Football cleats, Skates, etc. But when Derrick got his stuff the following year, his stuff always seemed a lot better than mines. I didn't like that at all. Here I was, good in all sports, the oldest, could do back-flips like a gymnast, beat up any kid my age, memorize the names of the first fourteen books of the Holy Bible, could fix almost anything electrical, and draw pictures in graphic detail. But Derrick got rewarded for trying to do the things that I could do so well. So, I set out to earn the love and respect (My Reward) from my parents.

The same store I sold weed at is the same store I stole candy from to sell at school. The 10¢ candies would sell for 25¢ at school. When the candy business became more profitable, I introduced my little brother to it and we started stealing from larger stores. Instead of taking individual items, we would steal the entire unopened boxes that were on display. From candy bars, lollipops, Now & Laters, bubble gum, and Saltalitos; to Chico sticks, Gummie bears, and jawbreaker candies. We filled our book bags and backpacks every day.

Derrick was in the 6th grade attending Long Fellow Elementary School, and momma had moved closer to her job at Memorial Hospital near Derrick's school. When Derrick was running for class President, I bullied some kids into voting him in as class President. Derrick was likable and smart, so he probably would've got voted in anyway, I just tried to do my part.

I attended Emerson Jr. High, which was located on the Westside of town. I had to ride my bike or catch the school bus because it was just too far to walk. Most of the black kids at

Emerson knew each other because they lived in the same neighborhood together. They were mostly Warlord Bloods or wannabe Warlord Bloods. They wore red clothes and red bandanas a lot and I couldn't stand them! Probably because I had a lot of bad experiences with some other Bloods in Inglewood, California.

My momma's other sista, Diane (Lady Di) lived there in Inglewood. She was the trendsetter and she used to put Jheri curls in my head, and she always bought me and Derrick things that the kids in Bakersfield hadn't seen yet. Her two daughters, Tracy and Tameka, were babies back then. When I would visit Aunt Diane, or when she would host a fight party for a Sugar Ray Leonard bout, I would play with the kids my age who lived in her Inglewood apartments. They were Bloods too. I would whoop on the kids my size and age. But the bigger and older kids would end up "puttin' hands" on me. I didn't bang yet, but those ass whoopins made me want to be a Crip. So, when the kids at Emerson Jr. High started trippin', I hooked up with two kids at the school that I knew were from the Eastside of town. They were both hella cool, as well another kid I hooked up with who attended Emerson as well. The four of us stuck together and would sometimes double-pump one another home on Beach Cruiser bikes.

During summer school, one of the toughest and most popular Warlord Bloods, named Big Squirt, pulled a gun on me. It all started when he saw me walking through the school with two fine girls. He walked up to us and asked the girls to give him a kiss. They both responded by kissin' me on the cheek and walking off with their arms around me.

After escorting the girls to their class, I headed to my own class where I was met by Big Squirt. He tried to "steal" on me, but he missed. I bombed on him with a cool two-piece in front of a lot of students and the next period, he came to my class and stuck his head in the door. He said he was gonna get me after school, and I said, "we'll see." The whole class was shocked that I wasn't afraid of him and they whispered amongst themselves.

The final bell rang to end the day, and I met up with my friends outside my classroom. Big Squirt walked up to me with a lot of other kids who were wearing red clothing and said, "What's up Blood?!" I responded by saying, "What's up Cuzz?!" Then a teacher came through the crowd to break us up.

CHAPTER 1

Gone were the days of playin' house with Bay-Bay, my cousin Christy, and the girl who lived across the street named Susie. I called her Susie Q because she was sweet and chocolate. When she made her mud pies she would take all of the sticks, grass, and rocks out to makes sure hers looked smooth. I didn't know how to tell her that I liked her. She was so sexy in her glasses, small waist, and big booty. I liked her so much I actually ate some of her mud-pies.

    I wasn't playin' with B.B. Guns, Go-Karts, or having meetings in the Clubhouse with June & Tip anymore. I had been rabbit hunting with my daddy, his friends, and one of his friends' son. I got a chance to shoot a real gun and I fell in love with the power it made me feel. My daddy and his friends would only let us kids shoot at the rabbits every once in awhile. We mainly just threw rocks in the bushes so the rabbits would run out into view to be shot. Jackrabbits are hella fast and could change directions in midair. One day while me and this kid were throwing rocks, he accidentally got shot by his own daddy. Blood was everywhere. They carried his lifeless body to the truck with a look of horror on their faces. Everything appeared to be moving in slow motion. I heard their cries as they begged the kid to "stay with us" and "don't die on us." But he had already left us. The kid was dead. It was the first time I'd seen a dead body up close like that. And I haven't been rabbit hunting since.

I tried to give my momma and daddy something to be proud of me for, so I put a lot of effort into my baseball skills. I was a natural who hated to lose. I won a lot of trophies and I loved the game. But, I'd have a fit and cry like a baby whenever my team would lose a game. I was good at a lot of things like boxing, football, board games, school work, making friends, and attracting girls. But, I'd lose interest in them all really fast. My love for the people and for the activities were genuine. I just lost interest in everything. Everything except music. Groove City was a mobile D.J. crew that would play music at local clubs, bars, and parks. They would have it crackin' at California Park every weekend. It would be packed with at least two-hundred people, and there would almost always be a fight but I would still go get my boogie on every weekend when Groove City showed up. I knew how to Pop-Lock and Breakdance too. I would even have practice and make up routines with other kids in my community. But when it came time to perform at Rollertown skating rink, I would be too chicken to actually dance. I'd show up in parachute-pants with different colored bandanas tied around my pants legs, and Coaster shoes on my feet. Yeah, I'd be lookin' the part, but I would never get out there and dance.

The Junior High and High school dances were cool, but as long as it was dark inside. I loved to slow dance real close to a girl with my hands on her booty. Sometimes I'd get smacked for that, but a lot of girls let me get away with it. Most girls smelled like Double-Mint gum and Curl Activator mixed with must. I never did understand why Jr. High and High school girls were so damn musty after only dancing to a few songs. I actually didn't understand a lot of shit back then. Like, why didn't I feel comfortable in public places around a lot of people?

I wore top of the line clothes and shoes. My momma had me wearing Calvin Klein and Jordache jeans, Penny Loafers with argyle socks and sweaters, Louis Vuitton and Gucci belts & wallets. But I just didn't feel comfortable in that stuff.

An old man named Vernon, who we called "Mack", was an old friend of my Grandma Le, and he had known my momma since she was a baby. Since momma's father was never in her life, Mack was like a father to her. Mack was a good, caring, and loving man. He often babysat me and Derrick, and he would pay us to help him clean his house and chop down the weeds in his yard. When Derrick and I were really young, momma would sometime leave us at Mack's house for two or three days without calling or coming by to check on us. Me and Derrick didn't care tho' because we loved spending time at Mack's. We would stay up late watching Johnny Carson and Mack would tell us stories about his time in the military and about his life working for the railroad company.

Mack had a couple of guns too. I would hold and examine his pistol while he and Derrick were asleep. It was a .22 and it was surprisingly heavy and cold. When I would put it in my waistband or in my sweatpants pocket, the weight of it would cause my pants to fall off my ass. One day I took his gun outside and pulled the trigger, "*Pop!*" My ears were ringing and the sound startled me. I had shot the rifles with my daddy in the past, but this was the first time I fired a pistol and it felt good. I wanted to shoot something. Anything. But before I could zero in on anything specific, Mack took the gun from me and told me to never touch any of his guns again.

The summer was almost over and school would be starting soon. Mack took me and Derrick shopping for school clothes downtown at J.C. Penney's and at Buster Brown shoe store. We were to get whatever we wanted. I ended up with a few pair of Levi 501's, blue suede Pumas, a Ben Davis coat, suede golf hats, Romeo's, Croaker-Sack shoes, Charlie Brown shirts, Dickies Coveralls, Chuck Taylors, and two blue rags. From that day on, I felt comfortable because I had clothes that made me feel, "cool."

Two weeks before school began, I was at 6th street park with a close friend and his brother. He had jokes and would talk about people so bad we would have to beg him to stop because our stomachs would be hurting from laughing so hard. We all played basketball and football, but some of us participated in other activities like shooting dice, selling weed, selling crack, and other illegal activities. While doing the "other activities" I lost my fat gold link necklace in a game of 3-Card Monty. This slick black ass nigga named talked me into putting my necklace up to his $400 cash. Of course I lost, but he did let me buy it back for $200.

A lot of us who hung out at 6th street park had been gettin' into fights with Warlord Bloods and decided it was time to form our own gang. So, we got together in the park and made it official. We swore to be Westside Gangsta Crips and pledged our allegiance to our neighborhood and to one another.

We met at the park the following day and discussed how we were gonna beat up any and every Warlord we crossed paths with. We even picked the nicknames we wanted to be acknowledged by. I told everyone to call me, "E-Loc." "E" is for Eric, and "Loc" is for Loco, which means crazy in Spanish. There was twelve original homies and if anybody say anything different, then they aint from my hood.

In the months and years to follow, there would be many more reputable homies to get put-on, and some who have even lied about the correct year they joined our gang; but I'm not gon' lie for, nor lie on anybody when it comes to my hood. And I'm not gon' get myself or nobody else "stretched-out" with a life sentence just to share my story. You dig?

6th street park was like a second home to us, and we'd hang out up there seven days a week. And on the weekends there would be people from all over the city in our park, and we welcomed them with open arms. After all, that meant more women to choose from, more money to win in dice games, more people to buy our weed and crack from, and a chance to be seen as a Westside Gangsta Crip.

When it got dark, everyone would drive to the Eastside and party at the Elks Lodge. Then, when the Elks would close, we'd travel down the street to The Randles Club, which was located on Lakeview Avenue. We called this street, "The Road." You could get anything on "The Road" and I mean anything. Like pussy, pills, heroin, cocaine, alcohol, guns, cars, jewelry, food, clothes... You name it, it's there!

When The Randles Club would close, we'd head south to the part of town known as The Country. Every city has an area they refer to as The Country and it's usually a bunch of rough niggas there. These Country Boys in Bakersfield were sho'nuff tough. In the area known as The Country, most of the streets were unpaved dirt roads so it would be dusty as hell out there at 3 o'clock in the morning.

The Cowboys Club would be packed like a can of sardines. Everyone would be using this as their last minute opportunity to take home or go home with some pussy. And if you took too long, you would miss out because there was usually a Country Boy and Eastside nigga fighting. This would then lead to gun shots and everyone scattering in a panic. The cold part is, nine out of ten times, the drama escalated behind two niggas trippin' over some pussy or a dice game.

A lot of the nigga from the Eastside were Mid-City Dancers or Midnight Stroller Boy Dancers, and both groups had become gangs. Since the niggas who lived in The Country were always into it with other gangs, they made it official and began referring to themselves as Country Boy Crips. The Country Boy Crips mainly hung out in the Watts Drive and Lotus Lane area and they were a force to be reckon with.

Around about this time, some niggas from the Los Angeles-Watts area, had moved on the Eastside. One of the kids who attended Emerson Jr. High with me, was one of them and him and his lil brother and big cousin were a couple of years younger, but they were two of the wildest.

After recruiting a few Bakersfield niggas who lived on or around E. 3rd street, they founded a new gang and called it Spoonie Gee Crips. The Spoonie Gee Crips who were born and raised in Bakersfield, pushed a cold line and they all had major "squabble." On any given day, they would be up at the high schools fighting.

I knew everybody from every side of town, so it was weird whenever my hood got into it with any other hood. A small city like Bakersfield forced us to come in contact with our foes on a daily basis. We literally lived "too close for comfort." It was even hard to identify the difference between the gangs who shared common areas.

The Midnight Strollers were considered to be "Country Boys" in the early to mid- 80's. Half of them would even represent both "Country & Strollers" whenever they "represented." Some of The Stroller Boys were always representin' both. Even today some of them still "push" both, and there was one who's responsible for the Stroller Boys becoming "Eastsiders". One things for sure...I know my history.

I've been around to see the start of Lakeview Gangstas, the 11th street Project Crips, and seeing the Mid City Crips become popular. I was always around niggas who had squabble, hustle, and boss-game. But most of all...they had heart! They say, "Birds of the same feather, flock together."

I was always trying to turn nothin' into somethin'. Me and my lil brother Derrick helped the old man Mack clean his house one last time before school started back. It was the least we could do after he'd bought us all of those shoes, clothes, and school supplies.

While Mack was in the kitchen trying to explain to Derrick how the rats were able to fit their bodies through the tiny lip of a pop-bottle, I was in Mack's bathroom tucking the .22 pistol into my waistband. When Mack tried to pay us for cleaning his house, I told him that he could keep mines because he had already done enough for me. Derrick gave me a strange look because he'd never seen me turndown any money. I usually didn't turndown nothin' but my shirt collar. So, my brother knew I was up to somethin', he just didn't know what. As soon as I made it home, I went into the bathroom so that I could look at my new gun in peace. I felt older, stronger, and tougher from just holding it in my hands. Derrick knocked on the bathroom door talkin' 'bout he had to take a dookie, so I tucked my gun back into my waistband and dashed to my bedroom.

We had a long mirror on our bedroom door, so I stood in front of it and lifted my shirt to see the .22. Yeah, I looked cool and couldn't wait for my homies to see me with it. I heard the toilet flush so I put my gun in my backpack and tossed it underneath my bed. I didn't count any sheep that night, instead, I counted the number of niggas I planned on knockin' down with my new gun. And...I fell asleep with a smile on my face.

CHAPTER 2

"Icy-E, Kid-D, and I'm Nest-T, we got the power to devour any rockin' M.C.'s so if you're down to hear some fresh M.C.'s, yeah listen to the sounds of E.S.D.!"

Yeah, me, Stanley, Deon, and Tray-Dog were always practicing our raps for our rap group and Tray-Dog was our human Beatbox. I would bust up laughin' when he would beatbox for a long time and have white foam in the corners of his mouth and spittin' through that missin' front tooth of his. We ended up recording a few songs, but it wasn't done right. We didn't have a recording studio or anything, so we used two boomboxes: One to play an instrumental beat, and One to record the beat, the rap, and Tray-Dog's beatboxing. We'd usually hear birds, airplanes, barking dogs, and coughing when we listened to the finished product. Talk about Low Budget...we had, NO Budget.

One day after practice, me, Tray-Dog, and Stanley made our way over to the apartments on "Q" & 36th street. Stanley's cousin and her friend were in the swimming pool dunkin' other young boys underwater. We didn't waste any time peelin' outta our clothes, down to our swimming trunks, and diving into the pool. I swam over to Stanley's cousin and grabbed her booty; then, I slid my fingers between her legs and pressed the bathing suit material within the folds of her young, hairy, pussy. She was a year younger than I was and she had a crush on me. I then swam over to her thick ass friend, who was much older than I was, and I did the exact same thing to her that I'd done to Stanley's cousin. But when I came up for air, I was slapped in the face with what felt like a million tiny needles.

Stanley's cousin big ass had splashed water in my face, causing me to swallow big gulps of chlorine water. I damn near drowned when her big ass grabbed me by my shoulders, jumped on me with her legs wrapped around me, and took me and her both underwater. I was mad as hell! Not to mention being out of breath with my nose stingin'. And this big healthy ass bitch was laughin' as if we both were enjoying it.

My play cousin, Andre, was at the pool too, along with Stanley's lil brother we called Tiger. There were two restrooms located near the pool, so we separated the two girls by taking them in separate restrooms. We ran "trains" on them until our knees were sore from fuckin' on the bare ground inside the restrooms.

After that day, I started fuckin' one of the girls everyday after that. Every morning when my momma would leave for work, the girl would show up ready to fuck and cook breakfast for me. She wasn't my "first" but she was the first girl I fucked in a real bed and laid up with.

My "first" was with this girl I was in 5th grade with and it happened at Bessie E. Owens school. One day after school, me, another guy, and two girls decided to all have sex. We were by the cafeteria outside on the ground, and the girls laid side by side. One of the girls had on burgundy silk-lookin' panties like a grown woman, and the other girl had on white cotton panties with blue and yellow flowers on them. The girl I was with put her hands over her face and was gigglin' and shit like she was the happiest lil girl on earth. I slid her panties to the side with one hand and slid my dick inside her. I pumped really fast, then I peed in her. The other guy still hadn't "did it" to his girl yet. He was too busy complaining about the holes he saw in her panties. She was embarrassed but they ended up "doin it" anyways.

Both of the girls were pretty cool. One of the girls was the fastest girl on the track team, as well as the "class clown." She was also a very good dancer and she could fight her ass off. And the other girl was one of the tallest girls who was more like a Tomboy. She acted like she wanted to whoop on me one day right before Halloween. I really didn't want to "see her" about nothin' at that time, and I was even thinkin' about payin' another kid some Halloween candy to beat her up for me. But I got outta the whole situation because she got sent home early for whoopin' on somebody else.

Both of the girls grew up to be successful, as the track star went on to become a High school basketball star and she also developed into a fine ass super thick woman. The Tomboy went on to become the founder of a gang, and later the owner of a Group Home for troubled youths. I often wonder if the three of them ever reminisce about that day outside the cafeteria. I know I do.

With our knees burnin' and fingers wrinkled from swimming, me and Tray-Dog headed to my mommas. On the way home, we stopped by Fastrip to get some candy and play a couple of games of Ms. Pac Man. We had our quarters lined up across the lower screen area of the video game, indicating the number of games we plan to play in a row. Then, four tall ass niggas came inside the store being extra loud and talkin' shit. We ignored them because they hadn't said anything to us yet. They were eating and drinking stuff that they hadn't paid for and continued to talk shit to the store clerks. They finally brought their dumb ass' over to where we were talkin' about, "Damn Blood, y'all sho' got a lot of quarters lined up." "That's enough to buy me a pack of bigarettes," another said. Tray-Dog was the one actually playin' Ms. Pac Man at the time so I told him this was gonna be our last game so I began collecting the quarters from the machine.

"What Blood say?" is what the oldest lookin' of the four asked.

"I think he said somethin' about yo' momma," blurted out by another.

Just then, I heard Ms. Pac Man get ate up by a ghost. So I picked up my backpack and made my way out the door with Tray-Dog at my heels. As I was picking up my bike, the four Blood niggas came outside and walked towards me.

"What you say about my momma lil nigga?" the oldest lookin' one asked again from a distance.

"Fuck yo' momma!" I replied as I hopped on my bike like a

BMX pro and pedaled my ass off. We left them in our dust.

When we arrived at my home, my momma was already there in her room talkin' on the phone. My lil brother had spent the night at Aunt Sivi's with my cousin J.J. I peeked in on momma. She was doin' a crossword puzzle, eatin' pumpkin seeds, watchin' T.V., and talkin' on the phone with a clear shower cap on her head. I asked her if Tray-Dog could spend the night but before she could answer, he had leaned over my should to ask her himself.

Momma let Tray-Dog spend the night but we had to agree to have her yard and house clean by the time she made it home from work the following day. We gave each other high-fives, cheered like we had just won somethin', then made our way to the kitchen. I grabbed some leftovers outta the refrigerator and warmed us up somethin' to eat. We had fried pork chops, macaroni & cheese, white rice with butter and sugar, buttermilk biscuits, and a pitcher of grape Kool-Aid. We took our plates of food into my room to eat and talk about how eventful our day had been, and about the niggas who had just chased us from Fastrip.

"I hope we don't run into them fools again," Tray-Dog said.
"I do," I said. "Because I'll bust a cap in their ass," I added.

I then unzipped my backpack and pulled out the .22 pistol and Tray-Dog started smiling like a Chest-cat and reached for my gun as if it were a toy.

"Let me see it?!" he asked excitedly.
"Hold on!" I told him as I took the clip outta the gun to make sure there were no rounds in the chamber.

Before I could hand it to him, he had reached over and snatched it outta my hands. Tray-Dog was crazy about guns just like I was. He wanted the clip too but I wasn't goin' out like that. I promised him that we'd go shoot it somewhere tomorrow because my momma would've tripped on me for bustin' caps at her place.

That night, I let Tray-Dog sleep with my gun under his pillow like he requested, but I kept the clip with me. Again, I counted the number of niggas I wanted to "knock down" with my pistol instead of counting sheep.

"Eric, open the back door," a faint female voice said.

Knock! Knock! Knock!

"Eric, open the back door," the faint voice said again.
"Who is that?" I asked half asleep. Then I recognized it was Stanley's cousin Tosha's voice. "I'm coming!" I yelled as I scrambled outta bed.

Tray-Dog didn't move and didn't hear a damn thang. He just laid there with his mouth wide open slobberin' on my pillow. I stomped my toe on the door-jamb as I hurried outta my bedroom and through the kitchen to let Tosha in. As soon as I opened the door, she put her arms around me and held on tight. It was way too early in the mornin' for this shit, but I held her in my arms for a brief moment anyways.
I sent Tosha to my momma's room while I grabbed the blankets off my bed, along with the clip to my gun. I spread my blankets on top of my momma's bed and fucked her in every position I could think of before fallin' back to sleep.
I awoke with Tray-Dog tappin' me on my shoulder, to find the blanket completely off of me and Tosha. Tray-Dog had his finger up to his lips, motioning for me to be quiet and for me to get up. I eased up with my clip in my hand underneath my pillow, movin' slowly so that I don't wake her up. Before I got all the way up outta the bed, I leaned close to Tray-Dog and whispered in his ear.

"Where's my gun at?" I asked.

He pointed towards my bedroom. I then pointed towards my bedroom too and silently mouthed the words, "Go get it." He went to get the gun and I followed close behind him. Once the gun was in my possession, I told him to go "handle his business" with Tosha, but I told him not to tell her I sent him.
I hopped in the shower to wash the smell of sex off of me, and when I got out, I find a steaming Tosha sittin' on my momma's

bed with a big ass butcher's knife in her hands; while Tray-Dog was in the kitchen eating a bowl of Frosted Flakes cereal, talkin' about, "Baby is trippin..." I told Tray-Dog to take a shower so we could get the house cleaned up. While he showered, I sweet-talked Tosha and pretended I was mad at Tray-Dog for "gettin" at her like that. She ended up cleaning the entire house before taking a shower herself and leaving.

  The yard was a mess. I paid this white kid $5.00 to do the whole yard. He was only 10 years old and had just moved next door to us from Oildale. Oildale is a predominantly white, poor community. Blacks would get chased outta there regularly, and if a nigga were to get caught out there, he'd most likely get hung with a noose. It was an unwritten rule growin' up, "Don't get caught north of the river."

  Me and Tray-Dog set out to leave when we noticed his bike's back tire was on flat. So, we double-pumped to the hood. I pumped him halfway there, and he pumped the rest of the way. We stopped at Norm's Market on 8th & "P" street, played a few video games, then made our way to 6th street park.

Tray-Dog's brother drove his Station wagon up to the park and had parked it at the apartments across the street from the park on "R" street. The park was crackin'. I wore some of my new school clothes knowin' that if my momma saw me in my new shit, she'd have a fit. I'd take them all off before I went back home, and try not to get the clothes dirty. But it never failed...somebody had touched me and left a Cheetos stain on my pants, somebody else stepped on my white Chucks, and then the weed & cigarette smoke kept blowin' my way. I was gonna have to wear these clothes I'd gotten dirty during my second week of school because the first week of school is when momma paid the most attention to what we wore to school. She'd make sure we were color coordinated. I wasn't takin' any chances, so I changed back into my play clothes and made it home before the street lights came on.

  Tray-Dog didn't get to spend the night that night because his momma said he had stuff to do at home. You know how mommas are...They're unpredictable.

That night I woke up early to Tosha bangin' on my window as usual. We fucked 'til around noon, cleaned up the house, then headed to 6th street park. I let her ride my bike while I walked along side of her. She was always talkin' about she thought she might be pregnant. I would mumble, "yeah right," under my breath because I knew she wasn't pregnant. But just to make her feel like I was concerned and believed her, I would ask, "What makes you think you're pregnant?" Then she would change her voice like she was tired, touch her stomach, and say, "Because my stomach be hurtin'." In my head I'd be sayin', "It damn sho' aint mine, and I ain't claimin' shit." She didn't have to talk that, "I think I'm pregnant," bullshit in order to ride my bike. I was always a gentleman when it came to females. But I was gettin' tired of her and was lookin' for a nice way to tell her not to come by anymore. I had a feeling she had been fuckin' other niggas too because her pussy wasn't as tight as it used to be. Plus I didn't get as hard or as turned on by her anymore, and my sixth-sense radar was alerting me the last few times we fucked. I thought I was trippin at first but my dick would get as hard as a rock for other girls. A man cannot tell if a woman has been cheating solely by how her pussy feels when he penetrates her. But, we men know when a woman has cheated because her guilt send waves to her pussy, and her pussy juices will let us know by deflating our erections. Just that simple.

I decided tomorrow would be a good time to break the news to her, and I'll even give her some dick one last time. When we got close to the park, I made her stop at Norm's Market so nobody would see us show up together. It was Friday and the park was already crackin'. I wore my black Dickies, Golf-hat, Croaker-sack shoes, and a long-sleeved black sweatshirt with Big E-Loc on the front in white letters. I mingled the crowd, shot some dice, sold a few rocks, and shared a bottle of Thunderbird wine & Kool-aid with Tray-Dog. I let ol' girl ride my bike home from the park, and me and Tray-Dog got in the Station-wagon with his brother.

Everybody was heading up to "The Road" on the eastside. It was fun up there. I was goin' in & out of The Randles Club because I was tryin' to sell all the rocks I had brought with me. I hung out with Tray-Dog on the corner of Lakeview Ave & Ralston Road.

You had to be aggressive to make some money up on "The

Road" because there were at least a hundred more niggas tryin' to make money too. As soon as I would stick my hand in the car to show the "Smoker" my product, there would be four to five more niggas puttin' their hands in the car too. We would be pushing and shoving, tryin' to convince the "Smoker" who had the biggest and best dope. Sometimes I'd lose my rocks because another nigga would bump into my arm while tryin' to sell his own rocks.

This one particular night, the "Smoker" in the car had slapped my hand, causing my rocks to fall inside his car. He even tried to smash off with my shit, but he didn't get far tho'. I unloaded my .22 pistol on him, causing him to crash into some parked cars. I was sure he was dead as I made my way to the wrecked car. The Smoker was slumped over the steering wheel just like in the movies, but I didn't see any blood. He was knocked unconscious. I knew his broke ass didn't have any money because of the scandalous move he'd just put down. Therefore I didn't bother searching his pockets. I just collected my rocks from the front seat and the floor of the car.

Still angry from what he had done, I tapped him on the head with the barrel of my gun hard enough to draw blood and awake him. He knew it was gonna be "curtains" and his eyes damn near popped outta his head as I squeezed the trigger. *Pop! Pop!* right in his face. I tried to shoot him again but there were no more "Pops" to be be heard, nor flashes to be seen. Still, I squeezed the trigger as if the gun needed to be squeezed harder for it to work. Nothin'! I was outta bullets.

The circus-like atmosphere had grown deathly silent. Everyone stood still, laid still, or held onto someone else for comfort and protection. I calmly walked through the crowd, motioned with my head for Tray-Dog to follow, and went inside the club as if nothin' ever happened.

The Randle's Club was for adults, 18 and over, but the club owners were not turnin' down no money. So, there would be people as young as 13 years old in the club on any given night. The police never came inside to check I.D.'s or anything back then. Hell, the police never got outta their patrol cars back then either. We would toss bottles, boulder-type rocks, and any other hard object at them if they even acted like they were gonna stop in the community. Every now and then, a brave or stupid cop would jump out of his patrol car and chase a Wanted nigga. But the onlookers would toss objects at the cop, trip him, or sometimes shoot at him to help the guy being chased, get away.

Things done changed. Now there are Gang Task Force and Super Cops with nicknames like Mario, who will come through the hood all by himself and enter a residence without invitation or a search warrant, and arrest a gang-banger. I mean, all by himself! But, I'll get into that later.

I never did get a chance to give ol' girl any "goin' away dick" because I ended up goin' to juvenile hall. I had three charges: Possession of narcotics, Trafficking, and Assault with a Deadly Weapon. I spent three days in the 200A unit of Kern County Juvenile Hall, and they put me in a holding cell for six hours. It was freezing in that mutha'fucka too. I think they turn the air conditioner up high on purpose. I balled up in the fetal position on the hard narrow bench. When momma didn't show up in six hours to pick me up, they fed me and processed me.

200A was quiet and clean like a hospital. An asian guy greeted me first, "Go ahead and take your clothes off and step into the shower," he said. I looked at him like he had shit on his face and I didn't make a move. He then got loud with me. "Are you deaf?" he asked sarcastically.

The Asian man was my height, but he outweighed me by nearly one hundred pounds. I wasn't scared though. In fact, I kept staring at this tight-eyed, bobble-head, mutha'fucka until I couldn't take it no more. I cussed his ass out. I told him to fuck himself and the showers. But he and a black hammer-head staff member took me to the ground and placed me in restraints, and I eventually calmed down and obeyed their rules.

For the five minute shower, the Asian man poured shampoo in my hair to kill any lice or bugs I might have brought into the facility with me. I told his dumb ass that I was only a kid, but even I knew that most black people didn't get lice. Our hair is too greasy.

The deodorant they gave me was some cream called Tussy. Before I saw the jar of Tussy, the Asian man asked me if I wanted some Tussy.

I said, "Hell yeah! Where is she?"

"No, Eric," he explained between his laughter. "Not pussy. It's Tussy with a "T". It's a cream-based deodorant," he further explained then handed me the jar.

The Asian Man laughed himself to tears. I, on the other hand, didn't find it funny at all. I was placed in a room and a green tag was taped to my door. The room was maybe 11 x 8 foot, and there was one long vertical window on the back wall with a horizontal window on the door. The window on the door was too high for me to look out of without me havin' to jump. There was no sink or toilet in the room. I banged on the door for what seemed like hours. "I gotta pee!" I yelled. But my pleas went unanswered. I laid by the door, placed my dick-head at the bottom of it and "pissed a river" into 200A's corridor.

I finally fell asleep, but I was rudely awakened and dragged outta my room through the pissy corridor, and into a padded room. Hell, I still didn't get a toilet or sink. I didn't even have a bed nor linen in the padded room. But there was a 1 x 1 foot square section in the middle of the room, so that I could handle my business.

Two days later I went to court and Momma was there lookin' like she wanted to kill me. But when the judge asked momma direct questions, she sure knew how to smile, put on her charm, and sound like a proper speaking white woman.

I got put on probation and was ordered to serve 8 hours of Work-Release. It was nothin'. The Work-Release was ordered because I had used a staple to scratch "E-Loc wuz here" and "W/S" on walls of the holding cell.

Tray-Dog and the other homies came by my house to see me and to hear all about my Juvie experience. I felt really cool and tough as I explained in detail what I'd gone through in the past three days. From the ride in the police car, to putting my personal clothes on the day I got released. And they hung onto every word like good students.

Two days later I got high on Sherm Sticks, which are cigarettes soaked in Phencyclidine (P.C.P.). I would sometimes smoke two or three sticks all by myself. That Sherm is some stinky ass shit, but I loved the "high". A lot of people who smoke it either get stuck and can't function at all, and then there are those who get so high they take off all of their clothes. For this reason, Sherm is often called "Butt Naked". I never did either of the two, but I would find myself in LaLa Land. I'd also do and say things that I couldn't remember doing or saying.

On this one particular day I was with a few guys and we were all on The Road sellin' dope and tryin' to hook up with some girls. They didn't like Sherm, so I would smoke with older niggas or alone. You could smell Sherm from a mile away. I'd keep a stick in my pack of cigarettes and take a few puffs on it throughout the day. But today my whole pack of cigarettes were soakin' wet with Sherm because I had stumbled upon a couple of gallons of Sherm in my Aunt Alma's backyard.

She had moved from the duplex connected to my daddy's, to a house five lots down on the same side of the street. She had Pit-bulls chained up in her backyard on one side, and the other half had a small tree and camper. It smelled like Pine-Sol back there too. When I first saw the one gallon jugs sittin' under the tree, I thought they were full of apple juice. But when I removed the Pine-Sol stained towels that covered the top of one jug, the distinct smell of Sherm filled my nostrils.

I had trouble finding something to pour some of the Sherm in, and I wasted valuable time tryin' to find somethin'. My Aunt Alma's neighbor jumped over the fence to where I was and took over. He's eight years older than me and he came prepared. He had already been planning to steal some of the Sherm, and had brought with him a funnel and a small glass apple juice bottle. In fact, he had been stealing the Sherm on several occasions prior to our encounter. He replaced the small amount of Sherm he stole with pure water, then he wrapped the Pine-Sol stained rag back on the jug and went right back over the fence and I followed him. He poured Sherm on all of the cigarettes in my pack, then laced me on the "Sherm Game". He taught me everything from pouring Pine-Sol on the ground to camouflage the Sherm odor, to packaging the "waste" (residue from Sherm a.k.a. K-Jay) so that I could sell it too. But I smoked mines tho'. Yep, I was a real live Sherm-Head.

Anyways, I had just split a rock sale with one of the guys and decided to take me a smoke break. When I finished smoking my Sherm-stick, I started walkin' through a vacant lot. I remember I was in LaLa Land, where I was stuck next to this two story house on a hill, and I was chained up with a Pit-bull next to me who was also chained up. Every time I tried to walk forward, I would end up takin' a step back, which kept me in limbo. I kept goin' from that scene to a scene where I'm inside a small hut and the roof is so low it's almost touching the top of my head. There are hundreds of people in the hut with me, but no one has a face and no one can talk. All we do is twirl a cigarette lighter in our hands like it's a baton, flick on our flames, and repeat it over and over again. The next thing I remember is seeing a bouncing bright light coming towards me and then I black-out.

    I awoke at my Grandma & Poppy's house on the floor of their den. I was soakin' wet. The first thing that came to my mind was the $1,400 I had in my pocket. But when I reached for my pockets, they were turned inside out, lookin' like rabbit ears. I almost passed out again. My chest was sticky from the milk that my Poppy forced down my throat, and my Grandma thanked the Lord for bringin' me back to my senses.

    I later found out that I had attacked several people on The Road, knocked out some guy, gave half of my $1,400 to some girls, and tackled a nigga comin' through the vacant lot on a moped. Sherm is a mutha'fucka.

CHAPTER 3

With my $1,400 gone, I had to get on the grind because I owed somebody that money and I didn't want to run into them without havin' their money in my possession. I didn't think they would kill me over their money, but I didn't feel right owing them.

I half hustle. A lot of the well known dope dealers throughout the town would offer to "front" me dope and would also give me good deals. But I would usually decline their offer and just purchase small amounts from them instead. However, I fucked around and let one of the guys "front" me three ounces. I only knew a handful of niggas who could afford to "front" me enough dope so that I could pay off this person and pay off whoever was willing to "front" me the dope. But half of them were closely associated with him, and I just couldn't let him find out I didn't have his money.

So, I went to holla at a couple guys who were both from Lynwood, CA. and claimed Pope Street. They were both Crips and wore Turquoise blue rags. They were also ballin' outta control. I didn't have to drive to Lynwood because they were already in Bakersfield havin' it their way in Bakersfield. I met up with one of them and he fronted me six ounces of hard white rocks. I chopped every ounce down into small pieces and put them in pill bottles. I would sell an ounce (rock-for-rock) everyday until I paid off everybody back.

I started trading rocks for a lot of different things like

jewelry, T.V.'s, VCR's, clothes, pussy, "head", and even rented cars from people who smoked rocks. We called them "Rent-a-Buckets". I once rented a Bucket from a Smoker and I couldn't drive it because I didn't know how to drive a stick shift. I just paid a different Smoker to drive me around in the "Rent-a-Bucket" and I paid him with rocks too.

I ended up in Juvenile Hall again. This time I was charged with Strong Armed Robbery, Cruelty to animals, Assault & Battery, Possession of a Firearm, and Grand Theft Auto. I stayed in Juvie for three days and was assigned a Probation Officer. Her name was Ms. Andrea Jackson. She was a light-skinned Black woman, who was very pretty, with a sexy gap between her teeth and I had the biggest crush on her. It was rare to see a Black woman in her profession, so I admired her and respected her to the fullest. She was sincere about wanting to help me and help other troubled youths get back on the right track.

Ms. Jackson was upfront, honest, no nonsense, and talked to me in a way that made it clear of her expectations of me. She knew when to be sweet and when to be stern. She single handedly convinced me that I could do anything I set my mind to.

I came from Juvie in full swing, ready to prove myself. I was picked up and driven to school by Ms. Jackson. She dropped me off right in front of Emerson Jr. High and told me to call her as soon as I made it home from school.

"Keep your hands to yourself!" she yelled as she drove off.

I walked into the school's entrance, through the crowd, and towards the Rally stand. My brother Derrick had rode the bus to school and was somewhere on the far end of the playground. He was in the 7th grade and this would be his first year in Jr. High. I shook hands and gave hugs to a countless amount of students I'd known. With my head held high, I stood lookin' out over the sea of students, listening to the cheer of the cheerleaders and to the roar of the crowd of students until... "*Blam!*" I was punched in the chest. It didn't hurt. I was more shocked than anything. It was him.

The nigga named Squirt. Panic set in quickly. The cheers and roars all fell silent. I froze in disbelief. All I could see was Squirt's lemon shaped head surrounded by eight other boys who wore red bandanas.

"You know I been lookin' for you," Squirt said.

Deep in my heart I knew I could whoop this boy, but my mind allowed me to see flashbacks of Ms. Jackson tellin' me to keep my hands to myself, flashbacks of my momma tellin' me not to have them white folks callin' up to her job, and flashbacks of my lil brother Derrick tellin' me to make sure I locate him as soon as I got to school. I looked him in his eyes, balled up my fists, and walked away from a fight for the first time in my life.

It would be the last time too.

Breakdancin', Pop-lockin', and Rap music was popular at the time. So was Michael Jackson, Prince, and New Edition. The girls at school would pretend a certain member of New Edition was their real boyfriend, and they would wear large buttons with the member's picture on it. Some would say Prince was their husband, while others would claim to be married to Michael.

We all had Jheri Curls, could do the "Moon-walk" dance made famous by Michael Jackson, and I'd be lyin' if I said I didn't put on a glitter glove, Penny loafers, and my homeboy's Michael Jackson jacket. I even did the kick, spin, and stood on the tip of my toes like I was tryin' to hold my pee. I was into everything that had to do with music and Momma could see my musical talent early on. She would buy me tape recorders, record players, and boomboxes. I would rap over songs by the Sugar Hill Gang, and Whodini. The song, "Five Minutes of Funk," by Whodini was my shit. I also use to love to rap to the song, "Flashlight," by George Clinton, and to the song, "So Rough So Tough," by Zapp.

I built my first show bike (low-rider bike) all by myself. I had the banana seat, long forks, sissy poles, lights, hooga horn, and music box. I used flour, newspaper, and aluminum cans to bond the frame. I had a Schwin and I used a car stereo, car speakers, and motorcycle battery to hook up my music box. I also put carpet on the outside of the box to give it a cool look. I did one project after another. I stayed busy.

  I got me a Paper Route job delivering newspapers door-to-door every morning. It was a lot harder than I thought it would be too. It's very difficult tryin' to ride a bike with a big bag that has thirty newspapers in the front and behind me. I improvised and hooked up my bag onto my handlebars, which I still found to be difficult. Then there's the crazy dogs tryin' to attack me on every street, and the Black Birds attackin' me from above. I guess the birds thought my Jheri Curls were worms or something. They would make a loud chirpin' noise that sounded like kisses, then they would swoop down at me. I'd drop my bike, the newspapers, and everything tryin' to get away from them damn birds.

  I had gotten the Paper Route job from a white kid named Jon who raced his bike at the YMCA's BMX racing track. I even got into the BMX racing thing for a while. I owned top of the line bikes like G.T's, Diamondbacks, Torkers, P.K Ripers, Skylines, and Mongooses. I had one cool white kid as a friend whom I hung out with a lot. Him, his brothers, and his parents were nice too. Me and him collected baseball, E.T, and Garbage Pail Kids cards.

  I participated in every extra curricular activity there was. When I learned how to sew in my Home Economics class at Emerson Jr. High, I made a pillow that looked like a boombox. But my real education would come from the streets. The School of Hard Knocks.

My cousin Roy was a well known, and well respected, gambler. He would win my money playin' 3-Card Monty, and shootin dice. It cost me $400 to learn about Six Ace Flats (Trick Dice).

  Roy was one of the best in town. He had a clean Chevy truck. It was tan, with a black phantom top, a dump bed, sittin' on chrome Deep Dish rims. Roy's nickname is Crafty Dog, and the name fits. His sister Renee (Nay-Nay) use to take me with her and her friends sometimes when I was really young. I remember when I was around 7 years old when Nay-Nay and her two friends took me to Winchell's Donut shop with them. They put a lot of donuts in the bag, gave the bag to me, then sent me to the car to wait for them. Nay-Nay is the one who introduced me to eating stuff like dill pickles with a peppermint stick candy stuck inside of it. The one who I first saw put salt on her lemon, and put hot sauce on Lays plain potato chips. My mouth is watering now from just thinkin' about it.

I remember when Nay-Nay first started dating her now husband Johnathan. He use to work at California park as an assistant with the recreation department. Nay-Nay was living a "stones throw away" from the park. One day me, momma, and Aunt Alma were on our way back from Zody's, and we drove to some nice lookin' apartments. We didn't go inside the apartments or anything, Aunt Alma just wanted to show momma where Nay-Nay and Johnathan were livin'. I was being nosy and asked, "Who is John?" Aunt Alma told me it was Nay-Nay's roommate. The way she said it made me think she was tryin' to hide somethin' so I left it alone.

I used to love goin' places with momma, Aunt Alma, and Nay-Nay, especially to the drive-in movies. Me and Derrick would hide on the floor of the car, and underneath blankets. It was so fun doin' stuff as a family, stickin' together, and getting' away with misdemeanor stuff.

Once Nay-Nay and Johnathan announced their engagement, we met Johnathan's son named Jason. He had grew up in the Bay area and he was a year older than me, and very likable. He was also pretty smart, really tall, and had skills on the basketball court. I remember Jason had stayed with us during the school's Christmas break, and the local high school basketball Christmas tournament was getting' ready to kick-off. I was still in the 8th grade, but I always went to a lot of the high school games.

Two days before the tournament was set to begin, momma sent me to K-Mart to buy her some pantyhose. She gave me $20 and told me to keep the change. Me, Derrick, and Jason walked to K-Mart as I only lived five minutes away. While at the store, I decided to steal the pantyhose, along with a record, and some candy. I made it all the way out the door when two plain clothed security guards began chasing me. I ran all the way to momma's, and pass her back door. By the time the security guards caught up to me, I had tossed all the stolen items over the fence, next door to momma's.

Momma and her boyfriend heard the commotion outside and came to my defense. Momma's boyfriend told the security guard to take his hands off of me. The security guard was apologetic, but he was also certain that I had tossed the stolen items over the fence into the neighbor's yard. Momma's boyfriend grabbed a flashlight and helped search for the stolen merchandise until they found the items. The police came and arrested me, but momma came to get me from Juvie within' a few hours. Momma "beat me" like a negro slave. She whooped me so hard and for so long that my feelings were hurt. Jason and Derrick sat in the living room during my beating and were both allowed to go to the basketball tournament without me. They had both stolen candy too, but I'm the only one who got caught.

The next day, momma's friend came to visit with her, and that's when I ended up going to the bathroom, and then back into my room. Then, I heard the lady ask momma why was I on punishment. What did she do that for? Because after Momma had told her what I'd done, she got so worked up again that she came into my room and whooped my ass again. That would be my last ass whoopin' from momma. I had asked my daddy to let me move in with him on E. 9th street, and he didn't hesitate, "Go get yo' shit and bring it to the house," were his exact words. Around this time my daddy was livin' alone so it was just gonna be me and him. I had my own room and could stay up as late as I wanted. I was only two blocks away from The Road now, and I'd go up there all the time to party and hustle.

My daddy loved to drink, and his favorite was Korbel brandy. But, like most alcoholics, he'd drink any and everything. He was also using cocaine at the time, but I hadn't seen him do it with my own eyes.

I was still sellin' weed and rocks whenever the opportunity

presented itself, then one day outta the blue my daddy asked, "Who are you sellin' dope for boy?" I just sat there like I didn't hear him. "You hear me talkin' to you!" he snapped. I wasn't gonna lie to my daddy, so I told him, "I get it from these guys," I explained.

Daddy told me to follow him into the kitchen where we sat down and had a man-to-man/ father-to-son talk. He started by tellin' me he didn't want me to keep secrets from him or do anything illegal behind his back. He also told me that he didn't approve or condone me sellin' drugs. But since I was already involved, he proceeded to show me how to go about it the "right way."

Up until this point, the only other time daddy spoke on drugs was when he caught me rollin' up real grass from the lawn and pretending it was a marijuana joint. That day he caught me in the act. He knocked on the window and motioned for me to bring the "play joint" inside to him. I was nervous as hell, but he didn't even get mad at me. He said, "Damn boy, you rolled the hell outta that; here, roll this up," and handed me a shoe box with weed and Zig-Zags in it. Later that day he had me roll a few more joints for his homeboy. But on this particular day, regarding the Rocks, daddy gave all the instructing and demonstrating.

Daddy pulled out a small, black, leather bag and emptied it's contents on the kitchen table. There was powder cocaine inside sandwich bags, wax paper the size of gum that had B12 in them, and a 6-set measuring spoon kit. He reached in the cabinet and brought down a bottle of rubbing alcohol, and a bottle of Korbel brandy. He then slid a chair up to the sink and stood on it so that he could reach further back into the cabinet. He came down with a Crown Royal bag that was purple and gold. In the bag was glass pipes, cotton swabs, and two seven inch pieces of wire clothes hangers that were bent on one end. He opened the refrigerator and grabbed a box of Arm & Hammer baking soda. Then, he filled a pot with water, sat it on the flames coming from the stove top's furnace, and let it boil while he prepared the cocaine. He took out a dinner plate and dumped some of the B12 packets. I didn't count the number of B12 packets he emptied into the plate, nor did I know the exact amount of cocaine he used. In our junk drawer, daddy grabbed a brand new Poker card and a straight razor. He used them to cut, mix, and fluff the B12 and cocaine.

He asked, "You ever seen powder cocaine before?"

"No." I said.

"Well, this is it," he said while handin' me one of the plastic bags full of cocaine.

I examined it through the plastic bag. It was snow white and looked a lot like flour to me.

"Go ahead and open it," he instructed.

I guess I took too long tryin' to get it open because daddy took it outta my hands and opened it for me. He smelled it, then stuck his pinky finger in it and sucked it off in one quick motion.

"Stick yo' finger in there and put some on the tip of yo' tongue," he further instructed me.

My tongue was instantly numb. I kept tryin' to taste it, but there was no taste aside from the initial aspirin-like taste. But now, I tasted nothin'. Just numbness.

Daddy reached into the sink and grabbed an empty Gerber baby food jar, rinsed it out really good, then took it to the plate of cocaine and B12. He used a measuring spoon to scoop the product from the plate into the baby food jar. Then, he used a tablespoon to transfer some of the boiling water into the baby food jar containing the cocaine and B12. It looked kinda pasty at first, but daddy added more water and few scoops of baking soda. He held the jar by the threads and held it over the simmering fire. As he swirled it in a circular motion, it caused the contents to swirl in the same motion. The oily lookin' mixture was in many different forms throughout the jar. But when each form would touch the other, they became "whole." After a couple of minutes of swirling, the different oily forms all became one solid form, appearing to be separate from the water.

Daddy took the creation to the sink and turned on the cold water. He let the cold water run on his free hand, then flicked his fingers over the mouth of the jar, allowing only sprinkles of cold water to enter. He said he had to do it like that so the jar wouldn't crack or break. He repeated the "sprinkle" technique until the jar had cooled enough for him to hold it in the palm of his hand. He then ran cold water into his palm that held the now cool jar. Then he held the jar above his head while shakin' it and examined the forming "rock" that appeared to be stuck at the bottom of the jar. He ran cold water directly into the jar containing the stuck rock until the rock broke free from the bottom of the jar and floated around in the cool water.

"There!" he said as he poured the water and the rock into his hand.

He tossed the rock onto a clean dinner plate. *Clink!* It sounded like he tossed a real cement rock onto the plate. I picked it up to examine it and I was amazed. Just that quick, daddy had transformed some powder into a solid rock form. I held it about a foot above the plate and let it drop. *Clink!* It didn't break. I did it repeatedly, but it still wouldn't break.

Daddy used the straight razor to cut the rock up into small pieces and showed me what one gram looked like. He said I should sell my grams for $40, and sell half a gram for $20 because everyone else sold their grams for $50 and half a grams for $25. He also told me to always be nice and respect my customers because an unhappy customer will take their business elsewhere and be quick to snitch on you if they happen to get caught up. But, a satisfied customer would come buy from you faithfully and would even protect you if they got hemmed up by a cop who specifically ask about you.

I took heed to all of the "game" daddy shared with me. Even the simple things he taught me as a kid, I still use them. Like, drying off with my face towel before using the large bath towel. And always keepin' nice lookin' shoes on my feet because daddy said that's the first thing people notice about you.

Daddy kept his afro forked out and he neatly trimmed his pork-chop styled side burns. Even when he wore a full beard, he kept it neatly groomed. He had a lot of tailor made suits with his initial "C" cut into the collar of his suit jackets. The closet was full of Stacy Adams, Leather boots with the zipper on the sides, and platform shoes. His bedroom, which was also his Den when he lived alone, was like a disco joint. There were beads hangin' in the doorway, a personal bar with a glass top, and two speakers with foam coverings. He had mirrors with gold leafing covering one wall, a large orange fishnet with different colored seashells inside it that hung on another wall, plus a large painting of a seashore on yet another wall. He had two end tables, a coffee table, two barstools, and a leather couch that folded out into a bed. He had a music system that consisted of a radio, record player, and an 8-track deck. He also had an album holder that stood in the corner of the room. It stood floor to ceiling, and held albums from artists like Dolomite (Rudy Ray Moore), Richard Pryor, and Redd Foxx. There were two black lights that made everything that was white in color, look purple. Steppin' into my daddy's den was like steppin' into a whole new world. When everyone else got Buick Riviera's, my daddy got himself a Buick Wildcat. He would get drunk as a skunk and burn rubber in that car like a mad man.

My daddy taught me how to build a house. From layin' the foundation, to the frame work, puttin' in windows, and hangin' doors. Between daddy and my Poppy teaching me to operate the lawnmower and edger, I became a real live Maintenance Man. However, none of the skills would be necessary in the line of work that I was into. But they would eventually come in handy later on in my life. For now, I was enjoying the fast money and all the excitement that came along with it.

I was pretty good at sellin' rocks. A lot of young niggas my age who were also sellin' rocks, didn't see very much profit because most of them were smoking the rocks themselves. The #1 rule is: Don't get high on your own supply. That old saying goes a long way. It applies to the fat kid tryin' to sell sweets, the alcoholic tryin' to sell beer, and the cigarette smoker tryin' to sell cigarettes. If I would've tried to sell Sherm, I would've stayed broke because I liked smoking Sherm.

The youngsters my age who were smoking rocks, usually crushed the rocks up and sprinkled it into their weed or stuffed it in the end of their cigarettes. Some called them Cavies, and others called them Primos. The shit has a loud distinctive smell. It's loud and strong like Sherm, and the best way to describe it is to say it smells like a sweet fart. I didn't like to be around anybody who was smoking that shit. And I would have a fit whenever I smelled it.

When I wasn't gangbangin', I would be doin' Home-invasion robberies or robbin' people at gun point. Yeah, I was a Stick-up-kid, but I really loved the Home-invasion licks. It was like shopping for free. We wold come up on jewelry, guns, money, rare coins, T.V's, and other appliances. I'd make sure I was the one who searched the freezer, cereal, and rice boxes, as well as the sugar and cookie jars. A lot of homeowners hid money and drugs in those places. I didn't share that information with my crime partners. That "game" was handed down to me by an O.G. who told me to keep that to myself. It was like my "bonus" from every lick we did. I was a busy body. I sold dope, hit licks, robbed people, attended school, wrote raps, and was gangbangin'.

School was almost over and graduation was near. This fat ass Blood nigga almost made me shoot his ass.

We were chillin' on the grass at Emerson Jr. High. It was me, my girlfriend at the time, and a few more couples, when he brought his fat ass over and started talkin' shit. My girl had a smart mouth on her and she said somethin' smart to him, and he said somethin' back. Then, she said somethin' that we all know is a no-no... She said, "Yo' momma!" He replied with, "Bitch what did you say?" But she didn't get to answer because he had kicked her in the eye with his Chuck Taylors. I jumped up to defend her, but everyone was holding me back and explaining how she was outta line for talkin' about his momma. I had my .22 with me too, but I didn't see him after school. In fact, it would be several years later when I finally did see him.

Momma bought me some gray dress pants, black Penny-Loafers, gray and maroon shirt, black belt, and a maroon colored tie to wear to my 8th grade graduation ceremony. Maroon is damn near red if you ask me. I think she did that shit on purpose. I was just glad to be graduating.

The graduation ceremony was held at the Civi Auditorium which is the same place a lot of the high schools held their graduations. I sat next to Andrea Nicholson because of our last names. We held hands and thanked God for helping us make it that far.

Afterwards, momma and her friend Wilma took me out to eat at Bob's Big Boy. It was cool, and it felt good to be making momma proud of me. Even if only for that one day.

CHAPTER 4

The summer was a hot one. If I wasn't spendin' the night at Tray-Dog's, I was over at Rod and Anthony's on Priscilla Lane. Rod, who we called R.J. was one year older than me, and Anthony (Amp) is a year younger.

We all use to live on 11th & "K" when we were babies. Me and Derrick lived in the shack, while R.J., Amp, and their older brother Dirk lived in the apartments across the alley from us. Dirk would sleepwalk and end up outside actually walking in his sleep. R.J. would always be climbing on top of shit like roofs, trees, and gates, and he'd be breathing and wheezing hard, while Amp rode his Big Wheel with his pamper full of shit.

They were my "play cousins" and I grew to love them as if we had the same blood running through our veins. I still do love them, and will kill for either one of them.

R.J. is responsible for me gettin' involved with the gang activities. We were all very good at playing baseball and should've all made it to the Major League. I'm serious! Amp is responsible for helpin' me learn how to take care of myself. We sort of raised ourselves in a sense, because our parents weren't involved in our lives as much as we needed them to be. My momma didn't want me living under her roof because I was in a gang and she felt like I was outta control. My daddy was too busy gettin' drunk or high to be there for me like I needed him to be, and I was officially living with him.

R.J. and Amp's mom was on drugs too and was always locked in her room whenever she wasn't at work. I called her Aunt Vicky. She accepted me under her roof and fed me. So, I'll always love and respect her and her husband Broadway. I call him "Unc". He was on drugs too, but he was always on major swole from lifting weights in prison.

Even R.J. and Amp's biological father, Clarence was on drugs. Clarence came from a wealthy family just like my own daddy, and was a "First Kid On The Block" type of nigga too. Our daddy's had a lot in common. They always lied to us about what they were gonna do WITH US and FOR US, and never kept a promise. I wanted a lot of things growing up as a kid, but more than anything, I just wanted a regular family and a normal life.

I got into a lot of fights towards the middle of the summer, mostly against Warlord Bloods. But, I also had fights against young Mid City Crips and Stroller Boy Crips.

One day I got into it with an older nigga who accused me of pickin' up his medicine bottle full of rocks while I was hustlin' on The Road. I think he picked me to accuse because I was young and relatively unknown. While I was tryin' to explain myself, he "fired" on me and he almost knocked me out. I pulled my pistol outta my pocket and shot his ass up. He "got in the wind" with the quickness, and only received through and through wounds. He was out of the hospital in two days, but then he came up missing.

I was arrested three days after ol' boy was reported missing, and booked for Attempted Murder. I stayed in Juvie fighting the case for a month, until it got dismissed. The victim, which was the only witness, was missing.

Two days later I started High School, and the first day of school was cool. Since I was living with my daddy, I had to attend East Bakersfield High (E.B). Most of my homies attended B.H.S. (Bakersfield High), but I knew a lot of the students at E.B. because I had attended Bessie Owens elementary school with them and had also met a lot of them at California park.

I had to ride on the school bus to E.B., and it was like a comedy show on wheels. Everybody was "cappin'" or "baggin'" on each other. And there was at least two fights at the bus stop everyday. Glenn Earl knocked out Bull; Big Head Corey knocked out Glenn Earl; Tamika whooped Neicy outta her shirt, and we all went crazy when Neicy kept on fighting while her ashy titties swung everywhere.

I'd ditch school during the lunch period just so I could have two lunch periods. I'd even walk the halls of Kern Medical Center, which was only a stones throw away from E.B.H.S. Sometimes I'd hang out at the hamburger stand across the street, or go to the record shop down the street. I'd even take girls to abandoned apartments and "do it" to them. But most of the time when I ditched, I'd just smoke weed or Sherm, and hang out listening to and telling jokes.

One of my daddy's girlfriends (Hazel) moved in with us, and brought her kids with her too. There was Larry (Booda), Yohantus (YoYo), Dean, and Crystal. We all lived in my daddy's lil two bedroom duplex. I was happy to be gettin' home cooked meals again, and not having to clean up the place by myself anymore. But, I didn't like losing my privacy or my own room.

Hazel and her kids came from Los Angeles. Larry was my age, YoYo was a year younger, Dean was five years younger, and Crystal was only 5 years old. All five of us slept in the same tiny room together. We had two sets of bunk beds: The two girls shared a bed, and us boys had our own beds. I would often sneak into the bed with YoYo and "do it" to her. We "did it" almost every night until one night after we "did it" she asked me to lay there beside her and hold her, and I fell asleep. What did I do that for? I awoke to my daddy's voice.

"Eric! Hey Eric!" he said.

"Oh shit!" I thought to myself. I didn't open my eyes but the orange glow from behind my eyelids let me know the lights in the room were now on.

"Eric!" he said loudly. But I still didn't move or open my eyes. I then felt his thumb press into my shoulder blade as he violently shook me and called my name again.

"Eric! Get Yo' ass up!" he demanded.

I finally opened my eyes, pretending that I wasn't aware of

where I was at. But he didn't care. He was mad as hell and I could see it all over his face. Hazel stood in the doorway peering at me over my daddy's shoulder. He dragged me outta bed, over YoYo, and onto the floor.

"What I do daddy?" I yelled just before he struck me with his double-holed, white, leather belt. *Woosh! Smack!*

"Don't whoop him Curtis," was Hazel's weak attempt to rescue me. But he dragged me outta the room, into the living room, and whooped my ass like I stole somethin'. That would be the last ass whoopin' I'd get from my daddy. My feelings were hurt because he whooped me in front of these people I had just met. They were my new family, but I still didn't feel it was right for daddy to whoop me in front of them. So, I planned to do something stupid to let daddy know that I didn't like them ass whoopins.

Me and Booda went to school lookin' for trouble. Booda wanted to beat-up some niggas who lived in the Projects, but they weren't at school this particular day. So we decided to see which one of us had the best knockout punch, by sockin' anybody that happen to come our way. We waited in the hallway and Booda tested his first punch. He didn't knockout anyone and neither did I. But we socked three students each and got in trouble for it. I even broke my hand on one of the kid's head and had to get a cast put on it. We both got suspended too.

While I was at the hospital gettin' the cast put on, the police came and took me and Booda too Juvie. We got out two weeks later and I was placed on House Arrest.

I got Shermed-out my first day home. I ended up in La-La Land again, with the same Pit bull and the same ole' hut. I woke up in Juvie and didn't know why or how I got there. But my probation officer told me that I had went to my momma's house to live with her and Derrick. She told me that me, momma, and Derrick were all in momma's bedroom when I attacked Derrick for callin' me a Sherm-head. She went on to tell me that I had broken every window at my momma's and pulled a knife on momma, Derrick, and the neighbors, and that momma had hit me in the head with a wooden table leg. I don't remember any of it. But I did have a bandage wrapped around my head that covered the stitches at the top of my head when I awoke in Juvie.

Daddy came to pick me up within' six hours and I was back out on House Arrest. Two days later I rented a "bucket" from a Smoker and refused to give it back. The car was a long ass LTD, and I drove the hell outta it.

I was Shermed-out one day and couldn't talk. Daddy was fussin' at me about the "rent-a-bucket" that I still had in my possession. But I was so high I couldn't explain to him why I was keepin' the car. I don't know why I couldn't form any words or why I couldn't make a sound. I just couldn't. I got so frustrated that I released the switchblade that I had hooked onto my belt holster, and I opened the knife exposing the sharp blade. Daddy kept on fussin' at me about how crazy and stupid the Sherm was making me act. I swung the knife down hard, stabbin' the kitchen table. I knew what I was doin' and could see what I was doin', but I had no control of what I was doin'. It was an out-of-body experience. I raised the knife high above my head and walked towards the bathroom where my daddy had went to take a piss. I stabbed the bathroom door really hard, punching a big hole in it with the knife and my fist. I then walked back into the kitchen and stuck the knife back into the table. Daddy ran outta the house and down the street to where his parents lived. I snatched up the knife and followed behind him.

My grandparents took too long to open the front door, and I was approaching my daddy fast. He panicked and knocked on their bedroom window. My "high" had come down and I wanted to tell him not to be afraid because I was o.k. now. But when I grabbed him, the knife was still in my hand, and it looked as if I was tryin' to kill him. Through all of the commotion I heard my daddy yell, "Call the police!" So I broke wide and I ran around the corner to where I had parked the Rent-A-Bucket and got in traffic.

The next day I awoke in Juvie, cold as hell, in the holding tank. I had more charges on me against my family members than anything. While I was in custody, the body of the missing person that I'd shot on The Road was discovered in the trunk of his car. I was charged with his murder. Before the body was found I had already been convicted of drug sales, Grand Theft Auto, and the crimes against my family.

I had been to the Camp Erwin Owens youth detention for boys. I failed the program and got committed to Kern Youth Facility. I was almost done serving my time when they hit me with the murder beef.

CHAPTER 5

"Sea-sick, C.Y.A. bound; If you can't swim, then you're bound to drown"...

I made a plea agreement for involuntary manslaughter, and was sentenced to the California Youth Authority (C.Y.A.). I was released from Juvie into the custody of a Tri-County transportation officer. I put on the same clothes I wore at the same time of my arrest. The officer then placed chains around my waist, arms, and legs. Each chain was secured with a small Master lock. I stepped onto the eleven passenger van like I'd done it several times before, and made my way to the back of the van. There were only four other prisoners on board, and all of them were male adults. There were two whites, one hispanic, and one black.

"Where are you headed to youngsta'?" the black prisoner asked me.

"Y.A." I said, tryin' to make my voice sound deeper than it really was. "Where're you goin'?" I asked.

"We're all on our way to San Quentin," he replied while sweeping his eyes in the direction of the other prisoners. "I'm Psycho Mike from Long Beach." He introduced himself, then stood to give me some dap as best as he could with his hands cuffed.

"I'm E-Loc from Bakersfield, Westside Gangsta Crips," I introduced myself.

I'm not sure where, but somewhere along the ride, a white female prisoner got on the van. She flirted with me and the others, but she got dropped off at the very next stop. I never did talk to the other male prisoners on the van. I dozed off and was awakened when we arrived in Sacramento.

The C.Y.A. reception center was called the Northern Reception Center Clinic (NRCC). I was glad to get off of that van and stretch my legs. Man! That was a long ass ride.

I was told to discard my clothes and was given brand new shit. I mean brand new everything! From wind-breaker jacket, socks, t-shirts and boxers, to Converse All Stars (Chuck Taylors). They sure knew how to put a smile on your face coming through the door. I was told to carry my bedroll across the yard to Company #2. That's the housing unit where niggas my age were housed. As I walked across the yard I heard several people callin' my name.

"E-Loc! Say E-Loc! What's up Cuz? Over here Cuz!" they yelled.

I yelled, "What's up?" back, but I couldn't see them because they were yellin' through their cell windows that were covered with mesh wire. I was smiling and lookin' all happy and shit. The staff member who was escorting me said, "Damn! I ain't never seen nobody be so happy to be here."

When I made it across the yard to Company #2, and walked through the dayroom towards the Y.C. Station, niggas were hittin' me up from all angles.

"Where you from Cuz!?, Where you from Blood!?"

The staff member shooed them away but they were still on me.

"Where you from?" they chanted.
I said, "I'm from Bakersfield Westside Gangsta Crips!"

It seemed like I heard and repeated the same shit a hundred times that day.

I was told the rules and led to my cell. The nigga in my cell happened to be a nigga from Bakersfield named Mike. He was from Mid City Crips. I had seen Mike on The Road a couple of times in the past, but I'd never done "time" with him. We ended up being cool cell-mates; we wrote Raps, played cards, and dominos.

One time Mike got a Care Package (Box full of food and candy sent in from family or friends), but the Care Package wasn't really meant for Mike. There was another kid with the same first and last name who was also doin' time in NRCC who the Package was actually meant for. There was cartons of cigarettes, shoes, sweatsuit, a camera, plus candy and food. Me and Mike split everything, destroyed the box, and considered this "Breakin' Bread" incident the beginning of our friendship.

We found out the other kid with Mike's name was a white kid. Some of his mail came to our cell a few times. We'd keep the stamps and envelopes that came, but we'd return the pictures and letters to the staff who would then get the mail to the rightful owner.

Mike put me up on game regarding the different words I could and couldn't use in the presence of other kids. Almost every cereal, food, or clothing brand was disrespectful to say around certain people. There was way too many rules in C.Y.A. for me. I'm talkin' about the rules the kids made up, not the rules made by the institution. For instance... If you drop your comb or hair brush on the ground or on the floor, you had to throw it away. If you drop your soap, towel, or bowl, you had to throw it away. If you failed to do so, you were put on The "L" (Leva), or put on The "Shine" (No one talks to you or accepts you). This basically meant no one could eat or drink after you, and you were not included in the "spreads" when groups would get together to celebrate special occasions like birthdays, holidays, or goin' home.

Most people on The "L" or "Shine" were people who were participating in homosexual activities, or were labeled a "Buster" because they were afraid to fight back when they were attacked. But you could be put on The "L" or on The "Shine" simply by eating or drinkin' after someone who's already on The "L" or The "Shine".

I wasn't turnin' down no fades though. The first and last time I'd done that was when Ms. Jackson dropped me off at school. I promised myself that I'd never "go out" like that again.

One day I was sittin' on the dayroom's soft back chairs watchin' t.v. when this big-head nigga with a missin' tooth introduced himself.

"My name is Powers," he said, extending his hand for me to shake.

"I'm E-Loc," I said.

He was sittin' directly in front of me. I had heard the staff sayin' the name "Powers" several times over the past few days. So, when he introduced himself as "Powers" I assumed that he didn't gangbang.

During the next commercial break he turned to face me again. This time he asked more questions. Like... What juvenile hall I came from? What was I locked up for? And making small talk. He finally told me he was from Sacramento, and that he was a Blood from Oak Park. I had never heard of them so I simply said, "Is that right?" Before I could tell him where I was from, he pointed at my left hand, where I had used a staple to scratch W/S on it. It was lookin' like an off-white & pink tattoo.

He asked, "What is that?"
I said, "Westside".
He then asked, "What is that, Rickets?"

I didn't answer him. I knew I had been "dissed", so I calmly got up, walked down my row of soft back chairs, went around to his row, all the way down, until I got to him. He was still sittin' down and was engaged in conversation with someone next to him. I didn't say a word. I aimed directly for his nose and followed up with a barrage of blows to his head. The staff sprayed me with mace and pulled me off Powers who was screaming like a bitch and holding his Snot-BOX. The staff cuffed me, put me in a golf kart, then wheeled me to a nurse station to rinse my eyes. I got a write-up and had to be in a single cell for three days. When I came out, I was sent to a different Company with older kids. I let the staff know I was a "Crip" and I wanted to be in a cell with a "Crip". But, instead, they put me in a cell with a guy who they said was a non-affiliate.

I used the door knob to open the cell door and let myself in. My new cell-mate had the cell lookin' clean with a blanket spread out on the floor as his carpet. He was layin' on the bottom bunk when I walked in and i could tell he was kinda tall because his legs hung pass his bed while his braided head was propped on his pillow. I saw the empty locker hangin' on the wall and began puttin' away my stuff. I was glad to have someone to talk to.

While unpacking, my new cell-mate asked me where I was from and I told him "Bakersfield." He then asked, "What's in Bakersfield?" I replied by sayin', "Crips and Slobs."

"What?!" he said as he sat up in his bed.
"Crips and Slobs," I repeated.

He swung his feet to the floor, threw-up a "B" sign with his hands and "screamed on me." "I'm Bleepy from Mad Swan Bloods!" he sternly said.

Then he stood up as tall as a tree, looked down on me, and served me with four or five quick blows to my chest, neck, and head area. I fought back but my lil punches didn't seem to faze him at all. It was already hard for me to keep my balance with the blanket on the floor. And this tall ass nigga had arms as long as a gorilla. I felt like I was fighting one of my uncles and it seemed like he was grippin' my head like a basketball while punching me repeatedly with his other hand. My ears were burnin', my lip was busted, and I was outta breath. I backed up to the door and kept my eyes on this nigga while I reached behind me in search of the door knob, but there was no door knob.

"Shit!" I said as I took a deep breath and rushed Bleepy.

I got a good punch in, but that only made him mad. I slipped on the blanket that was on the floor and went down on one knee. He hit me with a few more punches and tried to kick my head off, but he missed and ended up on the blanket next to me. I took advantage of the situation and attacked him with four hard punches to his head. He pushed me off of him and we were both back on our feet. We fought for what seemed like hours, but in reality it was only about seven minutes. We touched everything in that cell. The staff opened the cell door and wet us both up with mace. I was relieved because I was almost "outta gas" and didn't think I could fight much longer. The only one's to see the fight was me, Bleepy, and God. And all three of us knows that Bleepy won that fight.

Bleepy and I ended up fighting again when I came back to C.Y.A. the second time, and he won the second fight as well. I give credit where it's due. Even though I loss both of those fights, I still give Bleepy his props. His original nickname is Sleepy, but he referred to himself as Bleepy. I learned a lot during those two fights:

1.) Get off first.
2.) The pain you feel in a fight doesn't last long.

My last fight with Bleepy was the last I'd lose.

It was time to go to "Board". The Youthful Offender Parole Board was made up of three people who would determine how long my stay in C.Y.A. would be. Although the courts sentenced me to 4 years, the Board could let me out a lot sooner if they determined that I had behaved good. I was given a blue prison shirt to wear to Board. The exact same kind they wear in adult prisons. We referred to the prison shirts as "Board Shirts".

On this particular morning, I was allowed to iron my shirt. I put creases all over it in hopes of impressing the Board Members. A few days prior to my Board Hearing I was "schooled" by other kids about what to say and what not to say at my hearing. But I found out during my hearing that none of my preparation would be necessary. The Board only allowed me to state my name. They proceeded to talk more to the tape recorder than they talked to me. I can't remember all that was said, but I wasn't goin' home that day or any day soon.

Within weeks I was transferred to another institution. We rode in a big, black and chrome bus that was known as the Gray Goose. We would later change the name to Green Hornet once the buses changed their colors to green and chrome. We pulled up at the front entrance of O.H. Close School for boys. It looked like a school too. They made us "New Arrivals" sit in front of the Comm-Center.

It was early in the morning, so the kids were walking around the track, pass us, and to their classes. There were short and stocky, tall and skinny, bald and ugly, afros and braided young niggas steppin' outta line to "bang" on us and "hit us up". I banged back on them and stuck my chest out like I was the hardest nigga on earth. Some of them were saying, "You have a homeboy named such-and-such on Del Norte," or "Yo' homeboy named such-and-such is in the hole."

I got placed on a cottage named Glenn Hall. It was the cottage where the youngest kids at O.H. Close were housed. There were youngsters there for killin' their parents and for other serious crimes.

I met Claybo from Hoover Criminals, Gumby from Kitchen Crips, Huccabucc from Rollin' 60's, and Kilo from Southside Compton Crips, just to name a few. I had already met everyone on my cottage except for a few who were at work, and this one named Poonie from Pomona's 456. Everyone on the cottage kept speaking highly of Poonie and kept tellin' me I was gonna have to "get down" with him because he always wants to fight every Crip that moved into his cottage. "Oh well," I said.

When he showed up, I noticed how almost everybody ran over to him like they wanted to suck his dick or kiss his ass. It's one thing to acknowledge someone you respect, but to ride his dick? I ain't wit that.

Poonie made his way over to me and "hit me up." To everyone's amazement and disbelief, I banged on him. He didn't live in the dorm area like the rest of us. He and three more guys were housed in the honor rooms, which was reserved for those who were being good. But I think Poonie earned his room because he had been on the cottage for several years.

He told me we had to "get down" in his room as soon as it was safe to do so without us gettin' caught, but I refused to go into his room. Instead, I offered to fight him in any room other than his own, and he accepted my offer.

I sneaked into the vacant honor room and waited in a corner

for Poonie to show up. He stepped inside with his hulking frame and got into a boxer's stance. I wasted no time. I stepped into his range and let loose with multiple combinations. I think he hit me about four times, and I'm sure I connected with at least twenty good punches. I even busted his lip before somebody stuck their head inside the room and told us the staff was coming. We both made it back outta the room without gettin' caught. I walked out with my head held high and my chest stickin' out. I knew I won the fight and he knew it too. But he still came back up to me and said, "We gon' finish later on." "For sho,"' I shot back.

    The other kids on the cottage were acting funny and distant towards me. About an hour later I was told to report to the Y.C. station that's located in the center of the cottage. I was placed in handcuffs and escorted to a cottage called Inyo, which is The Hole. The staff who worked in Inyo wore shank-proof vests and were never around us without us being in handcuffs. Someone had told the staff that I was causing problems on the cottage, so I had to stay in The Hole pending investigation. I later found out it was another Crip who had told on me.

    While in Inyo I didn't have any contact with the free-world. I couldn't even use the phone to call my momma. I felt likes I was in a jail underground. My thin ass mattress was placed on a metal framed plywood bed, and the entire frame was connected to the cell next door to mines. If the kid in the next cell moved in his bed I could feel it from my bed.

    One day, I cussed out the staff and wouldn't stop yellin'. So, the staff put on their riot-gear and rushed into my cell. They stretched me out face-down on the wooden bed with my feet shackled and my hands cuffed behind my back. There was a hole at the head of the wooden bed where they pulled chains through and connected them to the cuffs behind my back. They then pulled the chains that were connected to the cuffs and my hands were pulled damn near to my head. "Momma!" I yelled at the top of my lungs. It hurt so bad I couldn't even cry. I stopped hollerin' and laid still. It didn't hurt anymore. Then all of a sudden some lil nigga in the cell next door started jumpin' up and down on his bed. With our beds being connected through the wall, every bounce caused my bed to knock the wind outta me. I started yellin' and screamin' again until the staff came to get me off of my bed. I could hear the lil mutha'fucka next door laughing his ass off. I made a mental note to fuck his lil ass up whenever I got a chance. I got outta Inyo after nearly a month and was placed on a cottage named, Del Norte.

Same shit, different cottage. I whooped on a few different people over the next ten months and didn't get caught. I went to Board again for my Annual and for Parole Consideration. I was led into the Board Room by staff and sat in a chair facing the three panel Board Members. After the formalities of an introduction, the female Board member asked me if I knew why I was there. I said, "Yeah, I'm here to get paroled." She cleared her throat and calmly said, "Let me tell you right now that you aren't leavin' here today or anytime soon." With that said, my hopes were dashed and I sank into my chair as if I deflated. The rest of the hearing was one big blur. I stormed outta there like a bat outta hell. I couldn't hold the big crocodile tears in. "*Bloop! Bloop!*" They came fallin' outta my eyes like raindrops. My feelings were hurt. I had been being good and being nice. I was suppose to get out today...

My counselor let me hang-out at the gym until I was all cried out, and I lifted weights until I was exhausted. Thirty days later, I got paroled.

CHAPTER 6

I rode the Amtrak train home because the Greyhound bus was on strike. I boarded the train in Stockton, California with a white kid and two Mexican kids who also got released the same day that I did. The train ride was cool. There was even a bar on the train where I bought a beer. One beer was really expensive compared to the store prices, but my system was so clean that it only took one beer to get me drunk. I was still tipsy when the train pulled into the Amtrak station in Bakersfield, and my parole officer, Ms. Kitch was the only one waiting at the train station. Ms. Kitch had known me for years because she was my probation officer a few months before Ms. Jackson was. Now Ms. Kitch worked for the state parole and I ended up on her caseload.

I was driven to juvenile hall by Ms. Kitch, and was housed there for almost two weeks. One day while in juvenile hall I was called for a visit. But, when I got to the visiting area there was no one there. I sat there for a few minutes wondering if momma was gonna show up or not. A few minutes later, two black men came into the visiting room and sat at the table with me. The two men introduced themselves as Ken and Lewis. Ken appeared to be the oldest of the two. He was in his mid-thirties, while Lewis appeared to be in his mid-twenties. I thought they were some type of detectives until they asked me if I wanted to get outta juvie. I said, "Hell yeah!" before they could even go into their sales pitch. They said that I could go live with them until I got myself together and was stable enough to live on my own. They both looked like they were "havin' money", eating good, and they smelled good too. Plus, I decided that if these two dudes had enough "pull" to get me outta juvie, they were worth goin' home to. Besides that, any place was better than juvie.

Five days after their visit, they came to pick me up as promised. Lewis had more of a casual look, while Ken loved to wear sweats and athletic gear. They picked me up in Ken's Mercedes Benz and drove to Stancliff Court. The house sat in a cul-de-sac. It was a four bedroom, two bathroom, single story, two-car garage home, with three trees, a fireplace, and a large, green grass field that sat over the backyard's fence. I didn't have any idea Ken and Lewis were taking me to a Group Home for boys until I got there and met a stuttering white boy named Robert.

"Wha-wha-wha-wha-what's yo' name?" he stuttered.
"I'm Eric," I exclaimed. "Wha-wha-what's yo' name?" I asked teasingly trying to mimic his speech.
He smiled and said, "It it it it's Robert!"

We shook hands and then he offered me a smoke. We walked through the kitchen to the back patio where we smoked two Marlboro cigarettes a piece. My head was spinning.

I later met Rochelle and Pat (Ken's wife). They were really nice people and they treated me and Robert like we were really part of their family. Pat's brother, Mike, worked the graveyard shift and he slept really hard. He snored like a big ole' bear too. I would fix my bed to look like I was asleep in it, then climb through my bedroom window and go hang out with my homies for a few hours before going to visit my girlfriend named Arika.

Arika lived kinda far away from the Group Home, but I'd still walk all the way over to her house late at night and she'd sneak me into her bedroom. Arika was a great basketball player and I loved her laugh. Back then I would've swore she'd end up being my wife because I was madly in love with her. She had short hair, when long hair was more popular, and she was athletic. Most guys didn't give her a second look, but to me, she was "fine". Not only that, but she was funny, smart, and crazy about me. She was my girl.

Arika told me that I was her first love, and claimed that I took her virginity. However, she was seeing another kid named Albert at the same time, and he claims that she told him he was her "first". I never did find out the truth. All I know is all summer long I was sneaking up to her bedroom "gettin' mines."

Ken enrolled me at South High School because that's the school district the Group Home was located in. I really didn't want to attend South High, but I ended up having a good time there.

It was my junior year. Everyone would hang out on the wall in front of the school "cappin'" and "baggin'" on each other. I broke up with Arika once I found out about Albert and started dating a pretty, black, cheerleader named Shelly. She was a sophomore and her parents were deep into church. She lived across the street from the school and was very popular, but she wasn't givin' up no pooh-nanny. So, I broke up with her and started seeing anot cheerleader/basketball player who was a freshman. Her name was Audrey, she was a fine, Filipino & Black, smart, sweet girl with long black hair. I was in love with her too. I took her virginity one day after school when we met at Greenfield Junior High. We held hands, kissed, and talked for awhile. I had already been pressuring her everyday to "do it" with me, and today she finally agreed to "do it". We found a spot in the hallway, and I laid my jacket down for her to lay on. She had on gym shorts so I got on top of her and pulled her shorts to the side.

"Hold on!" she said as she pulled out a hairbrush and clenched it between her teeth.

We "did it" and I walked her halfway back home then ran back to the Group Home. I was only suppose to be on a two hour pass. I hid the fact that I was living in a Group Home from all the kids at school. It wasn't any of their business as far as I was concerned.

It started getting hard to keep the Group Home a secret because we now had a total of six of us living at the Group Home. Plus, we traveled in a big ass Brady Bunch station wagon with the wood grained doors. I'd beg whoever drove us to school to let us out before we got in front of the school. They hired more black people to work at the Group Home too. There was Joanie, Avis, Milton, and John. And they were all hella cool. They would take us bowling, to the arcade, bumper cars, batting range, and to swim at Ken and Pat's home. They even took us shopping.

I played junior varsity football, but I wasn't a "starter". Our team didn't do well either because we were a relatively small team. I also played on the varsity basketball team and wasn't a "starter" either. I was the sixth-man. That really sucked. Our basketball coach, Mr. Washington, would fuss at me for talking while he's talking, or for being late to practice. I didn't take any sports stuff serious because I just didn't have a passion for them. I only participated in them at the time because it gave me an excuse to be away from the Group Home.

South High had a lot of the Country Boy Crips enrolled there, and a lot of them would come to all of the home games. This one kid named Loco Weed Lee would always sit in the bleachers at my basketball games and heckle me. He'd be clownin' and havin' the whole gym laughing. I'd be sittin' on the bench the entire game. With two minutes or less to play and our team down by twenty points, Loco Weed Lee would yell, "Hey coach! Put Eric Nichols in! Put his sorry ass in!" Even our coach would have to do everything he could to keep from laughing at me. I'd fight Loco Weed Lee after the game and Big Skeet would break us up. Hell, me and Loco Weed Lee ended up becoming good friends. That's what usually happened when two guys fought each other back in those days.

I helped my girlfriend Audrey campaign for her class presidential election and she won. Audrey was pretty, smart, and had a great personality. The seniors would see me and Audrey walking hand-in-hand down the school hallways and tease us about how cute of a couple we were. We would write "Eric loves Audrey" and "Audrey loves Eric" all over our Pee Chee folders and our book covers. One of Audrey's close friends was this Mexican girl named Erica. She was beautiful and a cheerleader too. She'd always flirt and be winking at me and shit. I would call her on the phone and ask her for advice regarding me and Audrey's relationship, and she'd always seem to have the right answers.

One evening me and Erica decided to meet at the large, green, grass field behind the Group Home. She brought two blankets and we got between them and fucked like rabbits. I walked her home from school the very next day and we fucked on top of a trampoline in her backyard. She ended up telling Audrey about everything, which broke Audrey's heart and eventually led to me and Audrey's break-up.

One of my basketball and football teammates named Ruben had a white girlfriend who looked similar to the blond Russian lady in the movie Rocky. Ruben was always too busy with sports to give her the attention she needed. I started counseling her and she would confide in me regularly. One day while at school, Ruben pissed her off. It was right after fifth period class. I caught her in the hallway looking frustrated, so I smoothly approached her and put my arm around her waist.

"What's the matter sexy?" I whispered in her ear.
"Ruben doesn't wanna be with me," she explained.

I looked her straight in her eyes and told her that she was too pretty to be crying over any boy, and that if I had an opportunity like Ruben, I would never let her go. She gave me a big hug, wiped her tears, and held my hand like she wanted me to take the lead. I led her alright... Down the street to Planz park and onto a giant robot slide, where I laid my jacket down on the sandy floor of the robot's head, and I fucked Carissa like there was no tomorrow. My knees were hurting from the sand, and my white Levi 501's were filthy. I didn't take my pants off while I fucked her. I merely undid a few buttons on my pants and pulled my dick through. Now I had a pink stain near my crotch section. I guess I made her lil pink pussy bleed. I had to walk back to the school with my jacket wrapped around my waist, and I headed straight to the gym to take a shower. I threw the pants away and called it a day. Every time I saw Ruben after that I'd get horny because I'd start thinkin' about his girlfriend Carissa.

When I was sneaking outta the Group Home, I would do a lot more than fuck girls. I was out "puttin' in work" for my hood and had the benefit of using the Group Home as an alibi if anything went wrong. I was also sneaking out late night to perform my music in the clubs. I'd win every Rap contest I entered, so they just started giving me the prize money to perform. I'd Rap at the Randle's Club, Cowboy's Club, Dolly's, and at the Y-Dub (YWCA).

This local D.J. named Thomas would rent the Y-Dub and have a dance there. He'd call it "T's Army presents..." Another local D.J. (Phresh Kutz) ended up becoming my personal D.J. and Producer. I made a song called "8-0-5", and he did the production using Ice Cube's sample from NWA's hit song "Gangsta Gangsta." I had a local hit and I'd rock the crowd with "8-0-5".

CHAPTER 7

"Me, Audrey, and Tray, cold chillin' on The Road; A Smoker pulled up in his Bucket tryna sell us some gold."

    I got a new girlfriend in my life, her name was Alicia. She was half black and half white, with light freckles. She was smart, funny, athletic, and had already had experience with boyfriends before I came along. She lived in the hood with her momma named Cheryl, who was a cool ass white woman with the soul of a black woman. Alicia's lil sister Alana lived with them too. I called her Bookie. She was super fine and had a major crush on my homeboy Locc... and their cousin Cherylinda had an even bigger crush on my homeboy Kid-D.

    When I would sneak outta the Group Home and go kick it with the homies, we would go on The Road, to 6th street park, to Taco Bell on Brundage Lane, and to every house party. By now, a lot of Warlord Bloods had turned Westside Gangsta Crips.

    Me, Kid-D, and Tray-Dog would go around town "courtin' niggas on". We were getting' deep too. There was NuNu, BooBoo, Biggie, L-Mac, G-Dez, E-Love, Halfdead, Willie-D, Fats, Amp, Pet-A-Moe, A.T., A.D., Sherm Loc, T-Bone, Bubba, K.D., Appletop, Baby Wes, D-Baby, Sugar Bob, P-Loc, Tiger, S-Loc, Pookie Moco Chip, Len Dog, Pud, Scruff, Big"D", Thunder, Bump, Scarface Dre, Breen Eyes, Tommy Guns, Mike-G, Reeco, Rob, Tone, Perry, Lil E-Loc, B.K.Blu, E-Baby, and Westside C.T. (Canal Team and Carnation Tract). Niggas like Baby Joe, Doolittle,

Richie Rich, Greg, E-40, Rayford, and Troy. I'm an original C.T. (Canal Team) nigga myself. The Canal Team would always compete against the Carnation Tract niggas in different sports. We got the names because the Carnation dairy was located between Union Avenue and "V" street, and the canal ran along the alley on "T" street. Brundage Lane and 4th street made up the other boundaries that outlined the area we now know as the C.T.'s.

I'm the first nigga from my hood with a lil homie named after him. Two young homies (Brian and Eric) came to me one day and said, "We both wanna be Lil E-Loc". I had known them both and knew they were both tough lil niggas. I use to make them go home sometimes when they would stop by R.J.'s on Priscilla Lane. But, I could tell they were both ready for this Gangsta shit, so I told them to fight each other and the winner could be Lil E-Loc.

The one named Eric won the fight so I took him with me to go "put in work", and made his introduction to the hood as Lil E-Loc official. Brian named himself Bri-Loc, and would eventually change his handle to B.K. Blu.

I was gettin' picked up by Kid-D and Tray-Dog almost every night. We'd go up to The Road to hustle and have fun as usual. I'd divide my time with the homies and with my girlfriend, Alicia. She didn't like for me to be out hustlin', and she'd be worried sick every time I'd go hustle. Many nights I'd come home from The Road, creep through her side gate, tap on her bedroom window, and have her let me in through the backdoor. She'd hug me really tight like a mother would hold her child. Her tears would wet the shoulder and chest areas of my shirt or coat.

When I would empty my pockets that were full of money onto her bed, and tell her to get however much she wanted, she'd slap the money to the floor, start crying all over again, and tell me she didn't care about the money. She just wanted me to be there with her.

We'd make love too. She wouldn't let me fuck her hard, fast, or rough. She'd say, "Why can't you just hold me for awhile? It's not goin' anywhere." I'd lay there holding her with my hard dick stabbin' at her butt-cheek, with a frown on my face. I didn't want to hold her, I wanted some pussy and some sleep. But, she'd make me wait until she was good and ready. Even while we laid there in the "spooning" position, I couldn't lay still. I would be slowly humpin and stabbin' at her butt-cheeks. I think all that dry-humpin' made her horny too, because she would be extra wet by the time she'd let me mount her.

"Take your time. Don't sex me like I'm some piece of meat. Be gentle. Slow down." is what she'd always whisper to me during our love making. She taught me how to "Please" a woman in bed. She's the one who let me know that a woman wants more attention paid to her body before and after penetration. In fact, Alicia's the one who helped me perfect my pussy-eating skills. Once I perfected my skills she would never again let me put my dick in her unless I ate her pussy first. Sometimes she'd let me eat her pussy and then come at me with that "Just hold me" shit. Talk about being mad...

I started kickin' it with the homies, Locc and J.B. a lot because Locc was always coming by Alicia's to see her lil sister Alana, and J.B. was always with Lace. Locc was one of the smartest niggas in the hook. He was named after his dad, and his his lil sister Lois, was named after their momma. Lois was fine and a couple of years younger than me, but I didn't try to holla at her because of my respect for Locc.

Locc had enough weights to fill up a school's weight room, and we would drive iron from time to time. J.B. was cock-strong and could sing really good. He was originally from New Orleans and had the accent to prove it.

The three of us would rob people on The Road. I always owned a gun after I got my first one. But Locc had better ones. He stole a .357 Magnum from his dad one day. It came in it's own carrying case, along with three different barrels, three different gun-stocks, and a scope. I loved using that gun. Sometimes we'd put .38 bullets in it. Locc was "the brains", J.B. was "the muscle", and I was "the stick-up kid".

Tray-Dog was still "my nigga". I loved goin' over to his momma's house on the hill by Kern Medical Center and make homemade french fries. He pissed me off one night, so I decided I was gonna walk all the way from the hill to the Westside. He begged me to stay but I was a stubborn lil nigga back then. My feelings were hurt too, so I started walkin' down Flower street with tears coming down my face, and a long ass kitchen knife in my hand. Tray-Dog caught up to me about eight blocks away from his house and blocked my path. He kept on tellin' me he was sorry and was making funny faces to get me to laugh. I finally gave in, accepted his apology, and walked back to his momma's house with him. A few days later Tray-Dog got hit by a car in a Taco Bell parking lot. We use to go to Taco Bell after the high school basketball games, and the parking lot was like the hangout. We whooped the driver's ass for Tray-Dog. Not long after that, Tray Dog got shot and killed while in a dice game on the Eastside. He wasn't the intended target. He and a few more homies were gambling in an area that was controlled by O.G.'s who were already feuding with another older nigga. The shooters were hired to scare any unfamiliar people hangin' out in the area, but Tray-Dog just so happened to get hit. I couldn't believe it. And I wouldn't believe it until I saw it for myself.

I went to his wake at Rucker's Mortuary and saw my nigga layin' in his casket with a blue Georgetown Hoyas jacket and Levis 501's on. He looked peacefully asleep to me, but his cold, stiff hands assured me that he was in fact dead. I kissed him on his forehead and said, "Damn cuz I'm gon'miss you."

The next day I went to his funeral at Mt. Zion Missionary Baptist Church in my hood. The same church I was baptized in, and the one that most of my family are members of. My grandma Olivia was ushering that day and the church was packed. Most of the homies sat close to the front near Tray-Dog's family, but I sat in the rear with my locs on. I wanted to view the whole funeral and not be a part of it. I was hurting for Tray-Dog's momma, Pat, hurting for his brother Kid-D, and hurting for the pain I imagined my nigga Tray-Dog must have suffered when he was shot. I wiped my tears with my blue-rag and placed it inside the casket with Tray-Dog and the rest of the blue-rags. I then gave his momma Pat a brief hug and kiss, shook Kid-D's hand, and got back in line with the other mourners.

Outside the church I got in the car with Tray-Dog's cousin named Erik. We called him Cherry. He's pigeon-toed like me and a few years older than me. And a lot of our "ways" are similar. For years, different people would tell me that I remind them of Cherry.

The funeral procession led us to Union Cemetery on the Eastside. I said my final "goodbye" and watched them lower his casket into the ground. I didn't go straight back to the Group home after the funeral. Instead, I went to my momma's house on "T" street. She had moved back to the hood. I sat in the room reading and re-reading Tray dog's obituary until momma came in and told me that I should go around the corner and talk to Kid-D because he was takin' it hard.

Kid-D's grandma lived around the corner from momma, so I went around there and chopped it up with Kid-D. I could tell he had been crying because his eyes were red and still wet. But, he tried to hold back the tears while he was talkin' to me. He didn't know exactly who killed Tray-Dog, but he knew the circle of people who could possibly be responsible. He told me what he wanted to do in retaliation of Dog's death, and I told him that I'd help him take care of it.

My return to the Group Home was very depressing for me. I felt like everyone who was mourning was in need of my support and I couldn't support nobody from inside the Group Home. The staff at the Group Home tried to console me, but they couldn't relate to what I was truly going through. Neither of them had experienced a violent death of a close friend or family member. So, the offering of condolences didn't seem genuine to me, and only irritated me. I felt like they were afraid of me and was only pretending to care about Tray-Dog's death, so that I wouldn't unleash my rage on them. I needed somebody to tell me they could understand my anger and pain, and someone to remind me that I had every right to be angry. I needed someone to offer me a hug and let me know it was okay to cry. But, no one did.

I held my composure in the presence of everyone, which only seemed to cause me to become even more angry. I didn't have anyone to rightfully take my anger out on, so I thought of a way to get removed from the Group Home without having to lash out at anyone. I grabbed a rope from the garage, tied it to a thick branch on the tree located on the side of the Group Home, stood on a chair, tied the other end around my neck, and jumped off the chair. I hit the ground feet first. The tree was too flimsy. I then stood there and waited for someone...anyone...to come looking for me. As soon as I heard footsteps, I slumped to the ground. My weight made the noose close tighter around my neck, and I was now on my knees.

"Eric!" Pat called out. "Er-ic!" she called out again as she searched for me. "Oh my God!" she screamed as she came from the backyard around to the side of the house and spotted me.

I watched her through my glossy eyes as she raced towards me. I was actually beginning to pass out from lack of oxygen when she held my limp body up. I can't remember who else helped her remove the noose from around my neck, but she saved me. I don't even remember how I got to the hospital, but I ended up at Kern Medical Center's 3B mental ward. The 3B ward was a lot like being locked-up in jail because I couldn't leave. The main door leading to the ward was always locked.

They gave me a gown and foam slippers to wear, like the rest of the patients. There were men, women, boys, and girls of all ages. There was only about twenty of us total. I was able to order my food from a menu just like a regular hospital patient, and my room was just like a regular hospital room. I also had a roommate who was a Mexican guy with really bad body odor. He was crazy for reals. He would do and say weird stuff like tell me he was the owner of the Oakland Raiders football team and he could sign me to the team. He'd even go as far as gettin' on the public telephone and pretend he was talkin' to lawyers about me joining the team.

His make believe conversations were extensive. Sometimes he'd be on the phone for house negotiating back and forth. Another weird thing he'd do is pack all of his belongings like he was goin' home, give me a stuffed animal, tell me to protect and feed it, then he'd go ask the doctor or nurse for milk and crackers. After eating the crackers, he'd crawl back into his bed, put his ass in the air, lay his head on his pillow, and instantly start snoring like a bear. That's when I knew I was in the wrong place.

Ken and Pat came to visit me and brought me a pack of Marlboro cigarettes. I wanted to leave with them, but I had to stay for a 72 hr. evaluation.

I had a fight with an old black man during breakfast my second day there. We were sittin' at the table eating when I noticed he didn't have coffee or cereal on his tray. But I had coffee and wanted some more sugar. I asked him if I could have his sugar, but he ignored me. I asked a second time but he just sat there with this blank expression on his face. When I reached for the sugar he karate chopped my hand like he was Bruce Lee. I immediately jumped up and socked his lights out. His old ass grabbed me and held on tight so that I couldn't "serve him" like I wanted to. Three big men in white coats came and gaffled me up.

I remember this white lady who didn't look like she belonged in 3B either. But, when I payed closer attention to her I could tell she wasn't quite wrapped tight. She would stand directly in front of me, then she'd squat down like a baseball catcher, exposing her hairy pussy. I saw her fat, hairy, pussy five or six times in one day. I even thought about inviting her to my room. That is until I saw her "throw a nutty" during pill call.

When my 72 hrs. were up, I was happy to go back to the Group Home. I realized the stunt I had pulled with the rag around my neck had really shook-up Pat. I felt bad because she was a really good person who didn't deserve to be hurt or taken through anything like I'd put her through.

I got my head together and got focused. I took a job at McDonalds so that I could get away from the boys at the Group Home more often. Plus, I wanted some money in my pockets. I was a cook, janitor, and a cashier. But, I mainly worked the grill flippin' burgers. I stayed greasy, and smellin' like a Big Mac and fries. I thought about robbing the place but I never saw enough cash worth robbing them for.

I kept seeing too many different niggas from rival gangs come to the McDonalds I worked at so I quit the job. Besides, how could I work when I still hadn't "put in work" for my nigga Tray-Dog?

CHAPTER 8

Kid-D picked me up down the street from the Group Home. We went to our hood for a couple of hours and then we went to "handle our business". I had a double-barrel sawed-off shotgun, and Kid-D had a snub-nosed .38 Special.

We parked down the street from where Tray-Dog had gotten killed at, and I saw two niggas smoking cigarettes, laughing, and talking to each other. I was in the passenger seat and Kid-D was driving. The two niggas tossed their cigarette butts and went back inside the apartment that they were standing in front of. We waited for a couple of hours, but nobody entered or exited the apartment.

My daddy lived nearby so I had Kid-D drop me off. Before he drove away I told him I was gonna creep back over to where we saw the two niggas at a little later, and I did. I took the "Sawed-Off" with me, and as soon as I turned the corner I spotted one of the two niggas in the front yard again. I quickly crossed the street to his side of the street and walked quickly up the sidewalk. The long sleeved Trench Coat I had on hid the bulge of the Sawed-Off that I held up my sleeve. As I got about 100 yards from him, he noticed me. However, he could not recognize who I was. He just kept watching me as I got closer and closer to him. I walked towards him like I knew him and knew where I was goin'. When I got 20 yards from him he asked, "Who is that?" and squinted his eyes to focus in on me. I didn't say a word, I just kept walkin' towards him. When I got 10 yards away I let the Sawed-Off fall through my hands until the taped-up butt of the gun was in the palm of my hand. Then I quickly raised the double-barrel and pointed it at his face. His mouth opened wide, but no words came out. His eyes opened even wider than his mouth. I thought they were gonna pop outta his head. Whatever he was gonna say was silenced by the deafening sound of the two simultaneous blasts that barked from the Sawed-Off. "*Boom!*" The force of the blast lifted him off his feet and damn near flipped him over. When he hit the ground I stood over him, and got a good look at his bitch ass. His once black face, was now pink and white like hamburger meat.

    I jumped on his stomach, causing piss, shit to escape his body. As I turned to walk off, the front door to the apartment opened and some nigga peeked his head out. I aimed the Sawed-Off at his face, squeezed the triggers, and nothing happened. I had already fired the only two bullets the gun held. He ducked back inside, and I "broke wide".

    Back at my daddy's place, I put the gun in a trashcan in his backyard, then I walked down the street to my Grandma and Poppy's to use their phone. Kid-D wasn't at home when I called, so I called the homie CoCo to come pick me up. CoCo didn't know I'd just shot somebody, nor did he know that after I called him to come get me, I had retrieved the gun from the trashcan and it was now in the backpack that I was carrying.

    I had him take me to my momma's on "T" street so that I could drop off the gun. He waited in his car while parked in front of momma's house, as I went through the side gate to the backyard. I used a shovel to dig a shallow hole, then I wrapped the gun in an old sheet and buried it.

    "Damn nigga! It took you long enough!" CoCo said as I climbed back into the passenger seat of his car.

    We drove to Queen Sheeba and hung out with Halfdead, Bump, Thunder, Willie-D, and Mob. After awhile me and CoCo got in traffic again and drove through the hood to do a lil "Hood Patrolling". Finally, we ended up at 6th street park. The homies BooBoo, M&M, Vada, D-Mac, Kid-D, R.J., J.B., Locc, Sugar Bob, and a few more homies were all up there. Not long after me and

Coco arrived, a car full of Warlord Bloods came through bustin' caps at us. Me and Coco ran to his car and chased after them. We were on their tail but Coco stopped in the middle of the street, got out, popped his truck, and grabbed his chrome .32 revolver. We burned rubber outta there but we couldn't catch them fools.

    The next day the news stations gave a description of the suspect wanted for the shooting of the nigga I nicknamed "Hamburger Face". I still hadn't told anybody about that "get down".

CHAPTER 9

B.H.S. was having a Talent Show on their campus at the Harvey Auditorium. It was poppin too. The homies Vada and Yorell did the "Peter Piper" song by Run DMC...

"Now Peter Piper pick peppers and Run rock rhymes..."

After the show we got into it with some Mexican boys who were being disrespectful. The homie D-Mac socked one first, then chased another one towards me on the auditorium steps. I knocked him out cold and then "did it movin'" before the Narcs moved in on us.

The following week I went to a House Party on Sandra Drive. This girl named Shannon was havin' a House Party and everybody was there. It was so packed that it seemed more like a Block Party. Me, R.J., Amp, A.D., E-Money, Pete-a-Moe, Kid-D, J.B., Locc, and Sugar Bob were all the ones I can remember from the hood who were at this particular party. But I'm sure there were much more there. We never did get a chance to actually make it inside the house. When we got up to Shannon's door, she didn't open it all the way or allow anyone inside but when she cracked the front door some, I was able to see a light-skinned nigga standing behind her. Just as I saw the nigga, the homie Sugar Bob tried to push his way inside, but was stopped by the door as it closed in his face.

Sugar Bob got mad and grabbed a metal trashcan from the

curb and threw it at the front door. At the same time, a lil nigga named Scooter from Mid-City Crips kicked a blue nissan truck that was parked in Shannon's driveway.

The alarm to the truck went off and then...*Pop! Pop! Pop! Pop! Pop! Pop!* I heard gunshots. I also saw a flash coming from the roof of the house and from the gate on the side of the house. I broke-wide like a Track Star. I was running side by side with the homie A.D...

"I'm hit!" he announced.

We both kept on running until we reached a fence across the street.

"I'm hit!" A.D. said again just before we both jumped over the fence.
"Let me see cuz!" I said, not believing he was hit.

He pulled the back of his pants down just below and there was a small bullet-hole in his butt-cheek. My nigga A.D. had been shot in his ass. I laughed on the inside, but I held it in. I knew he was gonna be alright. We walked towards our cars and saw another crowd forming. The homie E-Money was arguing with some big nigga. I don't know where the nigga was from. I stepped through the crowd, walked up to the big nigga, and knocked him out in front of everybody. The crowd went wild and the homies stomped his ass out.

The next day we found out the niggas who shot A.D. in the ass had also shot Scooter in his foot when he had kicked the Nissan truck. The niggas who did the shooting were from Los Angeles and they were 48th street Hustlers. They ended up gettin' "put on the hood" but A.D. never did forgive them. Kay-B, Sheldon, Pooh, and Chewy made Bakersfield their home.

The homie Sugar Bob was havin' it his way during this time. He had two Nissan trucks with ski-racks on top and major sounds in them. Plus, he had a fat dope-sack. He took a lot of homies to Sacramento with him to "Hustle" but I didn't get to go. I started spending more time sellin' dope than I did gangbangin'. If I wasn't with my nigga Chucc from the Eastside, I was with Pete-a-Moe and E-Money.

Chucc had "Boss Game" and was like a Living Legend. He had hustle, a lot of women, could Break-Dance really good, kept a nice car, was a trendsetter, and was very likable. He didn't gangbang, but he represented the Eastside because he grew up on the Eastside.

Chucc lived on S. Williams street with his daddy Big Rob, his momma whom we called "Sister", his lil brother Willie, his older brother Rabu, and his sister Lavena. Chucc's older brother named Eric got killed before I started hangin' out with Chucc. I use to spend the night over Chucc's, pay Big Rob $5 for a plate or bowl of whatever meal he made, then get up early in the morning with Chucc to go sell rocks. We would drive to an alley where we would have thrown our dope the night before. Chucc usually put his dope in a potato chips bag or a small brown paper bag, then he'd ball it up and toss it in the alley. Sometimes he would only check a few bags before giving up his search for his dope. He'd chalk it up as a loss and just buy more rocks to sell.

Chucc could sell a whole ounce (rock for rock) in about thirty minutes. Chucc had skills. The girls were crazy about Chucc. I use to drop him off at different female's house, and then pick him up a few hours later. One day we were takin' his Baby's momma named Porky home and they got into an argument. She made Chucc pull over and let her get outta the car so she could walk home, and me and Chucc drove back to his house without her. But, once we got there, he told me to go pick her up by myself and make sure she got home safe. I took her home too.

Porky was living with her momma in my hood at the time. Around the same time, I started fuckin' with Chucc's cousin named Kendra. She was thick, wore a lot of jewelry, kept her hair and nails done, dressed hella "fly", and lived in the Los Angeles area. Kendra had a lil more "game" than the average female her age. But she fell in love with me too fast and was always stalking me and poppin' up at every place I happen to be. I "shook her" and a lot of my other female friends to focus on gettin' money.

I was spending most days and nights at R.J.'s and Amp's on Priscilla Ln. I was basically living there. Pete-a-Moe, E-Money, and D-Baby would hang-out with us too. D-Baby had a Mexican girlfriend who lived directly across the street from R.J.'s and Amp's. Her name was Sherry. She was kinda funny-built with big titties, hips, no ass, and medium size legs. I could tell she was gonna end up being a "big girl" later on in life. She was cute tho', and her voice and facial expressions were sexy. I started plottin' to get in her panties the very first time I met her.

D-Baby was at least fifty pounds heavier than I was, but I wasn't the least bit worried about having to fight him if he wanted to "go there". I just didn't want to be the reason he and Sherry split up. So, I "got at her" on the "down low" and let her know I was interested in her. It started with a wink and a smile. I'd do that, and hold her hand a lil longer than I was supposed to every time I greeted her with a handshake. The handshake, along with the wink and smile, would make her blush every time.

One day I caught her in her front yard all by herself. I walked over to her fence and made some small talk with her. I ended up tellin' her that I wanted to talk to her some more in private because I had something important to share with her. She agreed to let me come over later when it was dark outside and her family was asleep. I called her on the phone before I went over to her house and let her know I was on my way. She met me at the fence and I hopped over it like I had springs on my feet. She led me to her bedroom window and told me to wait there while she went inside her back door to let me in through her window.

Her bedroom had lots of posters on the walls and too many stuffed animals on her bed for me to count. She wore a long t-shirt that hung down to her knees. I asked her for a piece of gum because she was chewing on hers so hard it made me want some. While getting me a piece of gum off her dresser, she pressed play on her Tape Player and the soft music of Shirley Murdock gave me goosebumps... "As we lay, we forgot about tomorrow as we lay..."

Sherry pulled back her blankets and sheets while I stripped down to my Birthday Suit. Damn! Sherry looked good in that t-shirt. She had her long hair pinned-up, her makeup on, and smelled like sweet perfume. Even her lazy-eye became sexy. We french kissed, leaving sticky, sweet, trails on each others neck and face. I didn't realize how big her titties were until she laid on her back and they fell on the sides of her body. They were like melons with baby bottle nipples on them. I wasn't a "Titty Man" but her titties made my mouth water. I licked, lapped, and sucked her titties like I was trying to get milk out of them.

Her pussy hairs were straight and long. I wanted to eat her pussy too, but I couldn't bring myself to do it, knowing that D-Baby probably fucked her that day or night before. Instead, I got between her legs and pushed my dick-head pass her long pussy hairs and into her wet, hot, young pussy. "Aye Papi," she cried in Spanish as I entered her.

I fucked her nonstop in every position for nearly an hour. I nutted in her too. She wanted me to lay there beside her and do some pillow talkin', but I wasn't trying to do all that. I had already got what I came for... Pussy! And besides, I didn't want D-Baby to catch us in the act. I gave her a kiss and a promise to return the following day.

I showed up at her fence the very next day as promised, but I didn't jump the fence. I told her we couldn't "do it" anymore because I didn't want to come between her and D-Baby. I could see the disappointment in her eyes and heard it in her voice. But, she said she understood, then turned and walked away.

It was Friday, so I went back across the street and inside R.J.'s and Amp's so that I could iron my clothes and get ready for the high school basketball game. The kitchen sink was full of dishes and there was a mildew smell. The plumbing was fucked up.

Pete-a-Moe, E-Money, and Vada were there too. Vada and R.J. were gonna go to the game together. They hung out a lot because R.J. was dating Vada's older sister Tonya. R.J. had a lot of girlfriends back then. Amp only had one. Her name was Teresa. She was a young, pretty, virgin, with long hair who came from a good family who lived in a big house. I use to walk with Amp over to her house so they could "do their thang". They both were madly in love with each other and I was happy for them.

Since R.J. and Amp's kitchen sink was always messed up, we mainly ate fast foods and cold cereal. Pete-a-Moe always had a damn toothache. We baked cookies and ate cereal while taking turns ironing our clothes. The can of starch was so big I had to hold it with two hands to use it. I never washed my Levi 501's. I just starched and creased them real good. The smell of dirty pants would hit my nostrils every time the steam from the iron heated my pants. The Levi 501's would be shiny lookin'. Pete-a-Moe's grandma, Ms. Bernice would sew in our creases for us too. She always hooked us up.

The B.H.S. vs. Fresno Edison basketball game was played at Bakersfield's Junior College (B.C.). These high school teams were rivals, and sometimes the rivalry led to violence. On this particular night there was a situation. Some halfbreed nigga named Chico from Fresno was the one who started the shit. I ended up chasing him through B.C.'s parking lot, over the News vehicle, and onto his school's bus. That nigga Chico had "wheels!"

R.J. and Amp's older brother Dirk moved in with their dad Clarence. Dirk was once the top high school Triple Jumper in the nation. He had good business sense too. He went to work for his grandfather, John Henry, who owned a Plastering company. Me, R.J., Amp, Pete-a-Moe, E-Money, and my brother Derrick had all tried working in the Watermelon fields "pitching melons". It was fun and hard work. But, working for the Johnson's Plastering company was the hardest job of my life. I would set up the scaffolds, mix the mud, and keep the mid-boards full of mud for the Plasterers. I got good at it too. I had a little bit of experience before working for The Johnson's because my Poppy's brother Wille Sr. (Uncle Wolf) owned a Plastering company and would let me work for him sometimes. I didn't have my own car yet, and I was tired of gettin' "Rent-a-Buckets" from Smokers and having to give them back.

I started selling dope for a nigga named Droopy. He was a tall, big lip nigga with major hustle. He was showing me "much love" until he went to jail for a dope case. That's around the time

Dirk decided he could use some fast money. Me, Pete-a-Moe, Amp, E-Money, and D-Baby all met with Dirk at the house on Priscilla Lane. Dirk had weed and rocks for us to sell. He weighed everything out with his triple beam scale and his digital scale. We bagged up our "work" and made our way to Patriot's park. It was light weight "poppin'" up there. When it got dark we would go over to The Chester Pines apartments with Kid-D and "serve". That is, until we got Raided.

    The police came from every where while we were in an upstairs apartment. Kid-D saw them first and yelled out, "Rollers!" which meant the police were in the area. We all scrambled, running into each other, and panicking. E-Money was on the toilet takin' a shit. He had diarrhea and the toilet was stopped up. He tossed hit rocks into the shitty toilet and ran for the bedroom window. Kid-D's girlfriend named Melissa, "threw-up" on top of the shit and rocks inside the toilet. I guess her nerves were bad.

    Kid-D was already gone, so I followed E-Money through the bedroom window and down a fire escape. We "got in the wind", jumped over a brick wall, ran through a Trailer Park, and went our separate ways. We could hear police sirens in the distance, so we laid low and returned to the Chester Pines apartments when it was safe. I can't remember if E-Money ever got his rocks back out of that nasty ass toilet, but we didn't go to jail that night.

The Road was always a place to make some money, so I started back going up there to "serve" regularly. My childhood friend Tip (Boss) saw me with a lot of money one day as I was passing through The Projects. I counted out a lil over $600.

    "Who's money is that?" Tip asked.
    "Mines," I replied.
    "Yeah right," he said sarcastically. "Where did you get all that money from?" he asked.
    "I got it from sellin' rocks," I told him.
    Tip then said, "You lying! If it's yo' money then let me have

some."

I peeled off two $20 bills and he was in awe. The next day I took Tip up to The Road with me. We were on our bikes on Ralston Street when this older kid named Headsacock walked up to Tip and grabbed his handlebars.

"Gimme this bike!" Headsacock demanded as he shook the handlebars.

"You better let my bike go!" Tip said, straddling his bike as he shook and snatched it outta Headsacock's grip.

Tip got off the bike, laid it on the ground, and then laid Headsacock down with a vicious "two-piece" to Headsacock's mouth. "*Cra-crack!*" Just that fast, Headsacock was on his back and had lost his tooth and his reputation as a Bully. Tip started servin' rocks everyday after that. I remember one day me, E-Money, Pete-a-Moe, and Amp were all on The Road servin' when Amp got into it with a Smoker that he was servin'. The Smoker got crazy and tried to attack Amp. When Amp tried to get away he lost one of his shoes and damn near got hit by the Smoker. It was funny as hell to watch the whole scenario unfold. I was bustin' up laughing so hard that I had tears in my eyes. Hell, I'm laughing now as I write this book.

Pete-a-Moe's momma named Che-Che had moved in the hood on "P" street. Me and Pete-a-Moe bonded because we always ended up attending the same schools together. But our families knew each other too. I love him like I love R.J. and Amp. Pete-a-Moe always thought I was hilariously funny, and crazy enough to do anything. And he was right. He was in my Metal Shop class back in the days when I was spinnin' on my back and hit my head on a workshop bench. "Ouch!" That shit hurt too. Pete-a-Moe laughed himself to tears while pointing at me on the floor in pain.

Pete-a-Moe's momma only had two sons just like my momma. And Pete-a-Moe was the oldest son just like me. His lil brother Allen was 4 years younger than us. Pete-a-Moe also had a lil sister named Sabrina and another lil brother we called Turtle. But they were his daddy's kids by two other women. Sabrina use to be one of my lil girlfriends too. I was messin' with her and her friend Roshawn. I even "did it" to both of them in the same week. I would go to Sabrina's while her momma was at work. We "did it" a couple of times, but I really didn't enjoy it because I was always worried about her momma coming home and catching us. I "did it" to Roshawn in my momma's garage, on a fold out bed. It was hella dusty in that garage and spider webs and junk was everywhere. While I was "doin' it" to her, my brother Derrick and our friend Tommy peeked in on us. They were suppose to watch us "do it" without Roshawn finding out. But Tommy said, "Uuuuuuuhh! She got shampoo in her pussy!"

  The friction from my dick and Roshawn's pussy, along with whatever type of powder she had on, made a foamy lookin' substance appear on my dick and on her pussy. Tommy started bustin' up laughing like he was watching cartoons. I pumped a few more times, busted a nut, and used Tommy's peeking as my excuse to get up and away from her.

I was still at the Group Home, but was able to get passes and spend weekends and holidays with my family. The Group Home staff even allowed my daddy's oldest son, Darren, to pick me up from the Group Home. One day my brother Darren, his high school Sweetheart named Cheryl, and another girl we called Red came to pick me up. They were droppin' me off at my momma's on "T" street, but momma wasn't home. I got outta the car, went around the back of the house, climbed through the window and came through the front door. When Darren asked me was I okay and if there was anything else he could do for me. I said, "Yeah, I want her," as I pointed at Red, who was scrambling outta the back seat of the car before my brother could reply.

  I fucked the hell outta Red in my momma's bed. It was bomb too. During this time in my life I had a few "square" school girls and a few "hoodrats" on my team. One night I was chillin' on The Road when this older girl named Kim called me over to her car. She was nice lookin' too. I had went to Emerson Jr. High with her younger sister LaShon, who was just as pretty and a lot thicker than Kim. Kim was at least 6 years older than me. At the time, other than Smoker bitches, Kim was the oldest female I'd hooked up with. She treated me like a man. When I would be shootin' dice, she would be right behind me stuffin' her pockets with the money I handed her. She would call me "daddy" and everything about her was "all woman".

The first time we "did it" she took me to a motel room. When she got undressed she had on bright red matching lace panties and bra. She looked delicious with the red lace contrasting off of her smooth caramel skin. I had already been taught how to eat pussy by Alicia, but Kim taught me everything else. We did it in the 69 position and took a bath together. She was fun. We went back on The Road so I could make some more money. She let me be "me", and she had my back.

I had my eyes on other females though. Especially this black and Mexican girl named Dooda. She was hella fine to me. Her hair and nails were always done. She always wore top of the line clothes and lots of jewelry. Her nose ring was sexy too. She was from Watts. Her brothers were Nukie and Pete from Spoonie Gee Crips. The same Pete who went to Emerson Jr. High with me. I use to always tell Pete to hook me up with his sister, but he would just brush me off or say, "Yeah okay." But he never got at her for me.

One time I was standing next to Pete on The Road when Dooda walked by. I stopped her and insisted that Pete let her know I was "cool". But I was too drunk and too young to get my point across. She was a year older than me, and young girls didn't want younger niggas as their "man". They wanted grown men. Plus, Dooda already had two kids by two older niggas who were havin' money. So, I didn't stand a chance.

CHAPTER 10

The Road was full of excitement. If Cripple-Leg Dre wasn't knockin' somebody out behind his girlfriend, then somebody was payin' a Smoker to do a ridiculous stunt for some rocks.

Smokers like Geechie Dan would get paid to dance, Payton would get paid to run head first into a brick wall, and Eddie would get paid to "cap" or "bag" on somebody until they ran off in embarrassment.

From the time I'd gone to C.Y.A. up until now, a few good niggas from different hoods had loss their lives. Like Sammy Cannon, Ronald Quick, Clayton Jackson, David Edwards, Eddie LaFore, and Derrick Jordan, just to name a few.

The Road was stomping grounds for everybody from everywhere. I had gotten real cool with Loco Weed Lee from C.B.C., the same nigga I fought against all the time at South High. He was wild and a "Rider" from his hood. I saw him losing a lot of money in a dice game one night, and he asked to borrow some money from me. I loaned it to him, and he won his money back, plus a lot more. Of course he "broke me off" proper. A couple of days later he asked to borrow some dope so he could make some money. I gave him some rocks, but he came back an hour later broke again. I gave him some more rocks and watched him walk down the street to some apartments. The apartments were new, and were built on the old lot where an old motel used to be. The old motel was called The Lakeview Inn. And when it was torn down there were a lot of skeletal bones belonging to humans found there.

I watched the apartment that Loco Weed Lee went in and I waited for nearly an hour. When I finally knocked on the apartment's door, my homie Baby Joe, and a big titty female answered the door.

"Is Lee here?" I asked.
"Naw he aint over here," they both said in unison, before quickly closing the door in my face.

I knocked again but they didn't answer nor open it, so I walked down the street to get Lee's Big Homie, Big Skeet. I told Big Skeet what had transpired and we walked back down the street to the apartments. This time Big Skeet knocked on the door and the same people answered with the same story. Me and Big Skeet turned to walk away, but we only made it to the curb before Loco Weed Lee came outta the apartment himself.

Loco Weed Lee and Big Skeet exchanged words like a big brother and lil brother. Then Loco Weed Lee started crying and saying, "I know you mad at me! But I can't help it! I'm sprung! Yeah I been gettin' high! Fuck it!"

He went on and on with tears and snot running down his face. Big Skeet cried with him and then hugged him. Shit, my eyes got all misty and shit from watching it all unfold. I told Loco Weed Lee that he didn't have to pay me back for the dope, and told him not to trip. But, he insisted that he'd pay me back anyways. A few weeks later, Loco Weed Lee got gunned down on The Road for sittin' on someone's car and then arguing with the car's owner.

One day this nigga name E.T. sold Scooter some Roast (fake dope). I'm talkin' about the same Scooter who got shot in the foot when A.D. got shot in the ass. Anyways... Scooter was sellin' the Roast not knowin' it was Roast, until a few Smokers came back demanding to get their money back. They even showed Scooter how the Roast had left black stuff on their crack pipes. So, Scooter gave them their money back. When E.T. showed up on The Road, Scooter got at him about the Roast and demanded his money back. But E.T. was a slim, 6'3" nigga in his early 20's, and he towered over the 4ft., 15 year old nigga named Scooter. E.T. laughed about it and even roared up on Scooter when Scooter was explaining how serious he was about his money.

    E.T. didn't pay up, and he didn't take Scooter seriously. Scooter popped up on The Road with a gun and shot E.T. a countless number of times. I watched E.T. run across the street towards Louie's Bail Bonds and sit between two telephone booths holding his stomach, as he rocked back and forth and grimaced in pain.

    Scooter, my lil brother Derrick, and Dirty Red were all in a car together when they got pulled over by the police in my hood near 6th street. Scooter and Dirty Red got sent to C.Y.A. Weeks later, I got arrested for the shooting of Hamburger Face, for Grand Theft Auto, and for possession of cocaine. I ended up beating the shooting beef because the victim was found with a fully loaded gun on him. But, I plead to the use of a firearm and shooting into an inhabited dwelling, and possession of cocaine. I got a parole Violation and got sent back to C.Y.A.

Doin' time in C.Y.A. as a parole violator was hella fun. I went to NRCC, just like the first time. But, I got sent to Karl Holton from there. I met the Rapper named C-Bo up in Karl Holton too. We called him Cowboy. A lot of niggas who lived in Northern California had the "Bo" on their nicknames. Like, Curty-Bo, Arty-Bo, and shit like that. I only had two fights at Karl Holton, but I did get to go to their "hole" on Yuba Hall.

    I was good when it came to academics, so I got sent to O.H. Close to work as as a Teacher's Aid. I was housed on Fresno Hall and worked in the library. Scooter, Dirty Red, Cadillac Dame, F-Boy, and Stan were the only niggas from Bakersfield up there with me. But we "held our own". I had a fight with a nigga named Frank from Fresno 107 Hoover because I accidentally stepped on a newspaper (The Fresno Bee). He claimed that by me steppin' on the newspaper, I was disrespecting the city of Fresno. There wasn't enough room in the tiny cell, but I did my thang.

After a couple of months I transferred to Preston, so that I could go to fire camp. But I broke a Mexican's nose on Pondarosa and got sent to Tamarack. After spending two months on The Rack, I got transferred to DeWitt Nelson. It was an institution for 13 to 24 year olds. Since I had a history of drug use, I was housed on Modoc in the drug program. I worked out with the weights regularly, got a few tattoos, and got into fights all the time.

I had a lil "game" when it came to bitches. But not as much as this nigga named Ronnie Bean from Sacramento's Oak Park Bloods, nor did I have as much as Young Stoney up outta Oakland's 6-9 Vill. I watched both of them get money, gifts, phone calls, and lots of attention from female counselors. My job in the main laundry netted me an opportunity to exercise my "game". There were six of us assigned to work in the main laundry's warehouse styled building, along with the three Free Staff who were our supervisors. They were all women. One black one with big eyes named Michelle was in her late-twenties. And the two Mexican ladies were in their early forties.

The place was big enough to get lost in. I would send letters in the laundry carts to the women in the women's prison (C.I.W.), which was only down the street. The women prisoners washed clothes for all the institutions in the area, including the three C.Y.A. institutions. And we folded clothes for all the institutions. The female prisoners would send me packs of cigarettes, dirty panties, pictures, and love letters. Sometimes two of us would get to work overtime, and this particular time I stayed back to work overtime, and I chose to work next to Michelle. She didn't have a cool shape or anything. In fact, she was sloppy-built, with Garfield eyes, and a frizzy Jheri Curl. But, I wanted some pussy really bad, and decided Michelle was worth fuckin'.

We were folding up sheets with the other guy who stayed back with me, along with the two Mexican ladies. I had to be smooth enough to tell Michelle what I wanted to do, without the others knowing. So, I made eye-contact with Michelle and mouthed the words, "when I go to the restroom, you go to the restroom". Her big ass eyes damn near fell outta her head. She got all nervous and shit, and was blushing like she had already gotten fucked by me. Michelle kept her head down, tryin' not to lose her composure. But, as soon as she looked up at me again, I looked at her and then looked at the restroom door.

I finally made my way to the restroom, complaining that my stomach was upset. I said that so that no one would suspect anything if I happen to be gone too long. I took a piss as soon as I got in the restroom, then I stood with my dick in my hand. Two minutes later Michelle brought her clumsy ass in there. I immediately reached for her belt buckle and helped her unfasten her pants. She pulled her pants down to her knees, so I turned her around and bent her over the sink. I aimed for her hairy hole and shoved my throbbing dick deep into her. I damn near knocked her down as I gripped her hips and slammed into her like I was mad. She even bumped her head on the wall as she held her breath and took all of my young hard dick. I skeeted in her and continued pumping until every drop had escaped me and entered into her. I moved her away from the sink, placed my swollen dick in it, and washed it off.

I left her in the restroom while she fastened her pants back up. I was glad we had to keep it a secret because I felt guilty for fuckin' her. I promised to visit her when I got out, and two months later I did call her from the Amtrak train station in Stockton. But, she didn't make it to the station before my train left, so we didn't get to hook up.

CHAPTER 11

My train arrived in Bakersfield on a hot summer day. This time my momma and Aunt Alma were in the crowd waiting for me. I wore all black, and was happy as hell to see them both.

I had turned 18 years old while in C.Y.A. and was now a "man". My momma still lived on "T" Street in my hood. The next door neighbor, JoAnn and her kids (Lil Jerry, Terry, Larry, Shawndia, and Tameka) were all happy to see me. I was happy to see them too. They had moved next door from Watts. I instantly loved them and felt like they were my family. JoAnn's kids ranged in age from 4 years old to 12 years old. Me and my brother Derrick affectionately called JoAnn our Aunt Jo. I still call her that to this day. We had an open-door policy with our homes. We all would come and go from each other's home like they were one in the same.

Aunt Jo's niece's, Sharmaine and Selena lived with her too. They were both a few years older than me, and they were hella cool. My first day home from C.Y.A. Was a day that I'll never forget. When I made it to the house, my brother Derrick was in the shower. I walked around the living room, kitchen, and bedroom and was amazed at how small everything seemed to have gotten. I saw Derrick had laid out his outfit for the day, along with his watch, jewelry, and wad of money. I didn't touch nothin'.

I barged into the bathroom and said, "Derrick! What's up nigga?" He pulled the shower curtains back just enough so he could see who I was, and I leaned into the shower to hug him. I missed my brother. He squeezed me like he missed me too. After he got dressed, he gave me some money and told me he was gonna take me shopping. We jumped in his Bel Air and went to the Valley Plaza Mall. He bought me a lot of stuff and he was picking my clothes out for me and letting me know the new styles. He also "put me up on" all the drama that had been goin' on and told me to call him by the name D-Mac from now on. I was trippin' off how much my lil brother had matured since I'd been gone. He had even been arrested and served time at Camp Erwin Owens. I was lightweight disappointed because I didn't want him to be classified nor recognized as being from a gang. But, it was too late. He was representin' Mid City Crips.

Derrick saw a skinny nigga passing by us in the mall who had spoke to me and kept walking.

"That's the nigga who pulled a gun on us!" Derrick said.
"What!?" I asked, lookin' in every direction.
"The nigga who just spoke to you," he answered.
"Come on!" I said as we quickly headed in the direction that the nigga was going.

We didn't catch up with him in the mall. But that same weekend we caught up with the nigga on The Road. It was jammed pack up there this night, and everything was goin' as usual, until I saw my brother chasing after some nigga. I joined the chase and discovered it was the same nigga from the mall. He ran down the street, back up the same street, through a yard, over some bushes, onto a porch, and banged on the windows and doors while hollerin' out, "Grandma!" I caught him with a few cool punches, but he was too frightened to be hurt by them. He moved like a gazelle mixed with rabbit. He dived off the porch, over the rose bushes, got back on his feet and sprinted back down the street. I gave chase and tackled his ass in the middle of the street.

He balled-up in the fetal position while me and Derrick "put hands on him". This triggered more fights this night and even led to some niggas to load their weapons. I personally noticed one reputable nigga from another hood loading his gun and saying, "Niggas is gon' quit jumpin' on my homies." I immediately ran to my homeboy J.B.'s car. He had a Gremlin with exhaust fumes leakin' on the inside of it. That shit use to have my eyes burnin', and I had to ride with my head hangin' outta the window. I had rode up to The Road with J.B. and Locc, and had left my .38 in the car.

I got my gun and posted-up in "the cut" so that I could wait to catch that reputable nigga who was talkin' that shit. I spotted him across the street talkin' to my homeboy Kid-D, who was just as big and who had a reputation just as big as the nigga I was plottin' on. I had already made up my mind to shoot this nigga as soon as he got in my range. He took too long to move, so I slowly started walkin' in his direction. I had my "thumper" out at my side in plain view. But, before I could reach the curb to cross the street where the nigga was, another older nigga stopped me.

"E-Loc, don't do that cuz! Come here let me holla at you," he said.

It was Big Day-Day from Mid City Crips who pulled me to the side. He saved me from catching a murder beef too because I was damn sho' gon' "Dome" that nigga who was across the street talkin' to my homie Kid-D. I didn't shoot nobody that night tho'. Instead, I got Shermed-out and dropped off at the house.

The next day I did a lil "Hood Patrolling" and spotted some Warlord Bloods living across the street from my momma's house. I couldn't believe it because Big-D and Big Al (two brothers from Los Angeles who were Crips) were living on the same street. They were two monster swole niggas with long perms and a lot of bitches on their team. I fucked with Big Al the most. He kept me full of tha' Old English 800, showed me how to charge bitches, and laced my boots when it came to Crippin'. So, I tripped out when I saw there was some Bloods living on my street.

I saw Antwon, Joker, and that nigga Squirt. They had on red belts, hats, and shoe laces. They even had red handkerchiefs hangin' outta their back pockets. I didn't like that at all. I lived on the block now. This was "my block".

I stood on momma's front porch and yelled out, "What's up Cuz!? What that "C" like!?"

I had dug up my old double barrel Sawed Off and my .22. I didn't care about the guns being "dirty" (used in prior crimes), because I planned on getting' em' even "dirtier". You dig? I almost caught Joker slippin' later that day, but my rusty-ass gun jammed on me.

The following day, Kid-D took me to patrol the hood, and we drove to where the Warlord Bloods hung out near 10th and 11th Street. Kid-D wanted to show me what the Bounty Hunter Blood nigga named Boss looked like. Boss' name had been "ringin'" while I was in C.Y.A.

We pulled up in front of some apartments where there were four Bloods standing next to three cars. I sat in the passenger seat while Kid-D did the driving. There was a new toy out called "Knockers". It was actually a new version of an old school toy. It's designed with two large marbles attached to a string. You're suppose to hold the string in the middle, wave it up and down, and try to make the big marbles hit each other. *Knock! Knock! Knock! Knock!* Kid-D stopped the car and stared at the Bloods.

"Do you know who I am?" Kid-D asked the group.

"Naw, who is you?" replied the dark-skinned one named Boss.

"You better ask somebody!" Kid-D said.

I noticed one of the other niggas had sat down in one of the cars and was searching for something. We didn't have any "heat" with us, so I told Kid-D to drive off.

A few days after our hood patrol encounter, Boss was up at 6th Street park sittin' in the cab of a Diesel truck. I smoothly made my way towards the diesel with my nickel-plated .32 revolver. The passenger side door was open and I could hear music blaring from inside. I leaped up the side-steps and was inside the truck within' a split second.

"West!" I sternly asked as I pointed my gun in the direction of the shadowy figures inside the sleep area. The curtains parted, and to my surprise, it was Boss and a female I knew well. She was one of my homeboy's sisters. "E-Loc!" she cried out in fear, clutching her young titties. Boss looked like a deer caught in headlights. The look of terror on his face was soothing to my soul. He knew at that very moment I held his life in the balance of my hands. "E-Loc!" the girl cried out again. "Please don't," she begged.

I snapped outta my killer instinct trance and shook my pistol at Boss like it was a finger. I also gave him that, "you-know-I-had-yo'-ass" look, before I backed outta the diesel cab and into traffic.

I started throwin' parties at my momma's house in the hood. I'd ride around town yelling out the car window, "Party on "T" street!" It would be packed too. I'd pay D.J. Donkey or D.J. Phresh Kutz, and charge a few dollars for people to get in my backyard to party. We had fun and it always ended with some niggas fighting.

My homie Kid-D had moved in a house on the south-side with his girlfriend Felicia. They lived on the corner of Melwood Drive and Lotus Lane, right in the heart of the Country Boy Crips neighborhood. Me and some of the homies would go over to Kid-D's to play cards, dominos, smoke weed, and get our drank on.

Melwood Drive had a lot of money comin' through, and I would see Country Boys like Big Mobe, Chief, Pedro, Ditto, F-Boy, Moan, Fox, Big Daddy, and Butch out there racing to cars and making money. My homeboy Kid-D use to sell his rocks out there too. But, outta respect for the C.B.C.'s, me and the rest of the homies from the Westside didn't sell dope out there.

A lot of new homies had gotten "put on" my hood. Even some niggas who were older than me started representin' The Dub. They were all riders too. With the addition of Spinks, P-Dog, Big Lou,

Big Dale, K-Swiss and others... We were getting' deep.

Kay-B, Pooh, Chewy, and Sheldon were the one's at the House party doin' the shootin when A.D. got shot in the ass. They joined the hood through the homie NuNu. A big family mixed with Samoan and black who grew-up in the hood were now "pushin" the hood too. Everybody called them the Fat Boys and the Gucci Girls. There was Big Homer, Ali Mae, Dave, Jerry, Peg, Annie, Helen, Lil Momma, Mac Tosha, and Mildred.

One night after I left The Road, me and the homies went out to the Country. We were hangin' out by Dolly's Club gettin' high and gettin' full on Old English 800's. My girlfriend Alicia had just had a fight with this white girl named Kay. They were both rollin' around in the dirt creating a cloud of dust, but I heard my girlfriend won the fight. Inside the club my homie J.B. knocked out some nigga from the Country, and there was a lot of pushin' and shovin' from the crowd. I was smack-dab in the middle of it, showing J.B. some support, when my girl Alicia got all on my back and started pullin' on me and shit. Talkin' about, "Baby come on, let's go, you don't need to be in that," as she was grabbin' my arm. I became irritated with the building tension, her naggin' voice, and the vulnerable position she put me in by grabbin' my arm. So, I jerked my arm outta her grasp and I screamed on her. "Get the fuck off of me!" I yelled into her surprised face.

I knew she was only lookin' out for my best interest, but, at that moment she didn't realize that by her grabbin' me she was distracting me and placing me in danger. Things calmed down a little, but the mood was one that had everyone on edge.

My nigga BooBoo was shootin' dice with a couple of C.B.C.'s and it led to an argument. Apparently nobody wanted to let BooBoo shoot the dice. It was his turn on the dice, but everyone in the game just stood there and didn't want to give him a fade. I didn't like that at all so I told BooBoo, "Fuck them dice homie! Tomorrow at our park can't nobody shoot no dice!" I made sure that everyone standing near the dice game could hear me before I left the scene.

That same night I spent the night at BooBoo's grandma's house on 8th and "T" Street. We took two females with us too. BooBoo kicked it with my cousin Danelle, and I kicked it with an older female known as Cricket. BooBoo's grandma was asleep in her room so we tip-toed across her wooden living room floor, to the other bedroom.

The next day 6th street park was jam-packed. Me and the homies had showed-up early that morning and strategically placed weapons throughout the park. Most were placed on the side of a big white house across the street from the park, while the rest were placed inside the pink trash-cans that were located throughout the park.

I had meant what I said about not allowing anyone to shoot dice in our park. The tension was building and the C.B.C.'s were grouping up. Since we were in our hood and in our park, you know we were the "deepest".

I finally got tired of lookin' over there at them niggas and I said to my homies, "I'm finna see what these niggas wanna do. I started walkin' towards the pack of C.B.C.'s and homies were right behind me.

"Yall niggas got a problem?" I asked with my chest stuck out.

"Naw we don't got no problem with the Westside, but I got a problem with one of yo' homeboys," a voice said from the back of the group of C.B.C.'s.

"Who is that?" I asked, as I looked through the crowd to locate the voice.

Me!" said the voice again as the group parted and a nigga named Country Boy Keith stepped out.

"Yeah, I wanna get-down with yo' homeboy Halfdead," he said.

My homeboy Halfdead was right there with us and immediately spoke-up.

"Oh, we can get-down!" he said while peeling outta his shirt and bouncing around like a boxer.

We all formed a circle with Keith and Halfdead both inside. I was on the inside of the circle, using my arms to hold people back. Keith and Halfdead started squabbin' and were goin' toe-to-toe, blow-for-blow, when Halfdead covered-up and started yellin',

"My eye! My eye!" I saw the homie Halfdead couldn't continue so I stepped in to make sure Keith didn't hit him again. But, as I took a step and a half, I walked right into the barrel of a shotgun. It poked me in my stomach and the nigga holdin' it said, "Hold up!"

It was a nigga named Laron. I pushed the gun away from me and instantly wanted revenge. I half skipped and ran towards a pink trash-can and grabbed a 12 gauge, the rest of my homies ran to grab their "heat" while the C.B.C.'s scrambled to get away.

The crowd of people went crazy when someone yelled, "He gotta gun!" I didn't have any good targets close enough for me to knock-down without possibly hittin' innocent bystanders. But, I still was bustin' in their direction. *Boom! Pop! Pop! Pop! Boom!* Gunfire went on for what seemed like hours. I dropped the 12 gauge after two shots and started bustin' with a .32 revolver I had. My hand was bleeding between my thumb and forefinger. Initially I thought I got hit with something of a large caliber.

"E-Loc is hit! E-Loc got shot!" is what everyone was saying.

I got dropped off at my momma's on "T" street and had her take a look at it since she was a LVN. There was a gaping hole in my hand.

"Let me see boy," momma said sounding like she wanted to whoop my ass herself. "Shit! You always gettin' caught-up in some bullshit!" she said while snatching my arm and leading me to the bathroom sink.

In the bathroom, momma ran cold water and told me to hold my hand underneath it. She pulled out a first aid kit, then grabbed witch hazel, peroxide, and iodine from the medicine cabinet. After she treated my wound she determined that I hadn't been shot after all. My injury had come from the hammer of a gun. The way I was holding the 12 gauge when I fired it, caused the hammer to bite-down on my hand. I knew I hadn't been shot all along, but, I didn't want to say anything because I was enjoying the attention.

My only other serious injury prior to my fake-ass gunshot

injury, was when I got hit by a car when I was coming from behind an ice cream truck at 10 years old. Now that was an 'attention getting' injury.

With my hand wrapped-up in gauze and an ace bandage, I went to Kid-D's house in the Country. He had gotten in touch with two of the C.B.C. Big Homies (Big Mobe & Big Daddy), and had arranged a fair fight between the Westside Gangsta Crips and the Country Boy Crips.

Big Daddy was a light skinned nigga with major hustle and a tough guy reputation. Me and him acknowledged one another as step-brothers because the rumor was that his sister Toni was supposedly one of my daddy's kids. And Big Mobe was married to Toni at the time and they also had a son together.

Since my hand was injured, my homeboy P-Loc volunteered to fight Laron for me. Everyone was in front of Kid-D's house in the middle of the street. P-Loc and Laron was chunkin' em', and we cheered them on.

F-Boy from C.B.C. pulled out his switchblade and snapped it open. *"Snap!"* Me and my homies were known to carry switchblades in holsters on our hip. We even wore the holster upside-down so that when it opened, the knife would easily fall into our hands. Hearing F-Boy's knife snap open, gave us an opportunity to pull out our weapons as well. *Snap! Snap! Snap! Snap!* I snapped mines open along with damn near every homie present. I sized-up the crowd with my "I-wish-a-nigga-would" look.

P-Loc won the three-round fight, then we all squashed the "beef" and went our separate ways.

Me and Pete-a-Moe went half on a '76 Cutlass Supreme, but he drove it more than I did. We ended up trading it in for a '76 Buick Regal. It was root beer brown, with gold flakes, major beat in it, sittin' on Straight Laces and Vogues.

I kept sweatin' the Blood niggas who lived across the street from my momma. The only one I was cool with was black-ass "G". We called him Ten Ounce in C.Y.A., but his new handle was simply "G". He use to be a Spoonie Gee Crip. That is, until some SGC's named No Good, Chinese, and K-9 came through "T" Street lookin' for some Bloods and accidentally shot "G's" grandma with some buckshots. From that day on, "G" turned Warlord Blood, and started gettin' his ultimate "bang" on.

My neighbors Lil Jerry, Terry, and Larry were playing in my momma's backyard and dug-up a few of my guns. That discovery made momma go hard on me about my gang activities. She said I was putting her and her baby (my lil brother Derrick) in danger, and then she gave me a choice. Either choose her and my brother, or the gang. I grabbed my belongings I had and moved in on East 9th Street with my Uncle Gleek.

CHAPTER 12

Uncle Gleek lived in a 2 bedroom house behind my Grandma and Poppy's house. He lived alone and was using drugs regularly. He had a job as an Insurance Agent, but it didn't last long. Uncle Gleek was also madly in love with Wanda, and they eventually got married and had lots of kids. But, after basketball and Aunt Wanda, his "love" was music. He's the one who put me up on Lakeside, BarKays, Rick James, S.O.S. Band, Cameo, Four Tops, Isley Brothers, Jackson 5, Temptations, and Earth, Wind, & Fire. He had a lot of 8-Track tapes.

My older brother Darren, who we call Nutt, had moved in the same time I moved in with Uncle Gleek. Darren is my daddy's oldest son; his momma name is Teri, and she married a Fireman named Big Elijah. They had a son of their own that they named Lil Elijah.

Teri and Big Elijah always treated me and my lil brother Derrick really good. We would spend the night at their house and do fun family things. When we were young, they took us on several trips, like Sequoia National Park.

Sequoia National Park was amazing. The trees were the tallest and widest I'd ever seen in my life. One of the trees had fallen and was used as a tunnel big enough for cars to drive through it. There was also a rock the size of a mountain. We climbed to the top of it, then came back down to have a nice lil picnic. They took us to Six Flags Magic Mountain and Disneyland too. Every time we traveled somewhere, Teri would make us these delicious sandwiches that we nicknamed Mc Nichols Sandwiches. They were "Bomb". My big brother Darren was only my half-brother, but he treated me and Derrick as if we all had the same mom and dad. Darren always acknowledged me and Derrick, and was always quick to defend us.

When I was a kid and went camping with the Cub Scouts, Darren was the one who came after me when I started walking home from the camp site. And when I didn't make it on big Elijah's traveling basketball team, Darren made sure his momma made me a warm-up suit like the rest of the team had. Mine even came with 'Sir Eric' printed on the sleeve.

Me and Darren have always felt really close. But when we both moved in with Uncle Gleek, we really developed a solid bond. Darren had just came home from playing basketball at a junior college in Sacramento. He was a very good point-guard in high school and won championship titles at South High school. But, in sports, it's all about being at the right place at the right time and it's "who you know" that 'll determine how far you'll go in your career.

Back at home in Bakersfield, broke, without a job, and a desire for finer things in life; Darren went down a path that led him to a much different kind of "game". The dope game.

I had already been doin' my thang for a few years now and had already built some clientele. My brother Darren, who we began calling D-Nutt, was new to the dope game, but he picked up on it fast. When we first moved in with Uncle Gleek, D-Nutt brought a big, blue chest that came with a lock and key. He gave me a key of my own, sat me down, and told me how things were gonna be from now on. I listened to him because I trusted his judgement, because he was older, and because he demanded that I listen to him.

D-Nutt started sellin' dope for Big Al and Wes. He was good at hustlin' and he learned how to cook dope the way daddy taught me, but D-Nutt was better at it than me and daddy both. He knew how to dry-cook it, microwave it, blend it with a blender, put 7-up soda in it, and he knew how to put vanilla flavor in it. He taught me how to "Chef" like him and showed me how to use Procaine to stretch or blow-up the rocks. But, the most helpful thing he taught me in the Dope Game was how to manipulate the customers with the amount of dope I sold them. He told me that most customers would rather get more for their money, and he broke it down for me like this: He laid out two pieces of rock cocaine, both weighing 0.5 grams, which was only worth $25 a piece. He then took one of the pieces and used a razor blade to chop it up into four tiny pieces. Then, he reminded me that the four tiny pieces weighed the same as the one small piece that hadn't been chopped-up. However, if the person buying the rocks had a choice, they would buy the four tiny pieces instead of the one small piece. I call it the "Micro-dot" remedy. It works too.

D-Nutt had been in a long term relationship with his high school sweetheart named Cheryl. The only other girl I knew of him dating back then was a fine ass Red-bone named Phillishawn. She was a couple of years older than D-Nutt, and ended up going off to Cal State Northridge for college.

One night while me and D-Nutt were up on The Road hustlin', a girl I went to school with wanted me to introduce her to D-Nutt. Her name was TuTu. She was a year younger than me and just so happen to be Squirt's niece. I saw D-Nutt coming out of The Randles Club and motioned for him to come to where me and TuTu were. I introduced them to each other and they begin calling one another on the phone everyday. One day TuTu came over to Uncle Gleek's and she brought her baby named Tia with her too. Tia was ten months old. Me, Uncle Gleek, D-Nutt, and TuTu were all sittin' in the living room chillin' and watching t.v., when all of a sudden.. *Do-Doosh*! It sounded like a t.v. fell in the bedroom. We all rushed into the room to find Tia's cute self laying on the floor looking up at us. She wasn't crying or anything. TuTu picked her up off the floor and inspected her, but Tia was fine. Once I realized the baby wasn't hurt I started clownin' and making jokes about the incident. I even nicknamed Tia "Do-Doosh".

I was in my hood one day visiting my momma when she told me about my cousin Roy's baby-momma named Tan moving in my hood. She also told me Tan had moved next door to her sister named Kam, who I'd always thought was the finest girl ever. Kam was five years older than me and already had two daughters. Jenaya was 4 years old and Mesha was 6 months old. I had the best girlfriend in the hood as far as I was concerned. Kam was super-thick with long hair, dimples, and a smooth caramel complexion. Only after we had sex, did I discover that her two kids were by my cousin Jerry. Jerry's momma Drusilla, and my daddy are first cousins. It was too late though... I was already in love with Kam and wasn't gonna stop being with her for nobody. My family tried to talk me outta being with her and even tried to bribe her into going back to Jerry. But, Kam was already in love with me too. She could cook good, was a great lover, she did what I told her to do, and she was a "Rider".

The small apartment we lived in sat behind a house on 4th street, and our parking lot was located in an alley. Kam was beautiful and I'd catch a lot of guys driving extra slow down the street tryin' to holla at her. I knew she loved the attention too, so I'd pop-up on her and the 'slow drivers', and I'd Loc-up on them.

"Get up outta here before I smoke yo' bitch-ass," is what I'd say to the slow drivers, causing them to burn rubber up outta there.

My homeboy BooBoo was fuckin' with Kam's sister named Tan. The same Tan who had a baby by my cousin Roy. So me and BooBoo ended up kickin' it a lot. One night Kam's cousin named Lavella came by our place all drunk and shit. My homies P-Loc, Vada, and BooBoo were there, along with my brother D-Mac. I stayed in the house with my girl, but Lavella was drunk, sittin' in her car, and talkin' about how good she could fuck. The next day P-Loc, my brother D-Mac, and Vada were all talkin' about how Lavella had sucked their dicks inside her car while parked in the alley. P-Loc even said he fucked her.

The drama started earlier in the day at 6th Street Park. The homie

Vada and his girlfriend named Dena got into an argument that led to her hitting him over the head with her shoe, as some older big head nigga held my homie Vada. I tried to get to his big-ass for puttin' his hands on my homie, but the crowd wasn't thick enough and there were too many witnesses. I was gon' "pop" his ass.

We all ended up leaving the park and going up on The Road where more drama followed. Dena attacked Vada again, but Vada didn't want to fight her back. There was a lot of pushing and shoving because Vada kept tryin' to get close enough to Dena so he could talk to her, but Dena kept on physically abusing him. Her homegirls, which included Lavella and her sisters and cousins, were all drunk and wanting to help Dena abuse Vada. But we wasn't havin' that. Lavella's boyfriend came up and tried to "bomb" on Vada, but Vada was too quick. He easily ducked the punch and squared-off with him. Her boyfriend was a lot taller and outweighed Vada, but Vada didn't backdown. They danced around the Liquor store parking lot like two boxers as the crowd cheered them on.

My homie Halfdead didn't like how the situation was looking, so he bombed on the boyfriend from the blind-side, "*Ca-rack!*" They locked-up like two pit-bulls and the crowd closed in on them.

Me and Vada started kickin' it real tough with each other after that. We got "fronted" some dope from Big Daddy and was hustlin' together. One night we had both just got an ounce of rock from Big Daddy and we were in the hood on Donna Ave. at Scarface Dre's house. Scarface Dre had some rocks of his own, so we all chopped up our dope and hid it in Scarface Dre's backyard. Scarface Dre drove us to The Road and dropped off me and Vada. Later that night when me and Vada returned to get our dope sacks we noticed that Vada's sack was missing half of his dope. We knew Scarface Dre had stolen the dope because us three were the only ones who knew about the dope being hid in the backyard.

Vada had a sad look on his face and was worried about what Big Daddy was gonna do if he didn't come up with the money. I insisted on calling Big Daddy immediately to let him know what happened, and to see if he could give Vada more dope to "Work it off". Big Daddy was more than understanding. We confronted Scarface Dre about stealing Vada's dope, but he denied it. Without any proof, we had to let it go.

While hustlin' on The Road I met many different niggas from different hoods. "The Real" always recognize "The Real" so I'd often hook-up with individuals to make money with.

Me, the homie Scruff, and a down-ass halfbreed nigga named Los-D from Mid City Crips had hooked-up. Scruff was originally from Arkansas, but he got "put on" my hood. He had major "hustle" and had the heart of a Gambler. Los-D had a little more "Game" than me, but I was more daring when it came to violence. Scruff was going back and forth to Little Rock, Arkansas gettin' his hustle on, while me and Los-D put our pennies together out here in Cali on The Road.

Our luck changed for the better when this big nigga from Bakersfield named Big Marv came home from Folsom State Prison. Big Marv was on Monster Swole. I mean he was huge. He stood 6'5" tall with 24" arms and a chest built like the hood of a truck. One day he was shooting dice with a few other niggas up on The Road, and he was the one actually rolling the dice when he "crapped out". The nigga who had Big Marv faded, attempted to pick up his winnings when Big Marv stepped on the money. The nigga looked up at Big Marv with a pleading look in his eyes but Big Marv told the nigga, "Back-up before I knock yo' ass out!" then kneeled down and picked-up the nigga's money.

Big Marv stood tall, shaking the dice in his strong right hand, asking niggas, "Can I get a fade?" But nobody wanted to place their money down against Big Marv's money because they figured it was a no-win situation. I pulled out my wad of money and peeled $20 off, and dropped it to the ground next to Big Marv's $20. He shot the dice and rolled a four.

"I bet you don't throw four for twenty," I said.

"Bet!" Big Marv said as he dropped $20. He shot the dice again and rolled an eight.

I said, "I bet you don't ten or four for twenty more," and I dropped another $20 on the ground. He followed suit, then shook the dice hard, snapped his fingers, and begged the dice to hit for him.

"Come on ten!" he demanded. But the dice landed on seven.

"Yeah!" I yelled as I bent down to pick up my winnings.

Big Marv stood-up with his foot planted firmly on my money. I paused to give him time to remove his foot, but he didn't budge. I stood up to face him when he said, "say youngsta, do you see that pole over there?"

Me and the bystanders all looked in the direction of the light pole that was at least two blocks away.

"Yeah I see it," I said.

"I'm gon' knock yo' head off yo' shoulders over to that pole if you pick up that money," Big Marv smoothly said as the crowd grew silent.

My blood boiled, and anger instantly swelled inside me. I bent down, grabbed the money, then snatched it from underneath his foot.

"You got me fucked-up!" I exclaimed as I looked him dead in his eyes. He just looked at me, smiled, and said, "I like that, you got heart lil nigga."

The following day while up on The Road by Footlongs Hamburger stand, a group of Gamblers and Dope dealers were hangin' out in the parking lot. I was there to order a couple of Chili Cheese Dogs, some fries, and a soda. Big Marv was the center of attention, talkin' 'bout how much money he got.

"I got a quarter of a million dollars at the house right now!" he claimed.

"You don't got a quarter of a million, you broke-ass nigga!" one guy said.

"Aw hell naw! You lying!" another said.
"Go get it then!" said yet another.

Big Marv jumped into his Impulse with the Porsche emblems on it, and sped away. He returned within' half an hour and pulled into Footlong's parking lot. He took out bindles of money and placed them on the hood of his car, along with two .45 caliber pistols. Everyone was in awe, and Big Marv rubbed it in their faces.

"Yeah, I can give this youngsta right here an ounce for $125.00 if I want to," he said while pointing at me.

I called his bluff by pulling out my money, counting out $125.00 and said, "Let me get it then!" as I held out the money in his direction. Big Marv sat down in his car and emerged with an ounce of hard-white. I was happy as hell. Ounces were going for $700 at the time, and there was a drought in the dope game.

Once I chopped the ounce up, and sold it, I told Los-D that it was only right for us to start buying our dope from Big Marv. After all, he did show me some "love". Every time I purchased some dope from Big Marv, he would "front" me the same amount that I'd purchase. If I bought an ounce, he'd front me an ounce.

With me and Los-D servin' on The Road, and Scruff taking trips to Arkansas, our money grew. Big Marv even allowed me to party with him at hotel suites with fine ass bitches. Older bitches knew that my pockets were "gettin' right" so they began trying to slide up under me thinkin' I was gon' trick my dick off. Once, this older bitch in a Z28 named Nia was on The Road hustlin'. I flirted with the bitch and she flirted back. She asked me what I had planned for the night, and I told her that I was gon' hustle all night. She said she was gonna be doin' the same thing too. She promised to holla at me before she turned in for the night.

I continued servin' my dope until just after 2AM when Nia approached me and said, "So, what's up?"

I couldn't believe it. I'd seen many different niggas try to holla at her in the past, and had seen her turn them down. But here she was givin' me action. I told her that I was done for the night and wanted to go with her. We got into her Z28 and ended up at a hotel. The bitch already had the room, and there was Louis Vuitton luggage and clothes everywhere. She took a shower first, then I jumped my stankin' ass in after her. When I got out of the shower she had just come back into the hotel room with a towel wrapped around her head.

"Where you been?" I asked.
"Oh, my homegirl and her friend are in the room next door," she explained. "Come on," she said as she walked back out of the room.

With a towel wrapped around my waist, I first peeked out the door into the night to make sure it was safe. I then quickly made my way next door. I made it just in time to see Nia disappear into the bathroom, and catch Big Marv with his head between the legs of a squirming and moaning redbone bitch named Lisa. Big Marv stopped his licking duties and smiled up at me with pussy-juice all over his face, before going back down on her. Nia came out of the bathroom and rushed pass me.

"Come on," she said, giggling and shit.

Something strange was definitely goin' on, but I couldn't quite put my finger on it. Nia and I did The Wild Thang and fell asleep in each other's arms. We only fucked a couple of more times after that night because she disappeared. I heard that she went to prison on a parole violation. I also found out that she was using cocaine during the times I was with her which explained why she kept going into the bathroom so damn much and never wanted me to come inside with her whenever she'd be peeing or showering. That bitch stayed on my mind for months.

CHAPTER 13

A couple of weeks after catching Big Marv eating pussy, he told me that I needed to start buying larger quantities of dope from him. And since there had been days when I couldn't find anyone who could sell me dope at a good price, I agreed. So, one day I went to Big Marv to buy nine ounces.

"How much money do you got?" he asked.

I told him that I had enough to pay for the whole nine ounces.

"No! How much money do you have saved up?" he asked.

At the time I was holding on to all the money that me, Scruff, and Los-D had been saving. It was $22,000, but I told Scruff and Los-D that we only had $18,000.

Big Marv said, "I'll give you a kilo, plus nine ounces for $18,000.

"Hell yeah!" I said with excitement.

The going price for a kilo was $17,500. So, we would be winning if we did the deal with Big Marv. He told us to meet him at 6th Street Park at 3 o'clock in the afternoon.

We made it to the park a little early and shot some baskets until well after 3 o'clock. We even waited until 4 o'clock, but Big Marv still hadn't shown up. I was getting a little pissed off because there was a risk involved simply by me having so much money in my possession. Back then, if you didn't have a check stub on you to prove the money wasn't drug money, the police would take your money.

Me and Los-D jumped in the dark blue Monte Carlo and drove east on 4th Street. As we passed in front of McKinley Elementary School's parking lot, we saw Big Marv in his imitation Porsche. We pulled into the school's parking lot and Big Marv pulled along side of us. He had his young son with him and didn't appear to be ready to conduct any business. He apologized for the delay and promised to make it up to us. He told us to meet him at the park again at 9 PM sharp, and said he'd be in a white Mercedes Benz.

At 8:59 PM me and Los-D pulled up at 6th Street Park. At 9:01 PM a cocaine white, big-body Benz pulled-up in front of us. Big Marv exited the Benz from the passenger side, while another nigga just as big as Big Marv got out of the driver's side. I didn't recognize the big, black, bald nigga, so I told Los-D to get out and make sure it was cool.

I had a brown paper bag with the money in it. I also had a .38 automatic in my waistband (the same weapon the government issue to the U.S. Servicemen and women).

When Los-D motioned for me to get out of the car, I adjusted the gun in my waistband, then exited the car. I placed the bag of money on the hood of the car and began taking the money out so that I could count it in front of Big Marv. I noticed Big Marv also had a much larger brown paper bag in his hand.

"You don't have to count it," Big Marv began. "I know it's all there," he added.

He looked around nervously as if he was being watched.

"This ain't cool right here, Big Marv informed me. "Let's go down the street and do this," he said.

I placed the money back inside the paper bag and got back into the car. The two big niggas got into the Benz and drove off as Los-D followed closely behind them. When we got inside the car Los-D immediately said, "something ain't right, these niggas is up to something." When we approached the four-way stop sign at 4th & P Streets, Los-D put the left-hand blinker on and attempted to abandon the entire deal, but I grabbed the steering wheel and insisted that we follow through.

"Man, I'm tellin' you E-Loc, these niggas is up to something," he said nervously.
"I'll smoke both of them niggas if they try to do anything fishy," I shot back. "We need this dope. I'm serious cuz, I'll smoke them niggas," I sternly said as I checked my gun to make sure I had one in the chamber and the safety button on "f" (fire).

We followed the Benz down 4th Street to Chester Avenue, three blocks down to 1st street, and turned right pass Sherry's Liquor Store, to Eye Street, and made a quick left. On the right hand side of Eye street, across the street from Taco Bell, sat a coin operated Car Wash. The Benz pulled into the Car Wash while Los-D pulled us into a parking lot next to the Car Wash. A short 3 ft. brick wall separated the two. Big Marv and the big, buffed, bald nigga exited the Benz and met us at the end of the short brick wall. Big Marv carried the brown paper bag full of dope, but I chose to leave my bag of money in the car. With Los-D's suspicion, I thought it would be best to at least see the dope before handing over any money.

"Let me see the dope," I said.

Big Marv opened the grocery store size paper bag and pulled out a large Zip Lock freezer-bag full of dope. It was one big solid piece. It appeared to be about an inch and a half thick, twelve inches long, twelve inches wide, and already in "rock" form. I tried to eyeball it's amount, but it was impossible. I would need a scale to weigh it and I knew where one was not too far away. I had been sellin' dope for several years and was good at it. I could easily eyeball an ounce, maybe even two, but not the big piece these niggas was trying to say was a kilo plus nine ounces. I told them that I couldn't tell how much dope it was, and I wanted them to follow me to where a scale was.

"I got a triple-beam scale at my spot. If it weigh-off I'm go' pay-off," I said.

The big, buffed, bald, nigga said, "I'm Double-M from L.A."

I said, "I'm E-Loc from Westside Gangstas."

He then went on to say, "You see that Benz right there?" looking back at his car, "that cost me $65,000 and I got another one that cost me $85,000. I don't get shit like that from bullshittin'."

Just then, a cop on a motorcycle hit the corner. Big Marv sat the bag of dope on the ground next to the brick wall until the cop passed us and disappeared. Big Marv and Double-M were in a brief conference exchanging what appeared to be heated words. Then, their attention was back on me.

"So what do you think lil homie?" asked Double-M.

"This is my life savings. I can't just give my money away like that. It looks kinda short to me," I replied.

"Whatever ain't there, I'll have Big Marv double it up for you," Double-M said.

Then Big Marv jumped in saying, "Whatever ain't there I'll triple it. That's on my momma."

Right then I knew all of the dope wasn't there.

"It should all be there," I said. Then Double-M jumped back in.

"So it ain't enough for you lil homie?" he asked.

I shook my head no and said, "Naw."

He waited for my reply, then calmly said, "I'll tell you what..." As he turned to walk towards his Benz, I said to myself, "Yeah, he's gettin' the rest of the dope. He was tryin' to test me." With his cellphone in one hand, and what I believed to be the rest of the dope in his other hand that was practically hidden from my view by his pants leg, he walked towards me. When he got about twenty feet from me, there it was...The barrel of his gun looked me dead in my face.

"Gimme the motha'fuckin' money!" he gnarled as he held the gun on me and looked at me as if he wanted to kill me. "I'm sick of this bullshit!" he said through seething teeth.

His curled lip, bunched-up wrinkles on his forehead, and beady eyes were enough to frighten anybody. I froze, then held my arms up in the air with my palms facing him. I would've reached for the sky, but I didn't want to raise my arms so high that my shirt would raise and expose the gun that I had in my waistband. That would've spooked him and caused him to open-fire on me. Having a gun drawn on you is an experience like none other. For a split second my entire life flashed in front of me. My mind really did envision different episodes in my life as if they were painted on a deck of cards and shuffled in my face. Everything flashed by up to that moment. Then I thought, "Damn, my momma ain't gon' even know who killed me."
Double-M didn't have to give me anymore commands. All he did was move that gun and I knew which direction to go in and at what pace to go.

"Please don't kill me. Please don't kill me," I begged in a whisper.

I felt drained and weak. My dick felt like it shriveled up inside me. My asshole got tingly, and it felt like butterflies the size of birds were in my stomach. Los-D was on the left side of me with his hands in the air too, looking like he'd seen a ghost. His body language looked like he wanted to run, but was uncertain. He then spoke up.

"Okay man don't shoot! We'll give you the money," he said.

Double-M waved the gun and we both knew that meant for us to walk towards my car. As we were walking towards the car I asked Big Marv, "Why yall doin' me like this?" He merely hunched his shoulders and threw his hands up in the air gesturing that he had no control of what was goin' on.

Los-D took what seemed like forever to get the bag of money from the inside of my car. Double-M had led me to the back of the car to face the trunk. I thought to myself, "Damn, this is it," and I could feel the back of my head get heavy. Los-D finally reappeared from the driver's side of my car with the brown paper bag in hand.

"Here." he said as he held out the bag towards Double-M.

Upon handing the bag to Double-M, Los-D stuck out his fist to give Double-M a "pound" like a handshake. Then said, "You didn't have to pull no gun on us man." Double-M replied by saying, "I'm not trippin' on you. I'm trippin' on that nigga," as he pointed the gun in my direction. I flinched and braced for the impact of the bullets, but he didn't shoot.

Double-M let the gun linger in the air pointin' at me, while walking away with the bag in his other hand. He continued to look menacingly at me for three or four more paces, then he finally turned his back to me as he walked around the short brick wall. Immediately my mind raced to thoughts of the .38 Automatic in my waistband. I could easily kill him now that his back was to me. But I didn't. I was still shook up and didn't trust my instincts. I was too weak to even go for my gun.

"There go that punk ass dope," Big Marv said, nodding his head in the direction of the brown paper bag full of dope that was still on the ground next to the small brick wall. Los-D retrieved the bag while I gathered just enough strength to make it to the passenger seat of my car. I was relieved, but my feelings of relief soon turned to anger. I pulled out the .38 Automatic, held it in my lap, and hoped like hell I could make it away from there safely.

Los-D jumped in the driver's seat, slammed the door, and tossed the brown paper bag full of dope in my lap. I didn't even look inside the bag because I knew it was short. Plus I wasn't in the mood. I just wanted to get the fuck away from there so I could regroup. I wanted to cry. My face and eyes felt like I was crying, but no tears came out.

"Don't trip," Los-D said as he pulled into traffic on Eye street. We made a left on Brundage Lane, then we headed east on Brundage Lane until we got to Madison Street, then turned right. My homegirl Felicia lived in a house on Madison Street. She knew how to fight like a man, was a good cook, and was good in bed too. Me and her had fucked a couple of times, but we mainly had a true homeboy/ homegirl relationship. I use to keep a lot of my guns at her house too. She had burns over some parts of her body, but she was thick with a pretty smile and a sweet personality. She was the only female who could come to any of my other girlfriend's place to holla at me at any time of the night.

On our way to Felicia's house Los-D said, "Feel up under the seat." I leaned forward in the car and reached underneath my seat. To my surprise, a lot of money came out and onto the floor of the car. I swept my hand under the seat repeatedly until loads of money was at my feet. I couldn't believe my eyes. Los-D bounced in his seat with the biggest smile I'd ever seen on his face.

"I didn't give them fools nothing!" he yelled. I then realized this was the money we'd had in our brown paper bag, our $18,000.

CHAPTER 14

I had been on an emotional roller coaster for real, and all in a matter of minutes. I still wanted revenge even though we had our money and the dope. By the way...the dope ended up only being a little less than a kilo. So, it was "short".

They didn't intend to rob us. They just wanted to make us buy something "short". Maybe they needed our $18,000 to put with their money so they could purchase larger amounts. I don't know. All I know is, they fucked up by pulling that gun on me. I wasn't gonna accept that. In fact, I made an agreement with myself to not hustle, fuck, or party until I got my revenge on them niggas. I wouldn't even let Los-D sell any of the dope we'd just got from them niggas. The homie Scarface Dre had popped up at Felicia's too. He kept on beggin' us to sell him four and a half ounces, but I didn't do it. I put the bag of dope in the top part of Felicia's bedroom closet.

I got dressed in all black. Black Dickies pants, black long-sleeved t-shirt, black Honcho boots, and a black Raiders cap. Los-D put on his black gear too. We grabbed our Brownie gloves and our 'Heats,' then got in traffic in search of a cocaine white Benz.

After driving around for several hours, we decided to call it a night, and we made our way back to Felicia's. Scarface Dre was still there, and had fallen asleep on the living room couch. I checked on the dope in the top of the closet, and it was all still there. Los-D laid down on the other couch in the living room, while I crawled into bed with Felicia. We didn't fuck. I fell asleep and slept like a baby.

The next morning I awoke to find Felicia and Los-D both fast asleep. But, Scarface Dre was gone, and so was some of my dope. Before I went to sleep the night before, I specifically noticed the large piece of dope didn't have any loose dope or crumbs in the large Zip-Lock baggie. I knew without a doubt that Scarface Dre had stolen some of the dope. I woke up Felicia and Los-D to show them what had happened. They both claimed they didn't know, see, nor hear Scarface Dre take the dope. We all agreed it was scandalous of him to steal from us, and also agreed not to allow him to come over anymore.

Big Marv was going around town telling everyone about the "Gun pulling" episode. He would say, "Yeah, the lil homies came to spend $18,000 but the thang was a lil short, so my boy had to draw down on them." Then he would laugh. Big Marv didn't know Los-D had handed Double-M a brown paper bag full of ripped up Lowrider magazines. Double-M had taken the bag from Los-D without inspecting it and had put it in the trunk of the Benz before hopping on the highway back to Los Angeles.

Me and Los-D had heard how Big Marv was bragging about how he'd done us. We also heard how a lot of niggas told Big Marv he "fucked-up" when they learned that I was one of the lil niggas who had been drawn-down on. I did my homework and learned that Double-M's momma lived in The Country on Melwood. I also found-out where Big Marv and his wife lived, where his parents lived, and the locations of a few bitches he fucked with.

I had Los-D drive me around all day everyday in search of Big Marv. Every time we'd show up somewhere, they would tell us that Big Marv had just left or had been there earlier. We fell asleep in the car outside of his house a couple of times while waiting for him to show up, but he never came.

I got tired of barely missing him. So, on the third day of searching for him, me and Los-D went up on The Road and hung out with the Gamblers who were shooting dice in front of Louie's

Bail Bonds. The Gamblers told us that Big Marv had been up there with them earlier. We waited for nearly two hours, then drove north down Lakeview Avenue and there he was! Big Marv was in his Impulse in front of Mr. Bennett's Barber shop. Los-D drove pass him, then made a u-turn and pulled right along side of him. I held the .38 Automatic in my lap. When Big Marv's eyes met mine, I threw my head up and said, "What's up?" He tossed his head back and said, "What's up?" too. Then he quickly exited his car and approached the side of the car I was in. When he placed both of his hands on the roof of my car and leaned down to talk to me, his eyes met the nozzle of my gun. He instantly went into panic-mode...

"Oh no youngsta! It aint like that! Listen man!" he spit out one after another. "Look the nigga Double-M is talkin' 'bout sending fifty of his homeboys out here to get y'all. He just want his money," he explained.

"Check this out," I began. "You tell Double-M if he sends another threat my way I'm gonna go in The Country on Melwood and smoke his momma." I then told him how I'd been looking for him, and even named all of the locations I'd been to. Big Marv had an astonishing look on his face.

I wanted to blow his head off right then on the spot, but the niggas down the street at Louie's Bail Bonds were all looking at us and I knew one of them fools would've snitched on me if I would've "did my thang". I thought fast and decided to talk Big Marv into meeting me somewhere soon. So, I got at him like I wanted to make peace and said, "Look man, I'll give you half of the dope back, but I aint givin' up no money." He was relieved to hear that. "But you gotta meet me at Queen Sheeba in twenty minutes, and you can't tell nobody I gave you half of the dope back," I added. He agreed, and we drove off. I didn't have any intentions on giving him anything other than .38 rounds in his punk-ass.

Los-D drove me to the hood and I spotted my homie Vada in 6th street park sittin' on a bench. I gave our hood call, "Yeeeeee!" and he came running towards the car. I opened my door and told him to get in, so he climbed in the back seat.

"Where y'all finna go?" he asked excitedly.

"Remember that nigga Big Marv you popped in the ass?" I asked.

"Yeah, what about him?" he replied.

"I'm gon' show you how to do it right," I exclaimed.

Vada had shot Big Marv in the ass one night on The Road. I'm the one who handed him the pistol and encouraged him to "pop" his ass. Even though Big Marv was my "Business Associate" at the time, Vada was my homie, and homies come first.

Me, Los-D, and Vada hit a few corners tryin' to kill some time. Vada jumped around excitedly in the back seat like a kid on his way to an Amusement Park. I finally told Los-D to pull up into Queen Sheeba's parking lot. It was 9:30AM. There was a Hostess cup cake truck and a Webber's bread truck in the parking lot blocking the view from traffic on 4th & "V" streets. We parked in the alley, but still near the parking lot. Los-D left the car in "drive" and kept his foot on the brake. Big Marv pulled into the parking lot, parked, then jumped out of his car. He was maybe fifty feet away when he started walking towards us. He had on white Chuck Taylor Converse sneakers, blue Levi 501's, and an off white thermal undershirt. He was huge. When he got halfway to me, he placed his hand underneath his thermal shirt to rub his chest and exposed the pistol he had tucked in his waistband. I guess he was trying to scare me, but it only made me want to kill his punk-ass.

"I'm killin' this nigga." I said without moving my lips.

"Naw don't do it." Vada said from the back seat.

"Not right now." Los-D added.

"Shut up!" I said through clenched teeth. "Fuck this nigga! I'm killin' this nigga!" I said again through clenched teeth, as I looked directly at Big Marv and then faced forward.

He was fifteen feet away and I counted his steps while looking at him with my peripheral vision. When he got close enough to touch the car that I was in, I quickly raised the .38 Automatic over the lowered window and squeezed off five quick rounds, "*Pop! Pop! Pop! Pop! Pop!*" The gun jumped in my hand

and Big Marv tried to run towards the back of the car. He moved so fast it appeared as if he was trying to slap the bullets down. Los-D was startled by the sound of the gun shots and released his foot from the brakes, then hit the brakes again, causing me to lunge forward a little in the midst of my shots. The car rocked and Big Marv laid motionless on the ground near the rear tire. I still had four more shots left, so I opened the car door, exited the vehicle, pulled my Raiders cap further down on my head, then slowly walked towards the lifeless looking body of Big Marv. I took a quick survey of my immediate surroundings as i made my way to "finish him off". His clothes appeared to be smoking and he was sprawled-out like he was already dead. I aimed my pistol at his head as I made my final approach and stood over him. I made one last survey of my surroundings and noticed a man wearing a safety harness on a telephone pole. He was looking directly at me. I immediately pulled my Raiders cap further down, turned, walked back to the car door and got in.

"Drive off slow." I told Los-D.

We drove down the alley, hit 4th & "T" street, and made our way to Pop-Locc's house on 9th street. I gave Vada the gun and told him I'd come pick it up later. Me and Los-D then drove to Felicia's to clean-up. I put all the clothes I wore into a black trash bag, and took a shower. Me and Los-D had agreed that if Big Marv survived the shooting, it would be Los-D's turn to shoot him.

We knew that most black patients were taken to Kern Medical Center (K.M.C.) because it wasn't a private hospital. So, we drove up to Flower street and went to a telephone booth located outside of a Liquor Store that sat directly across the street from K.M.C. I used the phone book to find K.M.C.'s phone number, and reached a lady in the Emergency Room. I told her that my brother Marvin had gotten shot and I wanted to know how he was doing. She told me that Big Marv had already checked out of their hospital, and that he had suffered through & through wounds. I later found out that while me and Los-D were on the corner at the telephone booth, one of Big Marv's girlfriends spotted us. She was at his bedside when he told her that I was the one who tried to kill him. So, he left K.M.C. with her and went to another local hospital.

The police kicked in doors at both of my parents', at my girlfriend Kam's, and was riding around in my hood showing my photo around. They also put me on a show that aired on the local news station, called Kern's Most Wanted. The Bakersfield Police Department and Kern County Sheriff's Department told my mom to talk me into surrendering because I was considered "Armed & Dangerous". I didn't "bite" though, instead, I laid low at R.J.'s and Amp's for a couple of days.

CHAPTER 15

My homie Kid-D came through and helped me bag up all of my dope. I knew I had to get out of town so I split the dope three ways with Los-D and Scruff.

I got tired of sittin' up at R.J.'s and Amp's, so one night I went up on The Road. I was on the corner of Gorrill street and Lakeview Avenue, hangin' out on the side of a store called B&M Market. Me, Kid-D, R.J., J.B., and Pop-Locc were all there when I noticed Scarface Dre's car parked in the parking lot of some apartments on Gorrill street. I told Kid-D that I was gonna rob Scarface Dre for stealing from me. Kid-D supported my decision, and even let me know that Scarface Dre was inside of B&M's. "Aw hell nawl," I said as I pulled out the .357 Magnum. The barrel was so long that it looked like I pulled out a rifle.

I sat on a parked car outside of B&M's with my arms folded so that the .357 was tucked under my arms and extended behind my back. There he was! Scarface Dre came out the front door of B&M's with a tall can of Old English 800, and a lime salt packet. He sprinkled some salt on his hand, took a drink of Old English, then he licked the salt off of his hand. He repeated the sprinkling of salt, then took another drink from the tall can, but when he brought the can away from his lips I was already grabbing a fist-full of his shirt and poking him in his ribs with the barrel of the .357. He nearly choked on the beer.

"Yeah mutha'fucka!" I said only loud enough for Scarface Dre to hear me as I escorted him across the street towards his car. He had a gray Caprice Classic sittin' on deep-dish rims, with a loud ass music system in it. It was a really nice car, but it wasn't worth what I felt like he owed me. He had betrayed my trust and I wasn't gonna let him forget that.

"E-Loc let me talk to you," he pleaded with me as I escorted him through the shadows of the night, and to the passenger-side of his car.
"Get in!" I ordered him while poking him in his ribs with the .357 to remind him that I was in charge.

He slowly climbed into the passenger seat and scooted over to the driver's seat, while I got in behind him with my gun still drawn on him. With his beer and lime salt packet still in hand, he went into his desperate attempt to lie by asking, "What did I do?"

"You know what you did mutha'fucka!" I shot back.
"I-I- didn't stea...," he began before I cut him off.
"Nigga! You stole from me cuz!" I said as I searched his eyes for the truth.
"Please don't kill me E-Loc," he begged. "Please cuz," he pleaded as tears poured out of his eyes. "I'm sorry", he said between sobs. "But please don't kill me," he begged again.
"Start this car up and drive." I commanded.

The engine revved to life and the buzzing sound of the twelve inch woofers filled the air inside the car. Scarface Dre sat there in a daze staring straight ahead. "Go nigga!" I demanded, snapping him out of whatever trance he was in. He broke down like a baby.

"Please don't kill me Eric," he pleaded again using my real name in hopes of winning my sympathy.
"Just drive!" I said as I sat with my back against the passenger side door to face him.

I propped my elbows on the seat's headrest and the

dashboard with the long barrel of the .357 pointed in his direction. I gave him a tongue lashing the entire trip. I let him know how much I loved him and how close I "thought" we were. This was my "play cousin".

We drove down California Avenue and he pulled into the parking lot of Jimmy's Arcade. I had already decided what I was gonna do to him, so after about twenty minutes of listening to his pleas, I instructed him to start the car up again and get in traffic. The Arcade was located in a shopping center so I had to get away from all of the bystanders. I directed him to hit a few corners until we ended up on a street with a lot of warehouse and office space. I made him pull into an unoccupied lot and instructed him to drive all the way to the back of the parking lot. It was there I ordered him to shut the engine off and hand me his keys.

"Please Eric! Don't kill me cousin!" he cried out.
"Shut the fuck up!" I barked at him. "I don't want to hear that shit! And stop calling me by my real name!" I added.
"Alright. You're right E-Loc," he muttered.
"Now put yo' hands on the steering-wheel and don't move 'em, or else I'm gon' smoke yo' ass!" I screamed on him. "You hear me?" I asked to make myself clear.

He nodded his head up & down to indicate he understood. I then opened the passenger side door without ever taking my eyes off of him, and stood outside the car with the .357 aimed at him. He closed his eyes and moved his lips as if he were praying. I hurriedly made my way around the front of the car and to the driver's side, where I opened the door and told him to put his hands on his head and step outta the car. He did as I told him, while silently mouthing the words, "Please don't kill me," and looking horrified. I didn't say another word. I let the gun do the talking, and waved it a certain way to let his big ass know where to go.

I led him to a twelve-foot high chain linked fence, and pressed him against it with my forearm. I went in all of his pockets and took cash, his wallet, and close to an ounce of rock cocaine. I also made him get on his knees and remove his shoes, where I found more cash. I ended up with $4,200 in cash, plus the rocks and his jewelry. While I was stripping him of his jewelry, he readily gave me every piece. He even started removing shit without me having to ask. "Here you go. That's everything. It's all yours." he rattled off.

"Lay down on your stomach." I said.
"E-Loc please!" he begged while on his knees looking up at me. "Please don't kill me! Please!" he cried.

This big'head, Herman The Monster built mutha'fucka reached out for my leg like he was trying to tackle me or something. So, I swung the .357 at his head and got off two quick rounds that sounded like a cannon. "*Boom! Boom!*" The shots echoed. Scarface Dre grabbed his head and balled-up in a fetal position, then was motionless. I had missed with both shots. I really didn't want to kill him anyways. I just wanted to teach him a lesson. And I'd done that. I made him get his ass up and drive me back to The Road where Kid-D and the rest of the homies were. I told Scarface Dre he should be thankful that I let him live, and that his car was now "my car" but I'd come pick it up later. I never did get the car though because I was too busy running from The Law.

PHOTOS

ERIC NICHOLS

(Mom, Eric)

(Eric & Derrick)

(Eric)

(Eric & Poppy)

LOC TALES

(Darren, Eric, Shon, Torrey)

(Eric Nichols)

(Eric, Torrey, Poppy, Curtis Jr., Darren)

(Leola "Grandma Lee" Burton")

(Aunt Sivi, Uncle Al, Grandma Olivi, Poppy, Uncle Glen, Aunt Elaine, Dad)

ERIC NICHOLS

LOC TALES

ERIC NICHOLS

CHAPTER 16

I met a fine ass light-skinned female named Lynell. She was mixed. Half black and half white. I was still with Kam, but Lynell was who I really wanted to be with. But, Lynell was head over heels in love with this nigga named JR. The first time I fucked Lynell, we was at her grandma's house in the garage. There was a love seat in the garage, so we ended up "doin' it" on the love seat. Lynell was two years younger than me, but she acted a lot older. We would sit up and talk all through the night about our future as a couple. We even discussed the names we would pick for our children and stuff.

Lynell and her cousin Sheila were pretty close, and were always hangin' out together. When Lynell's father died on a job related accident, I was there to comfort her. At the time, her mom Linda lived in SanJose, California.

Lynell didn't want me hangin' out on The Road or in my hood. She always wanted to take walks with me and be a typical couple, but I ran my own "program". I went back up on The Road, knowing that I was wanted for shooting Big Marv. I was selling dope one day when I noticed a black & white patrol car heading my way. I had already put my dope in a piece of plastic and toilet paper, and had placed it between my butt-cheeks, so I wasn't trippin' when the patrol car pulled along side me and two police officers jumped out.

"Put your hands on top of your head!" one of the cops demanded.

I did what I was told. The cop did a quick pat down search on me, then told me that I fit the description of a robbery suspect. They asked me if they could take a picture of me for their investigation, instead of taking me downtown. I knew I hadn't robbed anyone lately, other than Dope-Dealers and Drug-Users. So, I smiled for the polaroid camera as the police took my picture. I was relieved.

The following day while up on The Road, I got into it with a nigga who disrespected me. I was showing a Smoker how much dope I would sell him for $100, when this ugly ass nigga got in my business. The ugly ass nigga stole my "sale", and I couldn't accept that.

"You can't be steppin' on my toes like that!" I told Ugly Cuz.

"What do you mean?" he asked.

"You stole my "sale" nigga!" I barked at him.

"I can serve whoever I want to serve!" he shot back.

I didn't even argue with him. I skipped over to a vacant lot and grabbed the .357 cannon I had hidden, then I skipped back towards his ugly ass. He saw me coming and ran inside Nagi's Liquor store. I was on his bumper, and started bustin' the moment I walked through the front door. He dove towards the counter, but the slugs from the cannon knocked him into the potato chips display. *Boom! Boom!* He laid unconscious on the floor. The smell of gun powder filled the tiny store. I looked at the owner named Dave behind the counter and said, "My bad Dave". I ran outta the store, jumped a few fences, and ran to my Uncle Gleek's house.

The next day I met with the homie Kid-D at R.J. and Amp's house. Kid-D told me that it was best for me to go out of town for a little while because my name was "ringing". He suggested that I go with the homie named Baby Wes, who was two years younger than me, but carried himself like he was my age. Baby Wes' momma lived in a small town called Hanford in central California. It was about an hour and a half north of Bakersfield, and it sort of reminded me of Bakersfield, only it was a lot smaller. The black community in Hanford consisted of different territories like Amberwoods, Kings Terrace, and Home Gardens.

Baby Wes' momma had a new husband. He and his buddy had the Dope-Game in Hanford
sewed-up, and really didn't like the fact that I showed up with a lot more dope than they had. But, I wasn't there to step on their toes. I was merely trying to hide out long enough until it was safe for me to return to Bakersfield. But Baby Wes wanted the money and fame.

One afternoon I was shooting dice with a few niggas from Hanford. Most of them were from Hanford's Eight Tray Gangsta Crips. There was Dumpy, his brother Tony, Gee, G-Wayne, Fool, and Gee's step-daddy named Winston. We were shooting dice outside in the apartments parking lot on Jones street. I wasn't trying to move nowhere now that the dice were going my way. Winston picked-up the dice and walked over to an area he suggested. I told him to bring the dice back, but that only led us to argue. He stomped off to his house, which was next door to the apartments I was at. I jogged across the street to Baby Wes' momma house and retrieved my Tech-9. I saw Winston on his porch across the street with a long ass rifle. I didn't want to have long range gunplay, especially while I was at my homeboy's momma house. So, I walked across the street towards Winston with the Tech-9 in plain view. Baby Wes caught up with me and told me to go back into his momma's yard, then he scolded me.

"Damn E-Loc cuz. We are suppose to be layin' low, and you out here trippin'," he said. "Plus my momma gotta live here." he added.

He was right, so I let it go. But, I would never forget the old man named Winston. I made a mental note to add him to my "Bad News" list.

Baby Wes had a girlfriend named Valerie. We called her Val. She was one of the most popular females in the small town.

Her brother Big Money Meche had recently got killed in Oklahoma, and Meche's baby momma named Kenya was living with Val. I started fuckin' Kenya on Val's living room couch. She was "Square" but really cool and sweet.

One day Val found a bottle of Lice/Crab shampoo in Baby Wes' tennis shoes that were inside of her closet. She cussed his ass out too, but he told her that the shampoo was mines. I didn't like that at all because I didn't want rumors to be floating around like that about me. But, he was my homeboy, and I didn't want his girlfriend trippi' on him. So, I went along with his story.

A week later I went to SanJose, California to visit my ex-girlfriend named Arika. The same one that I was sneaking out of the Group Home to go be with. She was in college and living in a Sorority House with several girls. They were all interested in meeting me, and were fascinated by my Gangsta Mentality. I found their living arrangements to be interesting myself. It was almost like they were living in a Group Home, but without the supervision. Their bowls and their cups had stickers with their names on them. Their kitchen shelves and their refrigerator shelves had their names on them as well. At the time I wore my hair with a Jheri curl just like the rapper Eazy-E. The first night there I sat up late answering questions from Arika's roommates. When they finally fell asleep, I made love to Arika underneath her blankets. We "did it" nice and slow because she didn't want her roommates to know we were fuckin'. But, I noticed one of her roommates peeking at us anyway.

While we were "doin' it" I felt some biting and itching goin' on at the base of my dick and on my balls. I got up and went to the bathroom. Once inside the bathroom I looked at my dick and balls, but I didn't notice anything out of the ordinary. I still felt an itching and biting feeling on my balls, like a pin was sticking me. I grabbed my balls and inspected them closely, but there was still nothing visibly wrong. I then used my finger to feel my balls in the area that was itching, and I felt what can only be described as a hair-bump. But I still couldn't visibly see the hair-bump. I pinched the area where it felt like a hair-bump, then looked between my fingers. There it was! A tiny, almost transparent-looking spider-type bug. Crabs! My mind raced and I realized I had to have caught them from Baby Wes. 'But how?' I thought. I hadn't had sex with any of the females he was fuckin'. Unless he was fuckin' Val's friend, Kenya on the down-low. Nah! I believe I got them when Val washed my clothes with Baby Wes' clothes and the crabs somehow survived, and ended up in my thermal underpants.

I didn't tell Arika what I'd discovered on my balls. I just got dressed and told her that I had to make a quick run. There was a 24 hour drug store nearby, so I went there and purchased the same kind of Lice/Crab shampoo that Val found in Baby Wes' sneakers and I returned to the Sorority House to shower and use the shampoo. I ended up finding some more of the little creepy mutha'fuckas up under my balls, my scrotum, and damn near in my ass-hole.

The next morning I boarded the Amtrak bus to Sacramento, California.

CHAPTER 17

My oldest brother D-Nutt was at the station waiting, along with his homeboy C-Loc. They had been in Sac-Town for a couple of days already gettin' their hustle on. They drove me to a house in the Oak Park area where a guy named Corey lived. He and my brother D-Nutt had both attended Consumnes River College together, and had both played on the basketball team.

The house we were at was actually Corey's grandma's. My little brother D-Mac was also there with Crumb, Suavay, and Tee. They all came from Bakersfield to get their hustle on. D-Mac, Tee, and Suavay all had an apartment together on 65th street near the mall. D-Nutt, C-Loc, and Corey were all staying at Corey's grandma's house in Oak Park, on Orinda Way. Oak Park was a neighborhood full of Bloods. In fact, most of the black gangs in Sac-Town were Bloods, except for 29th & 24th Street Crips. There was probably a few more smaller Crip-Gangs out there, but I didn't know of them.

My brother D-Nutt had suggested that I get a motel room near the mall, and I was all for it until these two nice looking females came by Corey's to buy a half ounce of rock cocaine each. I flirted with them the moment they walked in the door.

"Hey baby, what's yo' name?" I asked the best looking of the two.

"Lorraine." she said while smiling at me.

The other one was named MeMe and I told them I was single and from Los Angeles. I always lied about where I was from just in case I had to kill somebody wherever I was at. I found out Lorraine had a 1 year old son and lived in her own apartment in a nearby town twenty minutes away from Sac-Town. The small town was called Rancho Cordova. I talked Lorraine into coming back to see me at Corey's later that night and she showed up with MeMe. Me and C-Loc left with them to Rancho Cordova and I ended up fuckin' that same night. C-Loc fucked MeMe too.

Lorraine was super cute and hairy. I made her my girlfriend, and even moved in with her. C-Loc moved in too. So, me and him got really close during this time. He was a cold killer, and was on Monster Swole. He had done a lot of time in C.Y.A. and was a well respected member of the Mid City Crips.

At the time, he was fuckin' MeMe on a daily basis, while I was fuckin' Lorraine. But, we both had our "real" girlfriends back at home in Bakersfield. His real girlfriend was Barbara, and Kam was still mines. It didn't take us long to learn how to "make things happen" in Sac-Town. The key to learning anything about any city or town, is to holla at the females there. Particularly the Hood-Rats, because they will gladly tell you everything. They know who's Ballin', Snitchin', Robbin', Ho'n, Pimpin', Smokin', Bangin', who's cool, who's scandalous, and who's real.

Lorraine was kinda popular in Sac-Town because she grew up out there, and her baby's daddy was a Blood nigga from Oak Park. He was in jail when I met her, so I never did meet him. But, I did meet his sister Olga. She was a cute, thick, red-bone bitch. She was half-black and half-Cuban, and she was "on me" the first time we met at Lorraine's. "Why couldn't I have met you first?" she asked seductively while looking at me with those "come fuck me" eyes. I'm a freak-nasty nigga myself, and couldn't resist her flirting. I started picking her up and taking her to my little brother D-Mac's apartment to fuck her. It was always fun and exciting with Olga because we were sneaking.

Lorraine introduced me to several more of her homegirls, and I put them all to work sellin' dope. I had C-Loc as my "right hand man", the bitches were making me rich, and niggas from my city who had major "weight", wanted me to put their dope in my hands. I rode the Amtrak train back & forth from Bake-Town to Sac-Town. I'd put all of my guns in a duffle bag, and put the kilo's of cocaine in another.

When I first started fuckin' with Lorraine I bought a lot of food and told her to invite her friends over to our place and I had her cook some jumbo shrimps. Me and C-Loc bit into that hard shit and looked at each other like we had a big secret. That was the worst tasting shrimp ever because the bitch forgot to take the shells off, and we were eating the whole damn thing. We laughed all day about that shit.

That same day I pulled out a bag of weed. It was some light-green Sess. At the time, I'd been having different weed like Ty-Bud, Indo, and Skunk. But on this particular day, all I had was some good-ass light-green Sess. It was some pretty good shit too. I tossed it all on the kitchen counter, all proud and shit, and told MeMe to roll-up a few joints. She opened the sack of weed and yelled, "Aw hell naw! They got Ban-Dingy! This is Bammer-Weed! We don't smoke this shit!" she ranted on. All the bitches there were giggling and laughing. I pulled out a wad of one-hundred dollar bills to silence their ass, and said, "Well, go buy us some mutha'fuckin' Greens then!" She did. And the shit she called Greens was what we called Indo in Bakersfield. What she got for $100 would've cost me $350 in Bakersfield. I had MeMe go spend $1,000 and I started taking the weed back to Bakersfield to sell at Indo prices. I made a lot of money and found out the weed business will get a man a lot of pussy too.

When it came to the "Coke Business", my brother D-Nutt had the most clientele in Sac-Town, and was probably making more money than I was. But, he also had more niggas to feed. I only had C-Loc to feed, and we ate good. I bought me a Caprice Classic, put 6x9's and 10" woofers in it. The niggas in Sac-Town called Caprice Classics "Mob Cars".

I started going out to the clubs in Sac-Town too. They had cool ass spots like Cocoa Palms and Ranch Royal. I used to run into stars like Eddie Murphy and basketball players like Wayman Tisdale. There were other athletes and stars that I wasn't quite familiar with, who were always drunk and had their arms around me like we were cool or something. I was hanin' it my way. I'd show-up in Bakersfield like I was Santa Clause, and buy my bitches shoes, jewelry, and clothes. I'd give momma some money and try to visit most of my family before getting back on that highway. When C-Loc's girlfriend named Barbara went to jail, I drove him to Bakersfield so we could pay her rent, watch her apartment, and make sure her son Nate was safe.

While I was in Bakersfield on one of my trips, I decided to go hang out with some of my homies. The first ones I ran into was G-Dez and Pud. They were in Pud's white Monte Carlo, and I got in the back seat while we rode around making weed and rock sales. I had that bomb ass Indo with me too. I wore two pair of underwear. Some briefs that I called "Butt Huggers" or "Thun-thun-thun-da-dums", and some boxers. I could put the weed in my crotch area and not have to worry about being caught with it. Anyway, we were riding down Virginia Avenue, and got pulled over. The cops asked Pud to step outta the car since he was the driver. After ten minutes of talking to him, they approached the car and asked me and G-Dez our names. I gave them a fake name, but it was one that I knew was "clean" because it was my cousin J.J.'s name. The cops made all three of us sit on the curb while they searched the car. Pud had given them permission to search. I don't know why he let them search. He wasn't on probation or parole. The cops found what appeared to be three or four rocks on the front floor of the car. They tested it on the spot and confirmed that it was in fact rock cocaine. The one cop who everyone called Mario pulled Pud to the side again to question him. The other cop, who was known as Indian pulled G-Dez to the side for more questioning too. After G-Dez and Pud got finished being questioned by the cops, they both sat back down on the curb beside me. Then Mario told me to stand up and he began doing a more thorough pat-down search on me than he'd done the first time. He grabbed my ass and felt up under my crotch, asking "What is this?" "That's my balls sir!" I said innocently. He felt between my legs again, "What do you have in there?" he asked again. "My balls sir!" I repeated. He moved me closer to the patrol car's back door, opened it, and asked me again what I had in my pants. I stuck to my story. He said he'd take me to Kern Medical Center to do a Body Cavity Search if I didn't give him whatever was in my pants. I still didn't give in. He got on his radio while I stood between him and the opened back door of the patrol car with the handcuffs still on me. "I got one transport to K.M.C. for a cavity search," he said into the radio. Static was the only thing I heard. He didn't wait for a reply. He just reached into my pants and pulled the weed out. He shoved me into the back seat of the patrol car then talked to G-Dez and Pud briefly before allowing them to drive off.

Mario and Indian were two well-known cops who basically crossed the line in order to nab suspects. Before the two came along, there was only one other cop bold enough to pull renegade stunts in the Black Community. And he was a Sheriff Deputy named McHale. There were two who came close, named Eindshink and Dickens. But, Mario and Indian were two bold cops. They drove me to the Bakersfield Police Station. But, on the way to the station they made small talk with me. I pretended to be afraid, and played the "Square" role.

"Please don't take me to jail sir." I pleaded with them. "My momma is gon' kill me if she finds out about this." I said making my voice sound like I was frightened.
"Well, you're in big trouble buddy." Mario said.
"This is a felony case." Indian stated.
I pretended to be even more afraid. "Please gimme a chance sir. I'm a freshman at Bakersfield College. I work at Kentucky Fried Chicken, and I've never been in trouble in my life." I pleaded with them.

Mario then tried to capitalize on what he thought was my fear, by saying...

"Unless you can help us find three people with the same amount of marijuana or more, you'll be going to jail for a very long time."
"But I don't know anybody sir." I said sounding more afraid. Mario then asked me if I knew Wilton, Ronnie, or Kevin. "I've heard of those names, but I don't personally know those guys sir." I said in my most proper-speaking voice.

We were getting near the police station so I thought of a quick plan. I could make up a name, have them take me to a location that would be impossible for them to see from their patrol car, get some weed, return to their car with it, and promise to help get a larger amount at a later date, I thought to myself.

"Excuse me sir." I politely said from the back seat as Mario pulled into the parking lot of the police station. "I know a Jamaican who has pounds of weed. He sold me the weed y'all found on me." I lied. The cops looked at each other like their silly "scare tactics" had finally broken me.

"Where does this Jamaican do his dealings?" Mario asked.
"I don't know the name of the street, but I can show you how to get there." I said matter of factly.

The cops then got out of their patrol car, went to the trunk, and put on their police jackets. They had flipped their jackets inside-out so that they would appear to be regular black jackets. They let me outta the back seat, removed the handcuffs, and led me to an unmarked patrol car. We all got into the patrol car and I gave them directions to some apartments near the Valley Plaza Mall. A good friend of mine named Phresh Kutz, who was also my D.J. at times, lived in the apartments. There was only five units, but there was also a high wooden fence around them so, the cops wouldn't be able to see the exact apartment unit I enter. The cops had already taken over $400 in cash from me when they first arrested me, so I didn't have any cash on me. They gave me two twenty dollar bills that were marked, and instructed me to purchase some weed with them. I went through the gates' entrance, pulled it closed behind me, and quickly made my way to apartment #3. The one Phresh Kutz lived in.

"Hey E-Loc!" he excitedly greeted me upon opening his front door. I shook his hand and stepped inside. I told him that I needed an ounce of weed, and that I'd pay him for it tomorrow. He didn't question me. He simply went to his kitchen cabinet and grabbed a handful of weed from the compressed remains of the pound of weed. He put it in a sandwich bag for me and handed it to me. I asked for another sandwich bag, and evenly divided the weed. I put one half in the bottom of my shoe and the other half in my pocket. I peeked out the window to make sure the cops hadn't come inside the gate.

"Who's out there?" Phresh Kutz asked.

I turned to face him, got really close to him, and whispered, "The police is in the parking lot waiting for me. They don't know which apartment unit I'm in because they didn't see which one I came in. I told them I was coming to see a Jamaican, so don't trip."

He looked at me with disbelief on his face. I didn't waste any time gettin' up outta there. I walked out the gate, closed it behind me, and got back in the car with the cops. We pulled off, hit a few corners, and I gave them the half ounce I had in my pocket. Mario handed me his business card and told me to call him the following day. I had them drop me off in the same exact spot they picked me up at on Virginia Avenue, then I walked five blocks to The Road.

In the Vernon Strong's parking lot I saw Pud and G-Dez mingling and selling dope as usual. When they saw me they both looked like they had seen a ghost.

"How did you get out?" Pud asked me.
"They never took me to jail." I said.
"What did they do to you?" G-Dez asked.

I then explained to them exactly what had happened. I tried to read their faces to see which one had told the cops I had weed on me, but I couldn't tell.

I went back to Sacramento early the next day. Lorraine's friends were good at selling the rocks I provided. I was purchasing one kilo at a time, but I'd also bring somebody else's kilo with me to sell too. My homie Bump had a big brother named "C" who was Ballin' outta control. So, I'd fuck with him and with other Top-Notch niggas like Weasel and Fontaine.

I was starting to catch serious feelings for Lorraine, and I wanted to include her in my life more than she'd been. My alias name was Chauncy and sometimes I'd go by Edward. I've used Chris, James, Elroy, and E.J., just to name a few. I believe the police records have me down for at least twenty-two alias names. Anyway, I wanted to make Lorraine my "main" girl, but I still wasn't sure if I could trust her or not. I came up with a plan. I had my brother D-Nutt's homeboy named Crumb get at her on the "down low". We and C-Loc set the bait by discussing Crumb in front of Lorraine. We talked about how he was the richest nigga in our circle, and we made up stories about the different cars and homes he owned. We "put a ten on it" then I gave Crumb her cell phone number and told him how to proposition her. It only took one telephone conversation, and she "bit". She agreed to meet Crumb at a hotel. I told Crumb that his reward for helping me discover if I could trust the bitch, would be a night in bed with her. I really didn't want the bitch after I found out she would so easily sleep with a nigga in my circle. I was still living under the same roof with her, and wanted to pretend like I didn't know about her and Crumb's night of fuckin'. But, I couldn't. I had feelings for the bitch, and I had to let her know that she hurt my feelings.

    Three days after she initially met with Crumb, I found out that she and Crumb had been meeting and fuckin' everyday for the past three days. Now I was mad about Crumb betraying my trust as well. I felt like killin' both of them, but my nigga C-Loc talked me out of it. But, that didn't stop me from confronting them.

    Crumb showed up at my brother D-Mac's apartment. We were all chillin', smoking weed, and playing video games. When Crumb came through the front door, my attitude instantly changed. My big brother D-Nutt got in Crumb's ear, then came to me and told me that Crumb wanted to apologize to me. I stepped out onto the balcony into the windy light-rain sprinkles of the Sacramento weather. Crumb followed. He immediately admitted to being wrong for what he'd done, and told me he didn't want any problems. I looked him dead in his eyes with my hands stuffed into my leather Raiders coat and my finger itchin' to pull the trigger of my Colt .45. The nigga babbled on and on about how much he loved and respected me. Then he said, "I know you wanna kill me. I know you's a killa." Then he looked towards the ground, shaking his head like he was telling himself that he fucked-up. I just stared him down, wanting him to say something that I could kill him for. But, when he looked up at me, all I saw were wet eyes on a pitiful-looking face. I walked pass him, back into the apartment, out the front door, and jumped in my car. C-Loc came running and I let him in the passenger side. I drove us to Lorraine's and we didn't say a word on the way there. I called her cell phone and found out she was out with some of her friends. I pretended like everything was normal and waited in her parking lot. When she finally pulled into the parking lot I became alert and enraged.

"Don't kill the bitch in the parking lot Dog." C-Loc said.

She didn't even notice my car in the parking lot. I got out of my car and approached her as soon as she exited her car. I shoved the .45 into her ribs and quickly escorted her towards her apartment's front door.

"Baby, What's the matter? Why are you trippin'? she asked with fear in her voice.
"Bitch! You know why I'm trippin'!" I exclaimed as I pushed her up against her front door. "Open this mutha'fucka!" I demanded.
"Okay baby, Please!" she said while fumbling to open the door. I led her through the apartment to her bedroom and onto her bed, face-down. I grabbed her by her throat, held her down with all my weight on her, and pressed the .45 into her temple.
"Bitch! Why did you fuck Crumb!?" I yelled. "Huh!?" I asked again. "Why you been fuckin' Crumb!?" I demanded. I couldn't hear her reply because my weight on her throat only allowed her to whisper. "Bitch! You hear me!?" I shouted again.

I let her throat go and grabbed a pillow. I placed it on her face to muffle her cries. As I sat on her with the pillow covering her face, she was no longer the girl I had feelings for. She had become some struggling bitch who betrayed my trust. I put the .45 up against the pillow and pulled the trigger. "*Boom!*" It echoed and left a deafening silence in the room. Everything seemed like it was in slow-motion. C-Loc burst through the bedroom door with the Mausburgh pistol-grip pump in hand.

"Nigga let's get up outta here!" he said.

I jumped up off the bitch, bumped into the door-jab on my way out, and into the rainy night. I drove us to a motel about two miles away, and got us a room for the night.

The next day I called one of Lorraine's next-door neighbors to find out what happened. She said she thought Lorraine's place got raided because there was a lot of police all over the apartment grounds, and Lorraine's front door had been kicked off the hinges. She also said one of the cops were at Lorraine's when she went by earlier that morning to check.

I later found out Lorraine had passed-out when I fired the shot into the pillow. Someone heard the gunshot, called the cops, and they kicked-in the door when Lorraine failed to answer. I finally got in touch with Lorraine later that night and we made-up. I decided that she couldn't be my main girl, but she could still sell dope for me but that turned out to be a big mistake too. Lorraine was the only one in her crew who would "come up short" with the money she owed for the dope-sacks I'd give her. I mean, she'd be "short" every time and had the weakest excuses. Then one day I caught the bitch in her bathroom smokin' my dope. I couldn't believe it. This fine-ass bitch was smokin'. I packed all my clothes, let her keep the furniture, and "did it movin'".

I moved in with Corey on Orinda Way until I could get my own spot. Corey's neighbor named Tiffany was fine as hell. She lived with her grandma and auntie, and was two years younger than me. I met her one day when she came to deliver Corey a message. She had on Capri pants, fluffy blue house-shoes, and wore her long hair cut with a "bob" on one side. She had a cool shape too. I started off by going over her grandma's to visit her. But, I'd talk her outta her pussy every time. I spent a lot of time with her, but stayed in touch with all of my other girlfriends.

One night I talked on the phone with my girl Lynell for four hours. She had pissed me off in the beginning of the conversation because she acted like she was defending Big Marv. "Why you shoot him baby? He's cool. He said he was gon' help me out," she said. But, after I screamed on her, she changed the subject. Lynell was always good at "buttering me up". She claimed she missed me a lot and wanted me to come home. She and her cousin Sheila were living together. Sheila used to be my homie Robert Earl's girlfriend.

Both of my brothers were already back in Bakersfield, along with the rest of their crew. It was almost Christmas, but I was "on the run" for all types of shit, and wouldn't feel safe in Bakersfield. Plus, the two cops named Mario and Indian were looking for me because I never did call them or help them "bust" anybody. But, I thought it would be fun to sneak into town and fuck Lynell. Fuck it! I got on the highway.

CHAPTER 18

When I got to Bakersfield I drove through my hood first, then went up on The Road. I saw both of my brothers standing by their cars parked across the street from Footlongs. I busted a U-turn and pulled up to them.

"What's up y'all?" I asked, smiling and shit.
"What you doin' out here?" they both asked in unison.
"I'm 'bout to go kick-it with Lynell." I said.
"With who?" they both said again in unison.
"Lynell." I repeated.
"Hell naw!" my little brother D-Mac said.
"She been fuckin' with Big Marv." he added.
"Yeah bro, don't fuck with her." D-Nutt said.
"Is that right?" I asked in disbelief.
"Matter of fact, that nigga Big Marv is across the street in a dice game." D-Nutt informed me.

I looked across the street at Footlong's parking lot and saw a group of niggas in a huddle gambling. I drove to Virginia Avenue and parked my car which was only one block away from the dice game. I popped the hood on my car and grabbed the same pistol-grip pump C-Loc had given me, then jumped the fence. I jumped another fence into someone else's backyard, then came out on Murdock street where I walked towards Lakeview Avenue and Footlongs. The streets was packed with cars bumper to bumper. I held the gun with one hand, draggin' the tip of the barrel along the ground behind me. I went through a maze of people and parked cars with people sittin' in them until I reached Footlong's parking lot. I was bent over walking, trying to stay low, and I peeked over every so often. I also came face to face with startled people sittin' inside the parked cars. Then I made my move. I drug the pistol-grip pump in one quick motion and held it in front of me as I charged at the dice game like a war veteran, then jacked the gun off to put one in the chamber. The clicking sound of the gun jackin'-off caused the crowd of gamblers to lay down in defeat. Some covered their heads, put their ass in the air, or balled-up in fetal positions. I made a quick survey of the immediate area, but I didn't spot Big Marv.

"E-Loc!" I heard my brother D-Nutt yell as he came running towards me. He pointed in the direction of some car tail-lights.
"There go Big Marv!" he shouted.

I ran around the corner and back to my car. I put the gun back under the hood and grabbed the Colt .45 from on the side of my car battery, then I got inside my car and got in traffic. I knew there was only a slim chance of me catching up to him, but I was prepared just in case I did.
After hittin' a few more corners I decided to drop-in on Lynell, who was at Sheila's. I knocked on the door and Lynell opened it without asking who was at the door. The shock and fear in her face instantly made me feel like she'd been up to no good, and that my brother's warnings about her were valid. She finally snapped out of her paranoid state and hugged me tight.

"I'm so glad you're home daddy." she said. Her voice and her tone were sexy like a Phone Sex Operator. "Come on in baby. Let me take your coat." she offered.

Her voice was hypnotic, and I peeled outta my coat without any hesitation. I handed my coat to her and she sucked in air like she'd been spooked by someone. The weight from the Colt .45 that was in my coat had shook her up.

"What do you have in here?" she asked whining.

I snatched my coat back from her and put it back on. Just then, Sheila walked into the livin room where we were.

"What's up "E"? Can I get a hug?" Sheila asked with her arms outstretched and walking towards me. I bent down to give her a brief hug. Lynell started going into her "I-want-to-help-you-do-right" role. "Daddy, you need to stay here with me and stop running around with guns," she said. She also said a bunch of other shit too, but it fell on deaf ears. I was once again faced with a decision to make regarding a bitch and her betrayal. Lynell stepped closer to me and asked me to hold her. But I stared into her eyes hoping she could see that she'd hurt me with her acts of betrayal. I spinned on my heels and walked outta there without saying goodbye.

I started fuckin' this short dark-skinned little bitch named Minisha. She was my age and already had one daughter who looked exactly like her. Minisha had a big head, but she was really pretty and I would call her "Big Head/Little Body". Minisha boosted clothes and when she would boost clothes, she would give them to me. The first time she boosted for me, she gave me a rayon and silk shirt. She told me that she had initially stole it for my homie A.D. but I guess he never came by to get it. He had plenty of bitches and he had started gettin' sprung on Pete-A-Moe's sister, Sabrina. The same one I used to fuck with too.

Minuisha lived off of Panama Lane with her momma and older sister. The first night I went over there I sat in the living-room talking to Minisha most of the night until her sister and their kids had gone to bed. She sat in an easy-chair while I sat on a sofa. The Springs on the sofa were old, so I sank into the pillows where I sat. While sitting on that chair, I kept feeling something crawling on me. First on my leg, then on my arm. I felt something on my neck and I swatted at it. Minisha kept thumpin' and flickin' shit off of the arm of the easy-chair, but she tried to be sneaky about it. She even acted like she was stretchin' her arms to yawn, and would sweep her hand on the wall near the easy-chair. Something dropped on my head and fell to the floor, but I didn't see what it was. I looked really good in the direction where I thought the object had fallen and I continued to stare. The whole rug appeared to be moving. I felt shit crawling all over me now, so I jumped up and clicked on the lamp.

"Damn!" I yelled.

There was roaches everywhere.

"Oh shit!" I yelled again.

They were deep as fuck. Roaches on the couch, ceiling, floor, walls, coming outta the t.v., the stereo, and on the tables and shit. I ain't never saw that many roaches in my life. Minisha didn't get excited or nothin'. I guess she was used to them.

"I can't stand these damn roaches, she said nonchalantly. "Come on," she instructed me as she motioned for me to follow her to her bedroom.

I was lookin' for roaches now. I walked by the bathroom on my way to her bedroom and saw roaches crawling on the sink. They were eating toothpaste and Ajax and shit. I ended up fuckin' her little ass and the pussy was good. But, I didn't enjoy it because I was too worried about a roach might crawl in or fall in the crack of my ass. After we fucked i promised to call her the next day and left.

On my way to my car I ran into her neighbor Anthony who was smoking Sherm in the parking lot of their apartments. I hadn't had no Loop in awhile and the smell of it made my mouth water.

"Let me hit that?" I asked.

He slowly handed it to me without saying a word. It was some good shit too. I got in my car and it felt like I was pedaling the car with my bare feet like on the cartoon show, The Flintstones.

I drove to Chucc's house on South Williams street. His cousin Kendra was in town so I figured I'd run into her over there. My "high" came down, but I kept the small piece of Sherm-stick in my ashtray for a later time. My homie Fats was over to Chucc's house along with Junkman, Henry, Lumbo, Benny, and Kay-B. We ate some of Big Rob's chili beans and barbecue. Everyone started leaving just as Kendra pulled up in her pink truck. Chucc's sister Lavina was with her as always, and they had just come from hangin' out on The Road, the same place everyone was on their way to. Chucc was laying on the couch sucking his thumb and talking on the phone. I thought it was his girl Leah because he had been seeing her a lot lately and was referring to her as "wifey". Lavina wanted to go back up on The Road so she talked Kendra into going back up there with her. I wasn't tryin' to be in public places because I thought I'd get arrested. So, I kicked off my shoes and stretched out on Chucc's bed in his bedroom. He finally got off of the phone all happy and shit.

"What's up my guy?" he gleefully asked.

Then he went into the small bathroom located in his bedroom and got in the mirror. He was putting curl activator on his little S-Curl. Chucc's hair was naturally curly because he was mixed with Indian. But he'd put S-Curls on his hair to make it look better.

"The square-bitch Tinisha is coming over," he said all enthusiastic and shit.

He brushed his teeth and slapped on some cologne.

"You can peek at us if you want to," he said as he raced to answer the knock at the front door.

It was her. I heard them embrace and then the door closed.

They didn't waste any time gettin' down to business either. I heard Tinisha giggle a couple of times, then it got really quiet in there. I tiptoed to the doorway and peeked around the corner. There they were. On the long couch. She had her eyes closed with one arm draped over her forehead and the other hand on top of Chucc's head, while his face was buried between her legs. He must have been an expert Pussy Eater because she started bucking her hips, fuckin' his face, and pulled a pillow over her face to muffle her cries. I could hear her pussy making a smacking sound as he greedily licked, sucked, and ate her pussy. She tossed the pillow to the floor after her body stopped bucking, then she looked over Chucc's shoulder and into my eyes. I froze for a second then ducked back behind the doorway. Chucc got up and came into the room where I was. He was smiling and blushing like he'd done something special. His face was wet with her juices and he smelled fishy. He acted like he couldn't smell himself, so I took another sniff to be sure my nose wasn't playin' tricks on me. *Sniff-Sniff!* I inhaled and the aroma stung my nose. I frowned up and leaned away from him like he had shit on his face.

"Damn cuz!" I said in disgust. "Her pussy smells like fish," I whispered so that she couldn't hear me.

Chucc fell-out laughing. But he didn't laugh out loud. He laughed so hard that his body shook and tears came from his eyes. I didn't think it was funny at all. Chucc finally recouped and walked Tinisha to her car. Kendra and Lavina both showed up an hour later. I took Kendra's thick-ass into another bedroom and fucked the shit outta her. Early the next morning I went back to Hanford with Baby Wes and took nine ounces of cocaine with me.

CHAPTER 19

Baby Wes' momma was mad about us gettin' all the money and for making it hard for her man to sell his smaller, less potent dope. Her husband was still one of the main Dope Dealers in the small town. I sat in her living room and heard her in the kitchen "checkin'" Baby Wes. She screamed on him real tough, then slapped the shit outta him when he tried to talk back. *Smack!* He came storming outta there with tears in his eyes and we "did it movin'" to Valerie's house.

Baby Wes told me it was "hot" in Hanford, and suggested that I stay indoors as much as possible while he goes around the small town selling the dope. I took heed and stayed in. For two days he didn't come by or call me. He had all of my dope and whatever money he'd made from selling some of the dope. I had a few thousand dollars on me, so I wasn't really trippin' on no money. I was worried about him and his safety. Plus, I also had a lot of people wanting to buy dope, but he had all of the dope with him. I grew tired of waiting for him to return, so I paid a nigga to drive me to Bakersfield and I went home to Kam.

Baby Wes finally called me and said he was on his way to my house. When he arrived he had the homie Sheldon with him. They had been shopping in Los Angeles, and Baby Wes had bought me some clothes and shoes with my money. He'd bought himself clothes too. I was a little pissed off at him for not letting me know he was going to Los Angeles without me, and for spending my money without asking me first. He told me he still had most of my dope and promised to bring it over later on. He and Sheldon left and I went back inside with Kam. I didn't sit long. I called a taxi cab to take me to the eastside so I could drop off some dope to my Uncle Gleek. While I was over there, my brother D-Nutt's best friend named June came by. June's little brother Tip was my best friend. The same Tip who was with me when I got my first piece of pussy. Anyway, I had June take me back home in his Volkswagen. I invited him in and smoked a few joints with him. Baby Wes called while I was there and told me he'd sold the rest of the dope and had my money for me. He also said he needed some more dope to sell. I told him over the phone that I was gonna be leaving soon, but it was cool for him to come by and pick up two ounces from my girl Kam. June told me that he'd just gotten out of jail and was broke. He also said it was his daughter's birthday and he didn't have any money to get her anything for the occasion. I didn't need to hear anymore. I gave him one hundred dollars and a quarter ounce of dope and I told him he didn't owe me anything. I gave Kam all of my dope to put up, and I let her know that I'd left two ounces in the bathroom under the plunger for Baby Wes. I told her that he was gonna come by later to get them. Me and June then got in his Volkswagen and headed back to the eastside.

I didn't make it back home until nearly 3AM. When I got into bed with Kam she told me that Baby Wes had came by to pick up the two ounces. I made love to her and was awakened with breakfast in bed as usual. Baby Wes called me around noon and said he was down the street from me and would be pulling up any minute. I asked him if he sold the two ounces yet, and he replied by saying, "What ounces?" like he didn't know what I was talking about. "I didn't even make it over there last night," he added. I instantly got mad and hung-up the phone.

"Kam!" I yelled for her to come to me. "You gave baby Wes that dope I left in the bathroom, right?" I asked her.

"Yeah Eric. Just like you told me to," she replied. "I know his ass ain't tryin' to say I didn't give it to him," she added.

"Yeah, he said he didn't come over here last night," I told her.

Just then I heard a car pull up. It was Baby Wes and Sheldon. I immediately went outside to get at him about my two zones.

"My girl said she gave them to you last night cuz." I stated. Before baby Wes could speak, Sheldon spoke up.
"He was with me all night E-Loc. I didn't bring him over here homie." Sheldon explained. "Cuz! That's on Tray-Dog rest in peace. I didn't come get two zones from baby!" Baby Wes said convincingly.

I stormed into the house, walked pass Kam, grabbed my .45 from my bedroom, then asked Kam again.

"Baby are you sure you gave this nigga my dope? Because he "put it" on Tray-Dog that he didn't get it." I explained.
"That's on my mutha-fuckin' kids I gave him that dope!" she yelled. "Why would I lie?" she cried.
"Well, one of y'all gone give me my shit." I said matter of factly while holding the .45 in plain view.

I walked her outside so that I could hear them both repeat what they had said, but in front of each other. They both had tears in their eyes, and Kam was hysterical.

"I ain't got to lie! He had on a black Beenie Cap and was in the same white Volkswagen," she explained.

Me, Baby Wes, and Sheldon all looked at her with confused looks on our faces. Then, a light came on in my head, "Aw cuz, it was that nigga June," I said. I apologized to Kam and Baby Wes, then invited Baby Wes and Sheldon in. I accepted the money Baby Wes had for me and then gave him some more dope to sell. I went looking for June, but I never did run into him.
As the days and weeks passed, I grew a little more comfortable and started back hangin' out. One day I was up on The Road sellin' dope. I had a hand full of rocks in one hand and money in the other. The Smoker I served had just walked away when I looked up and noticed an all white Company Truck driving

down Lakeview really slow. I made eye contact with the driver. It was Big Marv. Our eyes were locked on each other until he slowed down to a complete stop. I then noticed the white tail lights, indicating the truck was in reverse. I tossed the rocks into the air, stuffed the money in my pocket, and took off running towards a parking lot. I was trying to make it to the vacant lot where i had my gun laying in the cut. I ran fast, clear across the parking lot and "*Wham!*" I ran right into a thick wire that draped around the perimeter of the parking lot. I flipped, then landed on both of my hands, sliding like a baseball player head first as the gravel and glass embed into the palms of my hands. I got back on my feet and could hear the grinding of the clutch as Big Marv had trouble putting the truck in gear. I ran faster, nearly falling as I stumbled to the dusty vacant lot and to the newspaper with the brick sittin' on top of it. I snatched the newspaper and grabbed the Tech-9. I then ran to the street to see the white truck still in reverse, with Big Marv struggling to control it. I put one round in the chamber and pulled the trigger as I trotted towards the truck. *Pop! Pop! Pop! Pop!* I held the trigger and unloaded the thirty round clip into the truck. Holes appeared all over the truck, windows shattered, the side mirror hung loosely, and the front tire went flat. The truck lunged forward as the tires screeched. I couldn't see Big Marv's head anymore, but the truck sped off and I kept on bustin' at his ass until I ran out of bullets. I later found out he had been struck in the shoulder and chest areas. This nigga Big Marv truly had nine lives.

    I hung out at Minisha's that night and Baby Wes came through and kicked it for a while. Minisha was telling us about one of her "Fuck buddies" named Top Dollar. He was from Los Angeles' Menlo Gangsta Crips. His baby momma named Dooda had moved to Bakersfield while he was in prison, so he moved out there when he got out of prison. This was the same Dooda I'd been having a crush on and trying to convince to be my girl.

    Top Dollar was a buff nigga with a wide nose, Boss Game, Major Hustle, and a unique style. A few O.G. Crips from Bakersfield tried to run Top Dollar out of town, but he wasn't havin' that. He made it clear that as long as his son and baby momma was living there, he wasn't goin' anywhere. At the time, Top Dollar was havin' money and Low-Lows and shit. He had a lot of bitches on his team too. Minisha was just one of many. Anyway,

Minisha was telling me, Baby Wes, and a few of her homegirls about how Top Dollar was trying to make her sleep with another one of his bitches. She claimed that Top Dollar was a little-dick nigga who only wants to eat pussy. She said the same night she refused to have sex with him and the other bitch, he put her out of the bed and made her sleep on the floor. Then when he seen she was comfortable on the floor, he put Minisha's ass outta the room altogether.

The next day after Minisha had told us all of this stuff about top Dollar, me and Baby Wes went up on The Road to Footlongs. Minisha came running across the street talking all fast and shit, then asked for a hug. I gave her one, but I also noticed how her attention was focused across the street where she had come running from. So, I asked her what was she looking at. She told me that Top Dollar was across the street waiting for her to go back over there with him, but she didn't want to go. She also said he was mad at her because she had refused to rub some lotion on his back for him. Just then, her homegirls pulled up and told her to get in so they could leave. Minisha left. A couple of hours later, Top Dollar came over to Footlongs in his burnt-orange 65 Chevy. He jumped out with the fat gold Turkish rope necklace on and a pair of gold Door-Knocker earrings.

"What's up cuz?" he said in a super-cool voice.

We both greeted him, but Baby Wes didn't waste any time trying to "clown" him about all the shit Minisha had told us earlier. I really wasn't laughing with Baby Wes when he was repeating the things Minisha had said about Top Dollar. Baby Wes even went as far as to ask me what Minisha had said, like he couldn't remember her exact words. But, I didn't verify his story one way or another. I simply said, "I can't remember what baby said." It was no big deal to me. In fact, the shit Minisha claimed Top Dollar had did was some shit I myself wanted to do too. So, I really couldn't understand what the big deal was.

I spent the night at Chucc's house that night and was awakened at 2AM by Lavina. She told me that someone was at the door for me, so I walked to the door half-sleep to find Top Dollar there.

"Let me holla at you real quick." he said.

I walked back to the couch I had been sleeping on and put my pistol in my pocket before walking outside into the early morning darkness. I followed Top Dollar outside the front gate to a Rental Car where Minisha and another female waited.

"What did baby tell you about me Cuz?" Top Dollar asked.
"I don't know," I said. "I don't want to get in y'alls shit," I added.

Top Dollar kept on tryin' to get me to repeat what Minisha had said about him, but I didn't want to add fuel to the fire.

"You can tell him exactly what I said. I didn't lie on him." Minisha blurted out.

I was still tired and wanted to get back inside, so I finally told Top Dollar what she said.

"All she said was you got a little dick, love to eat pussy, tried to make her have sex with you and you put her out." I said it like it was no big deal.
"Yeah I said that," she admitted.
"That's on my son, this bitch sucked my dick." Top Dollar shouted. He walked up to her like he was going to hit her, then he stood over her and screamed on her, "Bitch I'll fuck you up!" he threatened.

Minisha walked away from him towards the fence, but he followed her closely. She reached to place her hand on the fence, but he snatched her arm away and spun her around.

"Bitch I'll fuck you up if you ever lie on me again!" he yelled in her face. She walked towards the rental car, pass me.
"Eric I thought you said you wasn't gon' let nobody put they hands on me?" she said sounding sad.

I was shocked because I did remember telling her that the same night the roaches were falling on me. She looked at me like she wanted me to defend her, and he looked at me as if he was waiting for some type of response too.

"I told you I wouldn't let nobody put they hands on you if you was my girl, and if you choose to be my girl I'll protect you," I explained. "So, who do you want? Me or him?" I asked.
"I want to be with you," she softly said.
Top Dollar leaned in a little closer like he didn't hear what she said. "You want to be with who?" he asked, sounding like he couldn't believe what he'd heard.
"I want to be with Eric," she said clearly.
"There it is," I said to Top Dollar. Then I looked at her, "Now you don't have to worry about him or no other nigga puttin' they hands on you." I told her.

Top Dollar got in the back seat of the rental car while I had a few more words with Minisha. I instructed her to call me later on since it was damn near 3AM. I gave her a hug, kissed her on the forehead, and went back inside Chucc's house to finish sleeping.

CHAPTER 20

The weeks that followed were spent traveling back and forth to Sacramento and Bakersfield. The Black History Pageant and parade were coming up. The pageant was usually held at the Civic Auditorium in Bakersfield, and it drew a big crowd. My cousin J.J. had won in his age category when we were really young. I wasn't gonna be a participant in the pageant trying to win a crown, but I was suppose to perform a rap song at the pageant that particular year. Although I was still wanted by the police, I still wanted to take a chance on performing at the pageant.

    This nigga I grew up with named Kyle talked me into going to the pageant with him. He was really cool with Chucc and was fresh in town from Texas. He'd been in Texas hustlin' and came home with a lot of money and a new candy green Amigo jeep, with gold rims on it. He picked me up from me and Kam's place in his rental car and we ended up on The Road at B&M's.

    When we got inside the store, Kyle went directly to the back of the store near the restroom area. I assumed he was picking up or dropping off money because when I came from the aisle, I saw him counting money. I grabbed a tall can of Old English 800, a Cup O'Noodle, hot sauce, and a row of Saltine crackers. As I was paying for the items, Kyle approached me and said he wanted to pick up his Amigo jeep from his momma's house. I got upset because we had just passed by his momma's house on our way to The Road. Plus, I didn't want to take any unnecessary chances riding around, knowing I was wanted by the police. So, when Kyle suggested I wait at B&M's while he goes to pick up his jeep, I agreed.

Damn near thirty minutes had passed and Kyle hadn't returned. I'd already eaten my food, drank my beer, and was on my second can of beer when I heard a car pulled up outside and static of a police radio. "Damn!" I said under my breath. "The rollers!" I said out loud as I panicked and pulled out my gun. I was standing at the counter in front of the register and an ice box full of Ice Creams. Just as I shut the glass door to the ice box, I saw a policeman out of the corner of my eye. I didn't turn my head to face him, but I could see that he held a gun in his outstretched hands.

"Why are you trying to hide your face?" the cop asked.
"I ain't tryin' to hide," I replied without looking his way.
"Go ahead and look this way," one cop's voice said.
A different cop's voice threatened me, "Go ahead and run so I can kill you," he said.

I then turned my head slowly and looked into the eyes of Mario and into the barrel of Indian's gun. I was caught. They cuffed me up, put me into their patrol car, and drove me to California Park.

"Where have you been James? And why didn't you give us a call?" Mario asked.
"I lost your number." I lied.
"I thought you were gonna be straight-up with us," he said.
"I am," I said, sounding innocent.

Mario then exited the vehicle and opened the back door where I sat in handcuffs. He pulled up the sleeves on my jacket to inspect my arms. He unbuttoned my shirt to inspect my chest. I knew he was looking at my tattoos.

"So, Eric, you know you're gonna get an additional charge for lying to a police officer, don't you?" he said.
"My name is James!" I exclaimed, not sounding very convincing at all.
"Cut the bullshit Eric!" Indian said. "We already know who

you are. It only took us twenty minutes to catch you," he added. "You should choose your friends more wisely," Mario stated.

    Someone very close to me had set me up to be captured. I was happy to find out during my booking process that I'd only been charged with possession of Marijuana, possession of cocaine for sale, and false I.D. to a police officer. I didn't know where the cocaine sales case came from because I hadn't been caught nor arrested for it. But, when I read the police report I was shocked to learn that I'd sold rocks to 3 Paid Confidential Informant named Eddie King.

    I had been indicted, along with over twenty other people. According to the police report, I had sold the informant $20 worth of rocks on two separate occasions. The report also stated that after Eddie King purchased the rocks from me, he drove to the police who were waiting several blocks away and gave them my description. The officers then stopped me and told me that I fit the description of a robbery suspect, and took a picture of me. With two counts of "sales" and one count of Marijuana possession, I was looking at some prison time for sure.

I was only in Kern County Jail for one week, then got transferred to the Lerdo Pre-Trial Maximum Facility to await trial. I was in a six-man cell that consisted of six beds, one shower, one sink, one toilet, one steel table, three walls, and steel bars. There was only four of us in the cell at the time. Me, a 40-something year old O.G. named Big Noch, another black in his early 30's named Ke-Ke, and a 40 year old white man. The tier I was on consisted of six more cells. There were two twelve-man cells, and the other cells were the same as the six-man cell I was in. Big Noch was in for a parole violation. He was tall, dark-skinned, with cornrowed braids, a wide chest, and twenty-one inch arms. He knew my daddy and shared a lot of "Game" with me about prison. Ke-Ke knew my daddy too, but he was on some selfish shit. He was in for shooting a guy named Mexican Rick with an AK47. Rick got shot seven times, but he survived. There was a lot more niggas on the tier that I knew, but I could only see them when we went to court, to the exercise yard, or whenever I was allowed to use the phone at the end of the tier. We were only allowed to use the phone for fifteen minutes per day.

One day me and Ke-Ke almost got into it over my phone time. He wanted me to use my phone time to call his girlfriend and deliver a message, but I had to call my girl Kam. When I came back into the cell after my phone call, Ke-Ke started talkin' shit and saying indirect shit. I didn't give a fuck about him being mad at me. But when I noticed him attaching a razor-blade to his toothbrush, he had my full attention.

"What you making that for?" I asked him.

Ke-Ke ignored me. He had been wolfin' shit to different niggas down the tier everyday. So, the weapon could've been for one of them. But, I knew he was mad at me for not making that phone call for him, so the weapon could've also been for me.

"Who you making that for?" I asked Ke-Ke again, but he still ignored me.

I told Big Noch how I felt about the situation and asked him if I would be wrong if I rushed Ke-Ke. Big Noch told me not to trip. So, I assumed he knew who the weapon was being made for. Big Noch was a member of The Black Gorilla Family, so I trusted his word.

Ke-Ke ended up wolfin' through the bars again and exchanging words with a nigga his age named Romel, who was in for a murder. He supposedly had killed a nigga over his girlfriend. He and Ke-Ke argued for an hour before Big Noch made them shut the hell up.

The next day a big, black, buff nigga named Dupree moved into our cell. He had a parole violation and would only end up staying in our cell for about a week. He had the biggest back arms I'd ever seen. He showed me how to exercise by using the table and the sink in the cell. I've been doing those same exercises all of my life and now have big ass back arms of my own. Dupree was from a Los Angeles Bloods gang called The Brims. But he, his momma, and his brother Sly had been living in Bakersfield for as long as I could remember.

Ke-Ke pissed me off one day when me, him, and Dupree were discussing gangs. Ke-Ke grew up on the eastside with all of the Mid City Crips, but he didn't actually gang bang. He had the nerves to say if he was gon' be in a gang, he would choose to be a Blood. I felt like he was only saying it to impress Dupree, and because Dupree was bigger than me.

Dupree was transported to prison within days and it was just me, Ke-Ke, Big Noch. and The Wood. Ke-Ke and The Wood were gambling with the cards one day and it led to an argument. The argument got heated when The Wood spotted a card on the floor near Ke-Ke's feet. The Wood accused Ke-Ke of cheating, then he struck Ke-Ke in the forehead with his filthy ass mechanic looking hands. Ke-Ke was startled and knocked off balance by the blow. He responded with three wild punches of his own, but they didn't phase the angry Wood. They both flung more wild punches at each other and were in my range. I stepped between them and hit The Wood on the chin, knocking him unconscious. I then picked-up his limp body, raised him in the air, and body-slammed him on the concrete floor. He regained consciousness, but he didn't get up off the floor. I grabbed his mattress, blankets, county-issued clothes, and dumped them in a pile next to him.

"You can't live in here no more." I told him.

Ke-Ke grabbed a hard, plastic, shower shoe and slapped The Wood in the mouth with it. The Wood just held his bleeding nose and mouth, and waited for the deputy to make his rounds. When the deputy came by for count, The Wood told him that he was "rolling-up". The deputy called for another deputy, and let The Wood out.

Later that night me and Ke-Ke were moved to The Hole. Pete from Spoonie Gee was in The Hole when I got there too. I would write letters to his girlfriend for him because I was a better speller than he was. One day while the nurse was passing out medication, a Mexican dude said something in Spanish to the nurse. She thought I said it so I got moved to a section in The Hole known as "Behind The Glass." The cells in The Hole are all Single cells. But the cells behind the glass are at the far end of the tier where a door can be closed to prevent any communication with other people on the tier.

Ten days later I was back in the cell where me and Ke-Ke had beat The Wood. The Eddie King case was looking like I could beat it because the key witness (Eddie King) was missing in action. He was actually addicted to cocaine and had disappeared. I was hoping he'd stay missing until my Readiness Hearing. Without Eddie King, there was no case.

One day during the early morning court announcements, I heard my name called. I was surprised because my next court hearing was supposed to be in one week. When the detention officer was putting the handcuffs on me I asked him what was I going to court for, and he said it was for my Arraignment. That meant i had a new case because I had already been to an Arraignment hearing for the Eddie King case. I tried to think of what it could possibly be, but my mind drew a blank. The bus ride from the Lerdo Pre-Trial Facility to downtown Bakersfield's Superior Court Building took twenty minutes. I got arraigned for the Big Marv shooting. I wasn't trippin' though because I knew that Big Marv was in prison doing a parole violation. Plus, I knew he would have to testify in order for me to get convicted of the shooting, and I doubted he would snitch on me. After all, he was a Dope Dealer, Bully, and a Convict. So, I just knew my case was gonna end up getting dismissed.

A few weeks later at my Preliminary Hearing, my attorney told me that the District Attorney's Office had a witness who was willing to testify against me. And that witness was the victim. The Pre-Preliminary Hearing was held at 8AM and the Preliminary hearing was set for 1PM the same day. I knew Big Marv was in Tehachapi Prison, and figured my case would get dismissed at the 1PM hearing.

Before my hearing was called, I sat in the courtroom talking to my attorney who told me that he'd been informed by the

Prosecutor that my victim was in fact in the building and ready to testify. During this conversation with my attorney, I noticed a copy of a hand-written letter in my file. I scanned it quickly and couldn't believe what I was reading.

"What is this?" I asked my attorney.

He didn't answer me, but he did flip the page so that I could see Big Marv's signature with his true full name.

"I ain't saying nothing else until you give me a copy of this letter." I said. I was shocked, angry, and couldn't believe it. This bitch ass nigga had really snitched on me.
The letter said that he was on his way to Queen Sheeba to shop for groceries when he noticed a blue car drive by him slowly with three people looking at him hard. It said we did a drive-by on him, and that I was the shooter. The letter ended by saying I tried to kill him, he feared for his life, and that he wanted justice to be served. He had sent the letter to the District Attorney's Office from his prison cell in Tehachapi.

My Preliminary Hearing was going to be held in a different courtroom, so I was placed in a holding cell with a few other prisoners who were waiting to appear in court. Junkman from Spoonie Gee Crips was in my holding cell so I showed him the letter Big Marv had written. Junkman read it in silence. When he reached the end of the letter and saw the signature, he looked at me then pointed at the wall to indicate that Big Marv was in the holding cell next door. Junkman didn't waste any time confronting Big Marv about the letter.

"Say Big Marv!" he yelled at the wall.
"What's up?" Big Marv yelled back.
"What's up with that letter?" Junkman asked him.
"What letter?" Big Marv replied.
"You know what letter!" Junkman shot back.
"You talkin' 'bout the one to the D.A. and the Judge?" Big

Marv asked.

"Yeah," Junkman answered.

"What about it?" Big Marv asked as if it was no big deal. "That's how I get down, and whoever don't like it can deal with it in here or on the streets," he added, trying to sound tough.

It grew silent for a minute because me and Junkman were whispering, making faces, and trying to understand what Big Marv meant by what he said. Then, Big Marv yelled through the wall again.

"I couldn't get him out there so I'm gon' bring him to me and get him in here," he said like it was cool.

We shook our heads in disgust. I couldn't hold my tongue any longer.

"Say Marv!" I shouted.
"Who is that?" he asked.
"Nigga you know who this is," I said with a serious tone.
"Oh is that you E-Loc?" he asked.
"Yeah nigga!" I replied.

That's when Big Marv went into his award-winning lines.

"Look homie, I wanted to help you get rich. I wanted to see you with a big house, new cars, and ballin' outta control," he rambled on.

Just then, the deputy opened the holding cell that Big Marv was in and escorted him to the elevator. I still couldn't see him, but I could hear the elevator open and hear his chains making noise with each step he took towards the elevator.

"Say Marv?" I shouted.
"Yeah homie?" he asked.
"Fuck you!" I shouted.

A few minutes later, I too was escorted to the elevator and

to my Preliminary Hearing. When the District Attorney called it's witness to the stand, Big Marv entered the courtroom in handcuffs, shackles, and a dark-red jumpsuit with CDC printed on the back of it. Big Marv sat in the witness seat, held up his right hand and swore to tell the truth, the whole truth, and nothing but the truth. When the D.A. asked him if he saw the person who shot him sitting in the courtroom, he responded by pointing directly at me and saying, "that's him right there."

I looked across the courtroom and into his eyes, but his bitch ass looked away. The Judge found "good cause" to bound me over trial. Kam came to visit me at the Lerdo Pre-Trial and told me she would stay in my corner no matter how much time I'd have to stay in jail. She even told me she wanted to be my wife. Just by her telling me those two things took a lot of weight off of my shoulders. I knew that it was gonna be impossible to beat the Attempted Murder case at trial, so I told my attorney to get me a good plea deal and arrange for me and Kam to get married on the same day of my Sentencing Hearing.

I got what I wanted, despite my family's pleas for me not to marry Kam. She became my wife.

CHAPTER 21

A week following my Sentencing, I was awakened by a detention officer at the Lerdo facility at 11PM and given a large, brown, paper bag to put my belongings in. I packed my letters, writing materials, and hygiene items, and a few minutes later I was led to a holding-cell where twenty other men were.

The detention officer gave us all a bag that contained the clothes we'd worn during the time of our arrest. We all sat in the crowded cell with the dry-ass peanut butter sandwiches, and soft-ass apples they gave us for breakfast.

At about 8AM, we were placed onto a bus and driven to the California Correctional Institution in Tehachapi, California, which is located about fifty miles east of Bakersfield. My ears got stopped-up during the ride as we changed elevations and made our way through the mountains where the large prison was hidden. The bus drove slow, down a road leading to the front entrance of the prison. The street was lined with normal looking homes that had prisoners doing yard work outside of them. Once we passed the small security booth and the large gate controlled by a Guard Tower, the bus pulled up close to a building. We were un-cuffed and unshackled as we exited the bus, and were lined up in a sallyport that led to the inside of a large building. Once inside, I noticed a control booth that sat two stories high with two armed guards inside it.

There were large signs throughout the building that read,

"NO WARNING SHOTS." The inside of the building can be best described as a warehouse with a lot of cells in it. The Correctional Officers (C.O.'s) on the floor instructed us to walk in a single file line towards an area that had ten 50 gallon plastic trashcans lined up.

Us prisoners were lined up in a large circle and was told to take off all of our clothing and toss them in a trashcan. Once we were all completely naked, the five C.O.'s on the floor stood facing us as one of them barked out orders.

"Raise your hands above your head! Arms out in front of you! Let me see those hands! Flip'em over! Let me see behind your ears! Run your fingers around your gums! If you have dentures, take them out! Open your mouth and lift your tongue! Bend over and run your fingers through your hair! Lift up your dick and balls, use your other hand to sweep under there like a baseball catcher! Turn around! Lift your feet! Left, then right one! I want you to squat three times on my count and cough every time you go down!" he said. "Down!" he instructed.

We all squatted and coughed three time in unison.

"Now bend at the waist, pull your butt cheeks apart and cough!" he said. "Spread'em! Let me see that ass-hole!" he demanded.

Immediately after we did our final spread and cough, some prisoners who were workin' in R&R dropped an orange jumpsuit and black Karate shoes in front of each of us.

"Get dressed!" the C.O. instructed us.

While putting on our jumpsuits and shoes, a lot of us were talking to each other.

"Shut the fuck up!" the C.O. ordered us. "Ain't no talkin' while I'm talkin'!" he exclaimed.

He then pointed out the different stations we were gonna

visit during our processing. There was the fingerprinting station, the property station, and the Photo I.D. station, and they were all ran by prisoners.

After we visited each station and received a T.B. vaccination from the nurse, we were piled into a holding cell to await our housing instructions. The prisoners who worked in R&R would come to the holding cell, call our last name, then direct us to an office where a lieutenant and sergeant waited to interview. They asked questions regarding my gang affiliation and briefly discussed my current offense. They told me they didn't "play that gang bangin' shit on their yard," and told me to stay outta trouble. I was excused and returned to the holding cell.

When this older white guy got called out for his interview, another Wood who worked in R&R came to the bars of the holding cell and told us that the next white guy to return to the holding cell was a convicted Child Molester. There was some brief mumbling and expressions of outrage and anger amongst us before the holding cell grew deathly silent, as we all waited for the next white guy to return. In prison, no one likes a Child Molester, a snitch, or a jail-house thief. Discovery of either one will cause an entire prison population to campaign for the death of the perpetrator. When the white guy returned, all eyes were on him as he made his way through the silent tension-filled holding cell, and sat in the back. We were on him like flies on shit. We beat him half to death for nearly five minutes. I'm sure the C.O.'s heard the beating too. But, like I said... In prison, no one likes a Child Molester. Not even the C.O.'s.

After all of us who were involved in the beating had cleaned ourselves up and calmed down, one of the prisoners who was working in R&R let the C.O.'s know that a prisoner in our holding cell had slipped and fell and bumped his head. Of course the C.O.'s knew what really happened, but to cover their own ass they went along with the slip & fall story. Minutes later I was called out for my T.B. vaccination shot. I walked into the small medical room and sat in a chair in front of an older Asian lady. She asked me if I ever tested positive for T.B., and I told her "no". She then picked up one of the many loaded syringes, and in one swift motion she stuck me in my forearm. She pushed the contents of the syringe just under my skin, leaving a small bump on my forearm.

"What the fuck was that!?" I asked her as I inspected the bump on my forearm.

"If you have no T.B. you fine. If you have T.B. then you die." the Asian lady plainly said.

I got up and walked back into the holding cell to further inspect the bump. I pressed down on it with my fingertip until the fluid underneath my skin came out.

"Say E-Loc!" someone on the outside of the holding cell said.

"Yeah!" I replied as I made my way towards the front of the holding cell.

"Are you E-Loc from eight-oh-five?" The prisoner in blue asked.

"Yeah that's me." I answered.

"These two bags are for you," he said looking down at the two bags of groceries.

I grabbed the bags and inspected them immediately. There was soap, lotion, deodorant, hair grease, toothpaste, Top Ramen noodles, cookies, potato chips, candy bars, coffee, Bugler tobacco, a Tupperware bowl, coffee mug, cans of chili beans, and cans of tuna. The Bakersfield 805 Mob had sent me the groceries.

It took nearly seven hours for all of us to get processed and housed in a cell. That night I slept like a baby because I'd been up all day and was really tired. Early the next morning I didn't hear the five minute warning for Chow-Release. My cell mate tapped on the bunk and I jumped down from the top bunk in record time. When I stepped outside the cell and onto the tier, everybody was already standing at attention and waiting for me. One of the C.O.'s walked down the tier inspecting everyone to see if we were properly dressed. When the C.O. got to my cell he yelled for another C.O. in the control booth to open my cell. He then told me to step back inside because I wasn't properly dressed. I didn't know what he was talkin' about because I thought I was fully dressed. But the C.O. looked at the top two buttons of my jumpsuit and told me I had to step back inside and button my jumpsuit all the way up. As soon as I stepped inside he closed the cell door behind me and I didn't get to eat breakfast. The cold part is, in prison, if you miss breakfast, you'll miss lunch because they serve breakfast and lunch at the same time. I didn't go hungry thanks to the 805 Mob who sent me the groceries. But, you can best believe I was prepared for breakfast the following morning. Hell, I even slept in my orange jumpsuit. When they opened my cell door I rolled outta bed like a Fireman and was one of the first to be on the tier standing at attention.

Later that same day, everyone who arrived at the prison with me had to go to the school area to take a TABE test to determine our reading levels.

Top Dollar, Pete, and a bunch of Smokers I knew were all there too. There was this one tall, ugly ass, black nigga who had titties, ass, and hips like a woman. I wasn't insecure or anything, but I just didn't want to be near his nasty ass. Top Dollar thought it was funny, and he used my dislike of the homosexual to get some laughs. He kept telling the homosexual to show me his titties, and then he'd start laughing. I would Loc-up and tell the homosexual not to disrespect me like that. I didn't want to see no titties on a man.

There was a Mexican homosexual too who was a hermaphrodite and was in a cell alone. He couldn't be around us normal prisoners, but we saw him walk to the shower and stuff.

A lot of shit you hear about prison doesn't really happen the way you think it does. Someone getting raped probably does happen every once in awhile. But it's highly unlikely. Mainly because there are openly gay men willing to have sex at any given time, with anybody. You would be surprised to see how many men participate in homosexual activities in prison. Half of them have wives and children who visit them regularly. And most of them are only serving a very short prison sentence. Some try to justify their actions by claiming to be only "charging" the punk or only gettin' their dick sucked. I don't know what goes on behind closed doors, but as far as I'm concerned, any man who participates in sexual acts with another man is either Gay or Bisexual. Like the old saying goes... "If you flip, you'll flop." I know some homies who are serving Life Sentences in prison, and they sometimes get their dick sucked by other men. I don't knock'em because of what they are up against, but I don't condone it either. To each their own. But, I don't give a fuck if I had Life in prison, I would never have sex with a man.

On my third day in prison the nurse came by my cell to check my forearm to determine if I had T.B. or not. And since there was no sign of a bump, bruise, or rash, I was told I didn't have T.B. The three days leading up to my T.B. Reading, I had been examined by the Dentist, Doctor, and Psychologist. All who had given me medical clearance, and made it possible for me to work in the prison's kitchen. There was a few O.G. homies from 805 Mob who also worked in the kitchen. Heavy-Hitters like Glenn Hunter, Thump, and Big Polk. I learned early on to pay close attention to my immediate surroundings and to listen carefully. An O.G. once told me that God gave us two ears, two eyes, and one mouth to do more looking and listening than talking. And I preach the same thing today.

  I watched the O.G.'s make knives/shanks out of everything from typewriter parts, plastic cups, plastic Hot-Sauce bottles, welding rods and aluminum cans, to rolled up newspaper covered in sugar and water.

  The prison yard I was on in Tehachapi was a Level-III yard and was mostly a Reception Center which is merely a temporary place until the prisoner gets classified, and then gets transferred to a prison that suits their needs. The Level-III yard in Tehachapi had five buildings on it. And buildings 3, 4, and 5 were for Reception Center prisoners. Buildings 1 and 2 were for the prisoners on the Mainline, and known as PWC's (Permanent Work Crew). The O.G.'s from 805 Mob used their influence to get me moved into the 1 Building, and on a PWC.

  The 805 Mob was made up of black prisoners who were

from Bakersfield, Oxnard, Ventura, Santa Barbara, and other small cities in California who's area code was 805. Everyone from those areas would hang out on the yard together, acknowledge one another throughout the day, and would embrace each other. I kept gettin' pulled over by C.O.'s because my pants were always sagging. There were zero tolerance when it came to gang banging on the PWC Yard. I was just being me, but I guess my youth, immaturity, my vocabulary, and my body language gave them a different impression. One day I was on my way to the yard and I greeted this big nigga by saying, "What's up Loc?"

"I ain't no Loc!" he replied in a nasty tone. "I'm a Piru!" he added.
"So what!" I shot back. "I'm a Crip!" I said proudly.

He stared me down, but I didn't bow down. He let it go, but he later hollered at my older homie Glenn Hunter. The homie got at me about it and explained that certain words were disrespectful to some people. I knew all about the "games" because I'd already experienced a lot in C.Y.A. But, I still had a habit of addressing everyone as either Loc, Cuz, or Nigga.

I spent most of my time on the yard in the weight-pile area. I wanted to get my body as big and strong as my heart was. A lot of knowledge is shared on the weight-pile too. I picked up some "game" from an O.G. Compton Crip named Big Woody. He only had one leg, but he was on Monster swole, and was well respected. I would come to appreciate all the "game" I was taught in Tehachapi because I was soon transferred to a prison in northern California. The prison was CTF (Central Training Facility), and it was located in Soledad, California.

CHAPTER 22

The bus ride to Soledad was similar to my trip to Tehachapi. But instead of the Kern County Sheriffs Department transporting us, it was the CDC (California Dept. Of Corrections) transportation officers, and they didn't play. There was two officers and one sergeant who were all armed and made it clear that they wouldn't hesitate to kill one of us if necessary. The sergeant sat up front with the driver, while another officer sat in a specially built cage in the rear of the bus next to the caged toilet. A big, tall, black, bald, officer who looked like an ex-football player gave us a speech.

"Look gentlemen, we have roughly a six hour ride. If you need to take a piss, use the toilet in the back of the bus one at a time. Keep the noise to a minimum until this bus starts moving. Once these wheels move, there is absolutely no talking. The driver controls the temperature and the volume on the radio, so don't ask. We want to have a real nice & quiet ride. If we gotta pull this bus over to remind one of you the rules, I'm gonna make you touch everythang on this bus. Do I make myself clear?" he asked at the end of his speech.

It seemed as if he'd said it a hundred times before. He kept sniffin' in between sentences though like he had a cold, runny nose, or something. This one smoked-out nigga sittin' next to me was mimicking the officer during the entire speech. The smoked-out nigga kept cracking jokes about the officer and was saying the officer was sniffing like he was on heroin. A couple of prisoners laughed and giggled and even made remarks of their own.

The tall-ass officer was walking towards the front of the bus when he heard the giggles so he spun on his heels and returned to the caged partition and peered through the cage. The smoked-out nigga seated next to me put his head down low and behind the prisoners seat in front of us and cracked another joke. That's when the officer unlocked the cage and came our way. The officer looked right into my face as he took his time coming down the aisle. He reached out towards me and I closed my eyes, bracing for whatever he was gonna do to me. I peeked out one eye and saw the smoked-out nigga seated next to me being lifted outta his seat, over my head, and carried off of the bus. I slid over in my seat to look out the window, but I couldn't get a good look at what they were doing to him. It looked like they were bending him up and stuffing him under the bus. When they brought him back onto the bus, they sat him in a cage by himself near the front of the bus. He didn't say a word the whole trip. In fact, when we got to Soledad, and had been in R&R for two hours, he still hadn't said a word. Whatever they did to him, changed him.

After we were processed and got interviewed by the lieutenant, we were housed in X-Wing. Soledad is an older prison with housing units broken up into "wings" and named after alphabets. There was A-Wing through G-Wing, X-Wing and Y-Wing. Then O-Wing was The Hole. I was housed in X-Wing on the 3rd tier all by myself. I looked through my cell door window and saw Pete from Spoonie Gee Crips. He had been transferred there a couple of days before me. That same evening, I got to walk to the Chow Hall for dinner and was amazed by the design of the prison and it's quarter of a mile long corridor. The dinner tray was overflowing with tasty food, and everything on the tray was at it's right temperature. Soledad fed me good, and most of the prisoners there were healthy and buffed. This was the first time I saw a lot of Bloods in one place, and they were all flamed-up. I did a double take when I saw this tall buffed Blood nigga come through the Chow Hall line and throw up the "B". He had on a bright, red baseball cap, red belt, a red flag hangin' outta his back pocket, with bright red Chuck Taylors on. His feet were hella big like a size 15, so his shoes reminded me of Ronald McDonald. I had never been around any Bloods who were openly displaying their colors. I expected the Crip homies to jump up and demand the Bloods to tuck in their flags, but they didn't. Everyone carried on as if everything was normal.

The following day I got a cellmate from Inglewood, California. He referred to his city as Inglewatts. His name was Lil Crayzo from 102 Raymond Avenue Crips. He had long braids, a slender frame, and was five years older than me. Lil Crayzo had just transferred from Folsom Prison. He knew a lot about the gangs and prison politics, and he "laced me" to the fullest. While he was unpacking his things, an older nigga came by our cell and slid some papers halfway under our door. I reached down to pick them up, but Lil Crayzo pushed me outta the way, nearly knocking me down as he kicked the papers back out onto the tier. He then got on the cell door with his face pressed against it and his lips near the small window as he screamed on the nigga who had left the papers underneath our door. He then turned to me huffin' and puffin' as he explained why he was so upset.

"Cuz! Don't ever accept no papers underneath the door!" he said. "You got C.C.O.'s and Blue Notes around here trying to recruit. If you would've picked up the papers, you would've been considered one of their comrades," he added.

I had already knew a lot about "Crips," it's protocol, it's original name (Cribs), and knew about Stanley (Big Tookie) Williams, and Raymond Washington. I even knew a little something about the Los Angeles gangc and the rivalries because of the time I'd done in C.Y.A. But, Lil Crayzo broke it all down for me.

After a few days of being on CTQ (Confined To Quarters) I went to Classification and was cleared to go to the yard. The long walk down the corridor leading to the yard was an adventure in itself. The corridor is a quarter of a mile long from one end to the other, and it's not a flat surface all the way through. There are too many highs and lows to count. There are several C.O.'s standing throughout the corridor pulling over the prisoners randomly and conducting pat down searches. When a Prisoner is told to place his hands on the wall, the prisoner's homeboys who are walking with him will stop to observe the pat down search and make sure the search is done in a respectful manner. At the end of the corridor leading to the yard is a metal detector, just like they have in airports. I had to take off my belt buckle and slide it across the table. We were usually allowed to keep our boots on while passing through the metal detector, but if the machine was turned up on high, it would "beep" with our boots on. Sometimes the metal detector would be so high the aluminum foil on a pack of cigarettes would make it beep.

The yard was hella big. The first thing I noticed was the regulation size professional boxing ring. As I walked further out towards the yard, I noticed to my left there was twelve telephones under a canopy like structure, with six telephones on each side, and a parade of prisoners dressed in bright red clothes. They were Bloods and Nortenos. To my right was the same telephone set up, but everything was like a sea of blue soldiers congregating with a sprinkle of purple in there. This side of the yard was for the Crips and Surenos. The Crips from Grape Street Watts wore purple flags, purple hats, and attire, which is why the sprinkle of purple was amongst the sea of blue. The telephones were split up amongst the gangs too. The six phones for the Crips were broken down like this... There was a Compton/Watts phone, a Hoover/Gangster phone, a Neighborhood/0's phone, an East Coast phone, Long Beach phone, and a non-affiliate phone. There wasn't a phone for Bakersfield Crips, but I damn sure wasn't gonna use the non-affiliate phone and give people the impression that I wasn't bangin' so I waited until I saw one of the other phones available and called my wife Kam.

I was extremely happy to hear her voice. It seemed like we had only been on the phone for five minutes when the C.O. in the gun tower yelled on the megaphone for us to clear the area. Every fifteen minutes the phone area was cleared to make sure no one was dead or seriously injured in the area. Those of us on the phone would simply tell the people on the other end of the phone to "hold on" while we cleared the area. It only took sixty seconds to clear the area and be permitted to get back on the phone. I talked to Kam for maybe ten more minutes when this nigga on the phone next to me tapped me on the shoulder and pointed at another nigga who was standing near the fence in the phone line.

"Say homie! You from Watts?" he asked. I shook my head 'no'. "Is you from Compton?" he then asked. I shook my head 'no' again. "Where is you from then?" he asked with an irritated look on his face.

I held up my index finger indicating for him to hold on a minute. Then I continued talking to Kam when the C.O. in the gun tower cleared the area. Again, I was met by the same nigga with the same questions. He tried to explain to me that I was on the wrong phone, but when the C.O. in the gun tower gave us the "O.K." to get back on the phones, I ignored him and ran to talk to Kam again. I could hear the nigga in the phone line wolfin' shit, but I ignored him. I told Kam what was going on and even let her know I was probably gonna get into a fight with the nigga. When the C.O. in the gun tower cleared the phone area this time, I walked towards the phone line and was met by the nigga again.

"Say cuz, why you..." he began. *SHACK!* I fired on him, and we locked up like Pit-bulls right up under the gun tower. I heard the C.O. yell, "Down on the yard!" through his megaphone, followed by two quick gunshots. The nigga dove to the ground, away from me and I dove the other way. I was quickly handcuffed and escorted off of the yard and to my cell. Since me and the nigga didn't live in the same wings, we were just put on CTQ status for ten days and received a 115 (Behavior Report) for Mutual Combat. At the 115 Hearing, I was found guilty and given sixty days loss of Good Time credits. But, I could get the sixty days back if I stayed disciplinary free for 90 days.

The 115 Hearings are commonly known as Kangaroo Court because it's not a fair system and really a joke. They only need the preponderance of evidence to find a prisoner guilty. So, if there's a 51% chance the prisoner is guilty, he will most certainly be found guilty at a 115 Hearing.

I finally got moved to F-Wing, which was known as Rider-

Wing because there was a lot of violence going on there. I was housed in a cell on the third tier with Twin from Watts Baby Loc Crips. I was only his cellie for a few days. Then I was cellies with Big Pete from Watts Baby Loc too. I was Big Pete's cellie for a couple of weeks and then I moved into a cell with a nigga from San Jose, California. His name was DA, and he was originally from Baton Rouge, Louisiana and had started his own gang in San Jose called The Dixie Crips. DA was hella cool. His older brother had a baby by the girl Minisha that I used to fuck with. The same Minisha with all the roaches.

I didn't have a job yet, and I wasn't in Education or Trade School, therefore, I wasn't allowed to go to the yard at night. During the few months I'd been at Soledad Central, I'd accumulated a lot of blue flags, blue caps, and blue tennis shoes. I even made me a pillow case out of blue flags, put blue cellophane on my lights, and my whole cell was True Blue. You could walk down the tiers in F-Wing and easily know who lived where, simply by the color their cells were decorated. Some cells would even have different gangs written on the walls with a big "X" over them, or 187 (penal code for murder) on top of them. One day my cellie DA went to the yard at night and a Tier-Tender came to my cell door asking if I had some tobacco for some nigga named Ducc. I didn't know what he was talking about because I hadn't promised anybody nothing. Just then, my cellie was calling my name from outside my cell window. He told me to roll up two Bugler cigarettes and give them to the Tier-Tender so he could pass them to Ducc. I got the tobacco out of DA's can of Bugler and did what he asked.

  The very next day the Tier-Tender came by my cell again for the same thing. When my cellie returned to the cell later that night, I let him know what I'd done. He said that he did tell Ducc he could have two more cigarettes, but he forgot to call me to the window to let me know it was O.K. to give them to him.

  The following day the Tier-Tender came by my cell again for two cigarettes for Ducc. I went to my outside window, but I didn't see my cellie anywhere in sight. But I went ahead and rolled up two cigarettes for Ducc anyway. When DA came to the cell later that night I told him about the two cigarettes again. But this time he got upset. He told me he didn't tell Ducc he could have any cigarettes today, and that he was gonna "check" Ducc for lying. I was upset about it too because I felt disrespected and used. When I was let out of my cell, I went straight to Ducc's cell to "get at him". He was wolfin' through the door and being a Cell Soldier. So, I told him to save all that tough talk for later, and we'll just let the moment his door open, be the bell. Big Slint from Grape Street Watts saw me on Ducc's door and he motioned for me to come here. I explained to him what was going on and told him that I wanted to fight Ducc and the Tier-Tender named Blacc. But, I wanted Big Slint to be present to make sure I got a fair fight. Big Slint set it up for me to get down with both of them on the first tier. I "put hands" on Ducc first, then I took a five minute break to catch my breath, and "tipped-up" Blacc.

News travels fast in prison. Most of the young Crips my age gave me my props and gave me my respect. But, I could sense a little jealousy from a lot of them too because their "Big Homies" were doing extra shit with me and not with them. Like, asking me to be their partner in a game of dominoes or to walk a few laps around the track with them. They would give me weed and let me drink pruno with them. Pruno is a jailhouse name for wine. With a few squeezed oranges, some sugar, and a few days of the combination sittin' in a bucket or in a plastic bag... I could make some bomb-ass wine. I even learned how to take the pruno, place a stinger in it, put a plastic bag over it with a small opening at one end, let the fumes drip into another container, and create another drink called White Lightening. It will look and taste just like Gin.

My cellie DA moved to a different wing so I ended up with another cellie. His name was Evil Wicked, and he too was from Baby Loc Crips. He was my age and was hella cool. He had just transferred from Solano Prison.

CHAPTER 23

Me and Evil Wicked became really close and did almost everything together. From working, to walking the yard together. He was there when I knocked my first C.O. Bitch. Her name was Ms. Patton, but I called her Sweet-P. She was a thick, almost chubby, black lady with a short, reddish colored Jheri curl, Chipmunk cheeks, and a cute smile. Her voice sounded like a little white girl's mixed with the voice of a porn star or phone sex operator. She worked 1st watch from 10PM to 6AM, and would make her rounds doing count as soon as she came on duty. I would jump up as soon as I heard her sweet voice.

"Top bunk, Top bunk," she'd say all sexy and shit. Then she'd go to the next cell, tap on the door with her flashlight and repeat it again. "Top bunk, Top bunk," she'd say so that whoever was laying in the top bunk would move to show they're alive. I'd stand at my door while she counted the 1st and 2nd tiers. Then when she'd get close to my cell I'd make Evil Wicked pretend to be asleep while I "got at her". I started off by complimenting her on how good she smelled, how pretty her eyes were, and how nice her body was. She'd blush, giggle, and give me that approving look. One night I told her that I had a lot on my mind and wanted to share it with her. I told her I wanted to put it on paper because I didn't want my cellie or anybody else to hear what I had to say. She said it was cool, so I wrote her a four page letter and gave it to her when she made her hourly rounds for count. And on the following round for count, she gave me a letter in response to the one I wrote her.

We exchanged letters every night and most of them were x-rated letters describing what we wanted from each other sexually. One night I wrote her and told her to get my cell unlocked when she let out the kitchen workers at 3:30 AM, so that I could go down to the C.O. Office and talk to her. She did. I slow-dragged so that I would be the only one left in the wing while the cooks went to work. As soon as it was safe I ducked into the C.O. office. The armed C.O. on the cat walk went back to sleep while me and Sweet-P tore at each other's clothes. She acted like she was in heat. She kissed and licked my face while pulling at my clothes and my dick. Her little chubby ass was too aggressive. I was having trouble taking off her belt and her pants, so I just grabbed the front of her pants and pushed them down. I was super horny and was determined to get up in there. I used my left hand to push her pants and panties just below her crotch, then I took my dick out of her hands and stuck it between her legs. I was squatting and trying to bend my dick up in her so that I could get inside of her, but she was making it difficult with her aggressive kissing and grinding. I finally felt my dick-head disappear into her hot, wet pussy, and in one full stroke I came like a mad-man. I was bucking and jerking, humping, and whimpering. Then my dick went limp. She was still kissing and being aggressive, but I was ready to get back in my cell. I was happy to have gotten away with fucking a C.O. without getting caught.

I ended up fucking Sweet-P everyday, five days a week, for the next month, then my world changed dramatically. First, my nigga Chucc got killed. They said he was winning in a dice game while his homeboy Henry was losing. Words were exchanged and a fight broke out between the two. Henry supposedly left to get a gun and returned. They said after he shot Chucc, people were trying to help Chucc get to the hospital, but was accidentally dropping him while doing so. It was September 1991. Chucc was dead, and Henry went to prison for murder.

My two homies from my hood (CoCo & Thun) hit the mainline, and I was hella happy to see them both. CoCo was locked up for shooting two niggas in their chest, and Thun was locked up for shooting at the police during a high speed chase. They both had 7 year sentences like me.

While they were still on CTQ I got moved to B-Wing in a cell with a nigga named Tee-Lee. He was a short and stocky older nigga with 20" arms, no neck, and a big-ass head. He had a bad attitude and came off as a Bully looking for any reason to start some shit.

Every morning he'd get up, make up his bed, wash his face, brush his teeth, make a cup of coffee, then sit in front of his t.v. I'd hear him, but I'd lay there until he finished doing what he was doing before I'd finally climb down from the top bunk. After washing my face and brushing my teeth, I'd try to make up my bed, but this big head mutha-fucka' would always be sitting, watching t.v., and in my way. Instead of laying back on his bed until I made up my bed, he'd sit there and force me to ask him to move outta my way. I had to make up my bed or else he'd go to the yard and tell all of the homies I was a Bumb who didn't make up his bed. And I was far from a Bumb. When I needed for him to get outta my way so I could make up my bed, I'd say "Excuse me Big Homie," all polite and shit. But, he'd still mumble under his breath, like I was really bothering him or something. He'd do the same shit everyday, so I let a couple of O.G.'s know about it. They told me it was just as much my cell as it was Tee-Lee's, and for me to keep on making up my bed every morning.

On this one particular morning I went through the same bullshit with Tee-Lee, but this time he had the audacity to tell me I needed to find a better time to make up my bed. He wasn't looking at me when he said it, but I was damn sho' looking at him and standing over him as I tucked in my sheets. 'I wish I could whoop this big nigga,' I thought to myself. I heard a C.O. coming down the tier unlocking cell doors, so I decided in that instant to take my chance. I reached back as far as I could and swung with all my might, delivering a solid blow to Tee-Lee's big head. Before he could react, I served him with fifteen to twenty quick punches to his head and face areas. He was finally able to get up off his bed and rush me, but I continued delivering quick blows even as he attempted to push me back against a locker and the cell door. He didn't punch me at all because he was too busy trying to block my punches and grab my arms. But, I "socked him out" until the C.O. opened our cell door and maced us. I was kinda relieved to see the C.O. because I didn't know how much longer I could keep that big nigga off of me.

As I was escorted down the tier I could see through my squinted, burning, eyes, a look of surprise on everyone's face. They couldn't believe a little nigga like me had come out of that cell a winner. My name began to "ring" all over the prison, and a few young niggas were eager to test me. A couple of days later I whooped on a nigga in the school's restroom for dissin' me in his rap, and that brought even more fame to my name.

The O.G.'s from Bakersfield were considered non-affiliates because they weren't Crips or Bloods. There was Big Brentwood, Al Monday, Skip, and Robert Earl. There was a few Crips from Bakersfield, which was my two homies CoCo and Thun, and Slicc from Mid City Crips, and Lil Rabbit from 805 Hoover. Every "set", gang, or city had their own crew, which were known as their "car". We had a Bakersfield/805 car, and we all stuck together. The Hoovers from Los Angeles made Lil Rabbit choose who he was gonna "ride" with. They told him if he was gonna be representin' Hoover, he was gonna have to function with the Hoovers. Lil Rabbit chose to function with the Hoovers and became a "Torpedo". This was around the time the Hoovers were rivals with most Los Angeles gangs and had began referring to themselves as Criminals instead of Crips. All of them except for the 52nd street Hoovers, who still referred to themselves as the Five-Deuce Hoover Gangster Crips.

Since I wasn't from Los Angeles, the set-trippin' and shit didn't apply to me. In my eyes they were all Crips, and I associated with Crips from San Diego to Sacramento. I even took pictures with as many as 200 Crips throwin'-up their set on the baseball bleachers at Soledad Central.

I participated in a lot of the activities Soledad had to offer. There was the concert-style Talent Shows, boxing matches against

Boxers who came to the prison from the streets, and the hard-hitting football games in the middle of the yard. We (Crips) planted grass and created a small picnic area around the old Mini-Canteen building. It was for Crips only. Me and the Bakersfield homies dug up a couple of benches and planted them in the middle of the yard. We claimed that area as ours and named it "The Patch" which is an old-school term used to describe the city of Bakersfield. We buried our knives in our area and would meet there everyday after we finished lifting weights.

The older homies from Bakersfield were some of the strongest niggas on the yard. They worked out on a smaller weight pile next to the bigger weight pile that everyone else used. They had better weights on the smaller weight pile, and other big, strong, niggas worked out on the small weight pile too. There was Big Meech from 9-0, Big River Rat from 11-8 East Coast, Big Will from Compton, Big Hogg from Rollin' 60's, Big Reese Cup from Long Beach 20's, Bimbie from 7-4 Hoover, Big Will from Harlem 30's, Big Chim Chim from Hoover, Big Pete from Watts Baby Loc, and Big Crip Dog from 1-20 Raymond.

I personally made it my business to lift weights at least five days a week. "If you stay ready, you don't gotta get ready." One day this nigga was laying on a bench lifting weights when another nigga dropped a 50 lb. dumbbell on his forehead. You should've seen all the blood running down his face. He got his "wig split" in a real way. The Woods and Surenos got into it and it led to some serious knife play. The Woods had real knives. I mean real switch blades, real hunting knives, and real store bought Ice picks, not inmate manufactured weapons like us Crips had. And I don't know what they were feeding those mutha-fuckas, but they were some big ass Woods.

There was always some kind of drama going on. If it wasn't gangs trippin' off of shit that had happened on the streets, then it was some drug deal gone bad, or some bullshit over a homosexual. There was this big, black, buffed, homosexual named Purple Passion. I couldn't believe his big ass was a homosexual until I heard him talk and saw him "switch" when he walked. One time I saw this square nigga trying to hide this little Hoodrat looking homosexual in his cell. The Square had on his robe and House shoes like he was really kickin' it with a female. Me and Evil

Wicked knew the homosexual was in the Square niggas' cell, so we gave the Square nigga a hard time. He had a sheet hung up so he could hide the homosexual, but I saw the homosexual's long ass feet stickin' out. Me and Evil Wicked was laughing hard and clownin' that day. The Square nigga was mad, but he couldn't do shit about it.

My wife Kam was visiting me every other week and bringing me weed every time she came. I had been listening to the Pimp niggas on the yard talkin' about how they make bitches pay them for their time and their conversations. I heard one Pimp say he didn't care if his woman was out there fuckin' the next man as long as she put money on his books and brought him some type of drugs on a visit. I began talkin' to my wife like I was a Pimp and even threatened to divorce her a few times while we were visiting. She would cry and get other women in the visiting room to sympathize with her. I was going hard on her and told her to charge every nigga that tries to get at her. She told my momma that I was trying to pimp her from prison. She was right.

CHAPTER 24

One day I got called to the Watch-Office to see the lieutenant. The lieutenant asked me if my wife was the type to play on the Phone or would she make up an awful story just to talk to me on the phone. "No," I said. The lieutenant then told me to call home using the phone in her office, while she listened in on another phone. It rang a few times then Kam's voice said, "Hello?" like she'd been crying.

"Kam, what's goin' on? Why you callin' up here?" I demanded. She paused for a moment, then softly said, "Baby, something bad happened to one of your brothers."

"What!?" I yelled into the phone. "Which one of my brothers!?" I yelled again.

'"Derrick," she said.

"What happened?" I asked in disbelief.

"He died this morning," she said.

"Don't play with me Kam!" I said in a serious tone. "What happened?" I asked again in disbelief.

"He got shot. They found him dead in yo' momma's house," she explained through her sobs.

I sat there with the phone to my ear, but I didn't hear anything else. I was numb and my chest felt like it was gonna explode. My head filled with blood, my face and nose filled with tears, but only one long continuous tear escaped my eye. I inhaled, then exhaled slowly as my surroundings became clear again.

"Nichols," the lieutenant said. "Nichols are you okay?" she asked.

I slowly turned my head to look at her and noticed she too had tears in her eyes. I nodded my head "yes," and blinked my eyes to release two crocodile size tears. I don't remember hanging up the phone, walking outta the Watch-Office, or how I got back to my cell. I was in a daze. The C.O.'s in my wing checked on me a couple of times that day. And my cellie Evil Wicked bugged me and let me cry on his shoulder. But, I refused to be put on CTQ. I didn't want to be stuck in no cell.

I kept trying to figure out how this could've happened to my little brother, and my mind kept racing back to our last telephone conversation. He had just bought me a t.v. and insisted on sending me some more money. He even said, "Ain't no tellin' how long I'm gon' be out here, so let me do what I can for you."

I thought about all the stuff we'd done together, all the secrets we shared, and how lost I was gonna be without him. I was his big brother, but he had a more mature way of dealing with things. When I'd think about doing something dangerous or stupid, he'd be there to warn me not to do it. When I'd forget to do something that momma had asked me to do, he'd be there to remind me. I always fought his battles. I'd help him hide his pissy blankets from momma when he'd pee in the bed. When he'd break something in the house trying to hit me, I'd fix it so that momma wouldn't know it was broken. I thought back to the time when we took a bath together and I peed in the tub. As soon as he saw that golden stream coming his way underwater, he screamed like he had been stung by a Bee. The only thing that got stung was my young ass and legs as momma whooped me with a switch. I even thought back to the time me, Derrick, and momma were in a laundromat washing clothes, and the entire entrance glass door fell on him, and caused him to have to wear a back brace. But one of the funniest memories I have is when me and Derrick were at a Card Party over Ronnette's house. The adults were in the living room and kitchen partying, while us kids were in Ronnette's bedroom turning the lights off & on trying to catch one another kissing. That's when I heard Ronnette's cousin named Pebbles say she needed to use the bathroom. I turned the lights back off and pulled Derrick out of the room. I told him what I'd heard Pebbles say about needing to use the bathroom. Then I suggested that me and him go to the bathroom before the girls do, so that we could hide in the shower and catch them on the toilet. We disappeared into the bathroom without anyone seeing us. But, Ronnette and Pebbles didn't show up. Instead, one of their Aunties came in and locked the door behind her. She was talking to herself all loud and drunk-sounding.

"Oh yeah! Lord I gotta pee," she said as if she was talking to someone in the bathroom.

I heard her unzip her pants, wiggle out of her jeans, drop the toilet seat down, then fart. Her fart sounded like a trumpet. I laughed through my nose, sending snot onto the shower curtain, and onto Derrick's hand as he tried to muffle my laugh. A loud pouring of pee followed the initial fart, as the Auntie "Oohed & Aaahed," while her pee continued to flow. My whole body shook as I laughed hard and Derrick held his hand firmly over my mouth. When her pee stopped, she farted four more times. Each with a different tune. Then she shitted. It sounded like her guts fell out. I heard the water splashing and she grunted in both pain and relief. I laughed harder, causing Derrick to punch me in the chest, pin me to the shower wall, and give me a look like he wanted to kick my ass. I laughed as more snot and tears escaped me, and my laughter blended in with the flushing of the toilet. We never did get to catch the girls in there because we got up outta there right after "Shitty Auntie" left. Memories are what kept me going, along with my faith in God.

I got a visit from a half-breed female my age named Millie, the same day I found out about my brother's death. My homie Thun had hooked me up with her, and she had rode up to Soledad with Thun's wife Sonya. When I got into the visiting room I told Thun, his wife, and Millie about the bad news I'd received. Millie asked me if I wanted to go back to my cell or be alone, but I stayed on the visit. I hadn't talked to my momma yet, so the bad news was still somewhat unbelievable.

    Momma had been out of state on a vacation when my brother was gunned down in her home. She was boarding a plane in New York when she got the news. My poppy offered to pay for me to attend the funeral, and I found two C.O.'s willing to escort me. But, the Warden wouldn't let me go because I was a Gang Member. I couldn't even say goodbye.

CHAPTER 25

After the funeral, momma came to visit me and brought me my brother's obituary. Now I knew he was really gone. Me and momma both stayed strong in front of each other and for one another.

      Shortly after that, a lot of drama jumped off on the yard. The Hoover Criminals and Raymond Avenue Crips went to war against each other, and my homie Thun almost got caught up in it. He actually almost got stabbed. One day after lifting weights, me, Thun, CoCo, and Slick were chillin' in the area of the yard that we named The Patch. Thun was acting distant and a little strange so I asked him what was wrong. He claimed it was nothing, but my homie CoCo felt the same way I did and said Thun was acting like he'd seen something. But, Thun kept denying it. I had already reminded all of them about the war with the Hoovers and Raymonds. And I told them it would be best not to socialize with either group today because I could feel the tension in the air. They all agreed, and we decided to walk a few laps around the track. Now, it was just me, Evil Wicked, and Thun walking laps. But Thun was walking about ten feet in front of us. On our second lap around the track, a nigga asked us if we had a light. He was closer to Thun when he asked, but I spoke up, "Naw, we don't got no light homie," I said matter of factly and we kept on pushin' around the track. On the third lap around the track, me and Evil Wicked were busy looking into my laundry bag for some fruit when I heard feet shuffling in front of me. It was Thun and the same nigga who had asked for a light. I didn't think much of it because Thun kept on walking. I figured maybe Thun and the nigga were horse playing or slap-boxing real quick. Thun suddenly slowed down when we passed by the water fountain on the far end of the yard and made our way by the tennis courts. Thun was visibly shaken. In fact, the rest of the half eaten apple he held in his hand shook uncontrollably, and Thun himself shook like a snitch at a Gangsta Party.

"Did you see that?" Thun asked through clenched teeth.
"See what?" I asked.
"That nigga tried to stick me," Thun said again through clenched teeth.
"Where?" I asked.

Thun stretched out his arm to show me a small pin-hole in the sleeve of his prison issued jacket.

"Let me see!" I demanded, as I assisted him in taking his arm out of the sleeve of his jacket.

His skin hadn't been penetrated but there was an ashy scratch on his arm. I was fuming mad. I led Thun across the yard and to The Patch where CoCo was. I didn't have to say anything because it was written all over my face.

"I told you that nigga saw something!" CoCo said as he shook his head pitifully at Thun.

I searched the entire yard by looking carefully from where I stood, and I couldn't spot the nigga who tried to stab Thun anywhere. I immediately dug up an ice-pick and a "Flat". CoCo took the Flat and I kept the ice-pick. A lot of Crips from different "Sets" came to holla at me and offered their support. Some even offered more weapons and suggested tactics to use in our efforts to retaliate. The homie Big Ace from Du-Rocc Gangsta Crips tried to calm me down and even gave me reasons why he felt I shouldn't retaliate. He said the "Hit" on Thun was an accident and a case of mistaken identity. But I found out that Thun was indeed the intended target. However, the "hitters" didn't know Thun was my homie, which I found hard to believe. I found out that Thun had witnessed one nigga give a weapon to another nigga. And to avoid any extra drama on the yard, the nigga who gave a knife to the other nigga, told the other nigga to "stick" Thun so that Thun would be moved off of the yard and unable to let anyone know about the little knife-passing he'd seen. The "Hit" didn't go right because the nigga they sent to do the Hit wasn't ready for the job.

    I was furious and wanted revenge. I felt like they played with Thun's life and I wasn't gonna let that go. As me and CoCo put together our plan of attack, Thun sat there looking terrified and pitiful. All the Crips who came and offered their support had made it clear that if Thun himself didn't make the first move, they were not gonna help us, which was understandable. A lot of them had much love for me and didn't want to see me fuck mines off for a nigga who didn't seem to want to defend himself. So, me and CoCo told Thun to stab the nigga who tried to stab him, and we would stab everyone else who was with the nigga. But, Thun just sat there scared to death. I asked Thun if he was scared, and he shook his head up & down indicating that he was. I couldn't believe this nigga Thun was acting like this. I gave him several options: Hit the nigga with a baseball bat, Hit the nigga with a dumbbell, or just punch the nigga and I'll put holes in him.

    Thun just sat there in a daze shaking in his boots. I wanted to slap his ass, but I loved him too much to make him feel more afraid than he already was. CoCo finally told me to walk Thun's scary ass off the yard. When they announced Yard-Crew workers unlock, I escorted Thun to the building and down to G-Wing. When we got to the wing, a female C.O. opened the door and asked us if we were Yard Crew workers. "Yeah," I said as I walked in passed her, and into the wing.

    Thun was so shook up, he didn't know how to talk or follow my lead. So she told him he had to go back to the yard until they call yard-recall. I looked over her head and into Thun's eyes as she searched for her keys to lock the door.

    "Don't go back to the yard," I silently mouthed the words to Thun as the door closed. He looked like he'd just lost his best friend. I got busy that same night sharpening my knife and the knife I made for Thun. I was gonna make Thun handle his business in the morning. I took my plastic toothbrush holder and burned two holes near the ends of each piece. Then, I put long shoe strings through the holes and tied the shoe string around my waist where I let the one half of the toothbrush holder hang near my dick. Then, I put my knives inside the toothbrush holder. I was able to carry my weapons and could stand a pat-down search because the C.O.'s hardly ever touched our groin area. I was also able to walk down the long corridor to the metal detector without getting pulled over. I'd been taught how to take knives through the metal detector without making it "beep". I just step completely over the small ramp located in the middle of the metal detector, instead of stepping on it when I walked through it. I had also placed a knife inside my boot, and it was killin' me by the time I made it to the yard. I'm sure my limp was noticeable as I made my way across the yard and to The Patch. I laid down on the ground near the bench and acted like I was just chillin'. Then I slowly but surely took the knives out. I handed CoCo and Slick their knives, and kept my own inside my coat sleeve.

    Some other Crips from Los Angeles, along with my ex-cellie Lil Crayzo pulled me to the side and told me that one of his homies had got stabbed in the neck. Lil Crayzo asked me to kick back so that he and his homies could handle their business first. I didn't want to lose the opportunity to get the nigga who attempted to "Hit" Thun, but Lil Crayzo seemed so passionate about him needing to get revenge. I didn't want to ruin their plans, and Thun was still afraid so I gave Lil Crayzo my word that I'd wait for him and his homies to handle their business. And they did.

CHAPTER 26

We were put on lockdown status and confined to our cells. We could only go to the Chow Hall and take a shower every three days. I had been writing more letters to the C.O. I nicknamed Sweet-P, and she'd always write me back. One night she had written me a sweet letter and expressed her concern about my emotional well being. I hadn't had sex with her since my brother's death, and I hadn't even bothered to ask her for any pussy since then either. Every time she and I would write letters, we would have to wait until she made her rounds at count-time to pass our letters. On this particular night I had written her, she had written me back, and I had written her again. But, I got sleepy and didn't feel like waiting for her to come back around for the next count, so I placed the letter I'd written her in the window of my cell door and then fell asleep. I awoke for breakfast to see that the letter was gone so I figured she had taken it during count-time, but didn't have time to write me back.

Later that day I was told to report to The Watch Office. The last time I was told to report there was when I found out my brother got killed. Now I wondered and worried what bad news I was going to receive this time. The lieutenant didn't waste any time questioning me.

"Do you know Officer Patton?" he asked me.
"Yeah I know her. She worked in my wing," I responded.

"Did you know her prior to you coming to this prison?" he asked.

"No," I said. "Why? What's up?" I asked.

"Do you know anything about a letter written to her?" he asked.

"Yeah, I wrote her a short note thanking her for being concerned about my well-being since hearing the news about my brother's death." I explained. "She's not the only C.O. who showed concern; I was able to thank the others because they all worked earlier in the day. But I left Ms. Patton a note because I'm usually asleep when she's on duty." I further explained.

The lieutenant believed my story since I hadn't said anything in the letter incriminating myself. However, for "safety concerns," I got re-housed in a different wing. My new cellie was an older nigga from West Covina Neighborhood Gangsta Crips. His name was Ken Dog. We were only cellies for a few days when they told him to pack all his belongings and transferred him to the North Yard.

It was the weekend so I used the time to rearrange my cell and prepare for my visit. I usually tied a string to my knives, placed them inside the toilet drain, and tied ink pen tops to the other end of the string to use as floaters. This way my toilet would appear to be empty, except for the water in it.

My cell door opened before I had time to clean up and put away my knives. So, I got dressed, put on some cologne, and placed the knives in the empty lockers inside my cell.

My visit went well. The halfbreed girl named Millie came to see me again. At the end of the visit, I was called to the back to be stripped-out all by myself. I thought maybe they thought I was bringing in some weed since I had done so on a few occasions. But today I didn't have any weed. Two male C.O.'s led me to the corridor, where a female Sergeant met us.

"You know what's goin' on, don't you?" she asked.
"No. What's up?" I asked.

"There were some inmate manufactured weapons found in your cell. Do you know anything about them?" she asked.

"Not in my cell," I said innocently. "You couldn't have found any in my cell because I'm the only one living in that cell, and I don't have no weapons." I added.

They escorted me to O-Wing (The Hole), and read me my Miranda Rights. It's routine for the prison officials to send a referral for prosecution to the district attorney's office in matters that are considered to be Felony Offenses. And possession of a weapon by a convicted felon is in fact a felony in the state of California. I was assigned to a cell on the 1st tier of the north side of the wing, near the end of the wing. The cells were single man cells, and were designed kind of like the six-man cell I was in while in Lerdo Max Facility. Only, these cells were a lot smaller.

After thirty days, I was allowed to have my food, hygiene items, and my t.v.. Smoking was allowed too, and the C.O.'s would give us some generic cigarette tobacco that was awful tasting and harsh. But, it was free.

It was mandatory for all young Crips like myself to participate in the exercise routines. Each of us were considered a viable part of a "Machine" and the act of us exercising together was our "Machine in Motion."

O-Wing was segregated. And the exercise yard inside The Hole consisted of sections of concrete slabs with one solid wall and three chain-linked fences lined with barbed-wire at the top. We had to wear yellow one-piece jumpsuits to the yard, but we could exercise in our boxer underwear. We only had handball and chess games. But, we were able to take pictures on the exercise yard to send to our families. When the Goon Squad (Prison Investigating Unit) came to talk to me about the weapons, I told them I wanted to exercise my Fifth Amendment Rights to remain silent. But, when the district attorney's office rejected the referral submitted by the prison, I decided to admit to possession of the weapon on one condition, to let my cellie Ken Dog go. Ken Dog had gotten gaffled-up from the North Yard the same day that I got gaffled-up from visiting. He didn't even know that I had the knives, so I was gonna let him off the hook anyways. But, I wanted to wait until the D.A.'s office made their decision to prosecute or not. Ken Dog was "short" to the house, so he was hella happy when I went to our hearing and took full responsibility for the weapons.

A couple of weeks later I had to go to another hearing (I.C.C.). At this hearing I received 360 days loss of good-time credits and was ordered to serve ten months in a SHU (segregated housing unit).

About two weeks after receiving my SHU sentence, a nigga moved into a cell next door to mines. I was asleep when he arrived, but I was awakened by his yelling down the tier. He was telling somebody about the incident that led him into The Hole with us. Apparently he came from Tehachapi Prison for attempting to stab somebody. But he really got my full attention when I heard him say that his intended victim was from Bakersfield. And when he said his intended victim was Big Rick, I got furious because Big Rick is my homie Pete-A-Moe's daddy. I didn't let my emotions get the best of me because I wanted to attack this loud mouth by surprise. I knew how to make a shank out of plastic from my CYA days. This white boy named Bino from Hoover, and this big nigga named Big Ant from Southside Compton Crips had taught me how to melt down everything from plastic cups to plastic hot sauce bottles. So, I emptied out all of the hot sauce from one of my plastic bottles and rinsed it out as best as I could. I used wet towels and t-shirts to handle the hot plastic once I set it on fire. I twisted and pulled the heated material into the shape of a knife. I used razor-blades to shave and sharpen one end. Then I tied strips of torn sheets around the other end to make the handle. My "piece" was ready.

I went over my plan of attack a dozen times until the C.O. announced it was time for yard-release on my tier. Since we were in The Hole, we had to go through the formalities of a quick strip-search before being allowed onto the yard. I rolled my shank up in my bath-towel, along with my extra pair of boxer underwear. I held the roll behind my back with both of my hands and stuck my arms through the tray slot so that the C.O. could put handcuffs on me. Once I made it to the yard, the handcuffs were removed. I waited until the C.O.'s were gone, and then I made my move. I caught Loud-Mouth stretching and preparing to do his exercises, then I "hit" him in the neck and face at least twelve times. He screamed like a bitch and balled up in a fetal position. I walked over to the fence separating the exercise yards and smoothly handed off the shank just before the C.O. in the gun tower yelled for us to get down on the yard. While the C.O. in the gun tower was focused on the Loud-Mouth, the shank was passed from one exercise to the next until it was tossed onto the roof. The Goon Squad came into the exercise area fully equipped with protective gear, batons, and Block Guns. The Block Gun was nicknamed Big Bertha because it's a big, black, shotgun, that looks like it can fire hand grenades. However, it only fires non-lethal projectiles. The Goon Squad didn't have to shoot or mace anyone on this day because we were all laying face down in the prone position. We laid there for what seemed like hours, as they scooped up Loud-Mouth, and took a lot of pictures of the crime scene. We all got strip searched and escorted back to our cells, and were interviewed the following day. I'm sure my interview went just like everyone else's... "No comment."

    A couple of weeks later I was transferred to Corcoran State Prison to serve my SHU term.

CHAPTER 27

We arrived at the prison in Corcoran, California around nightfall, and the bus pulled through three different gates before coming to a stop. Once we stepped off the bus, myself and two other prisoners were greeted by two Sergeants and six C.O.'s. We didn't go inside of R&R like I'd done on my last two rides. We were led through a tall gate, across the yard, and to a building that was designed as a special R&R building. Once inside, we were stripped-out and given a pair of boxer underwear, a pair of socks, flap-jap Karate shoes, and a one-piece jumpsuit with strings going down the front of it.

The C.O.'s were all 6' tall or better, and they had a zero tolerance attitude. I was advised to follow their commands at all times. And was told that any type of movement without their instruction would be considered an act of an attack on one of the C.O.'s, and would be taken down with great force. Words don't usually scare me but, I could tell by the way they "Man-Handled" me that they meant what they said. My beef wasn't with them anyways. As far as I was concerned, they were just doing their job, and I was doing my time.

I was escorted to my housing unit (4AlL). Also known as Bedrock, because of it's stone design. The two beds in each cell were nothing more than casket shaped stone blocks with two cubic feet sections cut into the sides of them that were used as a storage space. A three cubic-feet stone block at the back of the cell was suppose to be the desk. A three cubic-feet stone block near the toilet was used to place my t.v. on it, and I didn't get my t.v. or any of my other property until after I was there for thirty days.

The cell door was all steel with well over two-hundred dime sized holes in it. The most interesting thing about the cells were the light switch. However, these particular light switches were shaped like half of a ping pong ball. They were grey and they felt like really strong rubber. By simply touching the ball shaped rubber, the lights in the cell would come on. And touching it again would cause the lights in the cell to go off. The switch was designed so that you must also have shoes on to activate the light switch. Standing barefoot in the cell and touching the switch would not activate the lights. It took me awhile, but I found out that if I held my finger on the switch and jumped into the air, I could activate the lights.

With nothing but time on my hands, I learned a whole bunch of shit, and after I was classified, I was allowed to have a cellie. They moved me into a cell with this older nigga named Melo from Harlem 30's Crips. Melo had just transferred from one of the most dangerous prisons in California (Pelican Bay State Prison). He was hella cool, and had a lot of knowledge, but he was also a "Hot Head" and had serious beef with all the C.O.'s. We didn't get to be cellies for long because one day after we returned from the yard, he refused to lock up. I told the nigga it was a no win situation, but he didn't listen. He ran around the dayroom cussin' and throwin' fake ass nutty's for ten minutes. The tall, black, C.O. bitch in the gun tower told Melo to lock-it-up several times while she pointed the gun at him, but he still refused. She talked him into going to the door that led to the corridor, and it was a wrap. His dumb ass got right up to the door and she cracked the door open about one foot wide and two arms reached in, grabbed Melo, and snatched his ass off his feet. I didn't see Melo again, but I did write his momma a letter to let her know what had happened.

Later that night four C.O.'s came to my cell, gave me the letter that I'd written to Melo's momma, and told me to mind my own business, and then I got moved to 4A2R the next day. On my way to 4A2R, I got a chance to see Charles Manson. I didn't get a good look at him, but I did see he had stacks of mail in his cell. 4A2R was designed exactly like 4A1L. My cellie was this light-skinned buffed nigga named Rob-Dog from Long Beach, California. He was cool, but I could tell he was a Bully. His body language, behavior, and his tone of voice were all signs of a "Bully". I wasn't havin' that tho' and I nipped it in the bud by letting him know that me and him could fight instead of letting little shit lead up to a fight anyways. He looked at me like I was crazy, but he knew I was dead serious. We didn't fight. I'm glad too because I ended up liking Cuz.

    I finally got to order some food and hygiene items, and the C.O. opened every item I purchased and placed them in either paper cups or paper bags. My cookies were stale. He even opened each candy bar I ordered and placed them in a bag. All of my candy bars tasted like Paydays because salt and peanuts were everywhere. The Cup O'Noodles I ordered were all dumped into one paper bag and all the seasonings were at the bottom of the bag. When it came time to make a soup I couldn't tell what flavor I was eating. There was no comb, no razor, or no full length toothbrushes allowed. In fact, they cut my toothbrush in half when they gave me my property.

    The yard in the SHU was small, and the only activities were exercise and handball. The yard was maybe 30x15 yards with 15' stone walls surrounding it, and a C.O. in the gun tower watching over us. The yard was integrated and was usually racially balanced with two whites, two blacks, and two hispanics. Sometimes one of the races would have one or two more of their race on the yard. There was a small rotunda leading out to the yard. And in this rotunda, this is where our handcuffs come off and the electric operated door leading to the yard is opened. Most C.O.'s would instruct me or my cellie to actually step out onto the yard before the other was un-cuffed. But, I never obeyed their orders. When it came to shit like that, I'd be damned if I was gonna step out onto the yard with other races already on the yard. They would surely attack my black ass.

    At the far end of the yard was a shower. We would rotate shower times by race. Meaning one black showered, then one white, and then one hispanic. One day it was my turn to shower when this short hispanic fool tried to go ahead of me. He stood under the shower head and was getting ready to push the water button when I "got at him".

"I was next," I told him as polite as I could.

"Yeah, I know. You're next. After me," he replied.

"Naw, I was next. It's my turn now," I said with authority in my voice.

I looked at him the way a Pit-bull does when another dog gets near his food. When he turned his head in defeat, I took my eyes off of him. *Bam!* He bombed on me with an overhand right that slid down the side of my face. I was both mad and disappointed. Mad that this mutha-fucka' put his hands on me. And disappointed that I was slippin' and let my guards down in a hostile environment. His punch didn't phase me, so I countered with six quick blows to his head. A couple of my punches struck him in his elbows and forearms because he was trying to cover up. I could see my cellie Big Rob-Dog "puttin' hands" on the other hispanic, so I stayed focused on the one I was mixing up. Just as the hispanic fool went down, I heard the C.O. in the gun tower yell, "Get Down!" Instead of me getting down, I drop-stepped, then kicked the hispanic fool in his face like I was kicking a football. I was getting ready to kick his head off when I heard and felt the shot. *Boom!* I thought my whole shoulder and upper back was blown off. But the projectiles from the Block Gun only sounded and felt like it had done major damage. My right upper back and shoulder area was hit. There was a little bit of blood but nothing major. I received 90 days of good time credit loss and had to spend an additional 30 days in the SHU.

A few weeks later I got called for a visit. I was literally chained up with steel-linked chains and pad locks. I had five locks on me. On both legs, both wrists, and one around my waist. And to top it all off, I had chains connecting to my legs and waist, and to other prisoners who were in front of me and behind me. They too were chained up to other prisoners. With two C.O.'s on each side of us, we were escorted to the visiting holding cells, which were the size of a public telephone booth. We were only held there until it was time for our Visit, then we'd get escorted to a nearby cell where the actual visit took place. Although the actual visiting cell is larger than other visiting holding cells, they were still relatively small. There was one metal stool, a metal counter, and an intercom that was located too high in the cell for me to reach. One big window, two inches thick, with wire running through it, is what separates the prisoner from the visitors. On the visitor's side of the window, was a metal counter, a phone, and a couple of plastic chairs. The entire SHU visiting room was like this. I was so happy to see my momma and my wife Kam, that I had to hold back my tears of joy. They didn't. They were both smiling and crying but I had them laughing after awhile. After they left, they both came back to visit me again the following weekend. This was the time I met Charles Manson and even held a brief conversation with him. "Charlie" is the name I'd heard several C.O.'s call him.

On this particular morning, me, and two other guys were being escorted to our visits, while Charlie was also being escorted. The C.O.'s didn't have Charlie chained up to us. He was off to the side with his own escorts, but he was chained up like us. When we made it to the SHU visiting holding cells, I was locked in a cell next to the one that Charlie was in. He was really short. A lot shorter than I thought he'd be. The swastika tattoo on his forehead was faded, and I had to look really hard to see it. He was frail looking to me, but those rosy red cheeks and bulging eyes would brighten up every time he thought of something clever to say. Then his eyes would take on a hypnotic quality like Santa Clause, as he'd share his thoughts. He looked me dead in my eyes and blurted out, "Rich people don't know how to spend money. They will spend $65,000 on an automobile but are afraid to spend $6,000 on a bed; And a bed goes into your home and will last a lifetime," he added as he shook his head in disgust. I didn't know what to say at the time so I just shook my head too and chuckled a little. I never did understand what he actually meant by all of that. But, over the years I've sometimes thought of what he said, and think maybe he's right. Kam and momma were able to see Charles Manson too because on the day that he said all the stuff about rich people, I told momma and Kam to go two booths down and see Charlie. Sirhan Sirhan was also in Corcoran's SHU too. I saw him on a visit one day, but I only spoke to him without any conversation with him. He too was a lot shorter that I imagined he'd be.

After going before the Committee, I was told that I could be released back into General Population.

CHAPTER 28

It felt like I was getting out of prison because the SHU is a prison within a prison. I ended up on Corcoran's Level-III, on the B-Yard. The atmosphere was like a breath of fresh air. While I was in the SHU I had stayed awake nearly four days watching the L.A. Riots, and the subsequent "Gang Truce". So, to actually see Crips and Bloods functioning together was unbelievably beautiful.

There was only six other niggas from Bakersfield on the yard, and they were all off the eastside. There was Fonzo, Mo-Bounce, Blue, my step-brother Booda, and his uncle Gary, who had a Life Sentence.

I was getting visits regularly from Kam. I even hooked-up my Aunt Diane with this O.G. nigga named Larry from Compton. We called him Big Hub. We both got visits regularly, but I was bringing weed in every time. I sold some of it, but I smoked most of it. My wife Kam had started failing to send me money, stopped making it to visits, and didn't send me anymore packages. Her letters weren't the same, and she didn't sound the same on the phone when I'd talk to her. I hadn't heard anything about her and another man, and I didn't think she would actually cheat on me. But, my gut feeling told me something just wasn't right. One day while I was talking to her on the phone, I told her that I'd heard she was messing around with another nigga. She got really quiet but she didn't admit or deny it. I then asked her if she loved the nigga, and to my surprise, she said "yes." I damn near fainted. My head Spun and my heart felt like it had broken into a million pieces. I was crushed.

> "Who is he?" I asked her.
> "You don't know him," she replied.
> "What's his name?" I asked.
> "His name is Paul," she finally admitted.
> "I thought you loved me," I said, sounding pitiful.
> "I do love you Eric. But I love him too," she replied.

I didn't hear anybody in the background, but I assumed he was sitting next to her because she was boldly telling me she was involved with another man.

> "Who is that?" I asked, although I hadn't heard anybody. She was silent. "Who is that in the background Kam?" I asked. "Let me talk to whoever that is over there," I demanded.
> "Hello?" a deep voice said on the other line of the phone.
> "Who is this?" I demanded.
> "Paul," he answered.
> "What are you doin' at my house with my wife?" I asked him.
> "Your wife?" he said, sounding like this was news to him. "Baby didn't tell me she was married," he explained.
> "Yeah Cuz, that's my wife," I told him.

I was hurt and mad, but I couldn't be mad at Paul because he was only doing what any man would've done. So, I got at him like a real nigga is supposed to.

> "Check this out Cuz, from man to man, Crip to Crip, I ain't trippin' on you." I started off saying. "Whatever you do, don't stop Kam from taking care of me or from visiting me, and don't put yo' hands on her daughters." I added.

Paul agreed to everything I said then he put Kam back on the phone. I told her I was hurt and disappointed, but I still loved her. She told me she loved me too, then she hung-up.

She visited me a few more times and brought me some

weed, but when she failed to make it to our Family Visit, I had to let her go. I divorced Kam, but I continued to love her.

My nigga Casper from Neighborhood Compton Crips was my "Road Dog," and he called me his "Road Puppy." He was locked up for murder, but he already had 10 years in, and had a release date. He would go on his Family Visits and bring back weed too. Since he worked in PIA (Prison Industry Authority), I didn't get to hang out with him in the daytime. I lifted weights every morning five days a week with D-Bone from Nutty Blocc Compton Crips, and with Baby Smokey from 8-3 Hoover. We were all 21 years old, had heart, and had much respect for one another.

When I first hit the yard, my step-brother Booda was hella excited to see me. I was happy to see him too, but not as excited as he was. I soon found out why he was so damn excited. He had been "having words" with a few of the other Crips in our building, and didn't feel like he had anyone to watch his back if he wanted to take a fade with one of them. But, with me being there he knew I'd have his back. Booda immediately started walking around with his chest out and with a chip on his shoulders. He even got into a shouting match with this fine ass C.O. bitch who happened to be the R&B singer Karyn White's sister. She was working in our building's gun tower. Booda acted like he was gonna throw his cup of coffee at her, so she drew-down on him with the Mini-14 and told him she was gonna bust a cap in his ass.

A few times the same C.O. worked in the kitchen area where I also worked. I would flirt with her and engage in very personal conversations with her. One time I watched her go into the staff restroom. When the door was closing she gave me an inviting look. But, for some reason I didn't trust her, so I didn't go in. She did me like that two more times too, but I didn't bite.

I met an O.G. from Bakersfield named Big Teeney. He had a Life Sentence and had already been in prison for 15 years. He was on the C-Yard, but we met in the visiting room. We took pictures together and chopped it up. On one visit, the Porter/Camera-man, who was a prisoner, got smart with Teeney and they almost went to blows, but I wouldn't let it go down in front of our families. The nigga was housed on my yard, so I took the fade for Teeney. I would go to the Muslim Service on the C-Yard so that I could chop it up with Teeney once a week, even though I wasn't Muslim.

    When my victim (Big Marv) hit the C-Yard, I shot a kite over there asking the 805 Mob homies to "roll him up". But, they took too long to handle it, so I went to a Muslim Service with a shank so that I could bust a hole in Big Marv. Everyone felt the tension as soon as I got there, and they had Teeney "get at me". He asked me not to attack Big Marv at the Muslim Service because it would ruin future programs for the Muslim Community. I had to respect that so I left it alone and took my ass back to the B-Yard. I was disappointed that Teeney didn't roll-up Big Marv, and I never went back to another Muslim Service.

My step-brother Booda was always in some bullshit. He had hooked-up with a Norteno he knew from C.Y.A and had gotten some weed from him on credit. Which is a very big "no-no" in prison. The Norteno gave Booda ten $10 caps of weed which are small bindles that are big enough to roll-up three $5 joints out of each one. The Norteno only wanted Booda to pay him $40 for the ten caps of weed, and he had given Booda more than enough time to pay him. I didn't know Booda was doing business with the Norteno or with anyone else. But, I did wonder where Booda was getting the weed that he kept firing up with me and Casper.

    Then one day, while I was on my way into my building, I overheard Booda arguing with two Nortenos. Booda called them all kinds of punk mutha-fuckas and threatened to fuck them up. Before I could get over there to them, the Nortenos had started walking away. My nigga Casper had walked up at the same time I confronted Booda about arguing and threatening the Nortenos. Booda tried to downplay the situation like it was no big deal, but I watched the Nortenos closely and even pointed out their obvious actions to Booda and Casper.

The Nortenos walked to the sit-up bench on the other side of the yard and sat down. I could see them digging in the dirt with their bare hands, and then they cuffed and stuffed what I believed to be shanks. Casper and I immediately went to our designated table, which was only about twenty feet away, and we dug up our shanks too. The Nortenos weren't bullshittin'. They walked directly back towards us. I could see the fear in Booda's eyes as the Nortenos got closer and closer. When they got twenty feet from us I asked them what was up and I took a couple of steps towards them. The tallest one spoke up and gave me the story about the ten caps of weed. He went on to say he had two knives on him and wanted to give Booda one so that he and Booda could battle it out like men. I told him Booda was my brother and it wasn't gonna go down like that. I asked Booda on the spot if what the Norteno was saying was true. And when Booda admitted it was true I told the Norteno that he would be paid before yard-recall, and he was to never do business with Booda again. Booda stayed in some shit. He even got into it with niggas who were in our "Car" (805 Mob).

Blue from Mid City Crips wanted to stick Booda, but I wouldn't let it go down. Booda got into it with Fonzo, and when I tried to get between them, Booda "fired" on Fonzo. Booda got into it with so many different people so many times, that I got fed up with his shit and had to get in his ass myself. I put my t.v. under my bed so that it wouldn't get damaged while I whooped his ass. I had fucked him up before when we were both a lot younger, so I knew I could win. I really didn't want to whoop on him but if I didn't do it, the whole Crip Car was gonna end up rollin' him up off the yard.

I let Booda come all the way into our cell then I closed the door and "put hands" on him. He started crying and shit. Not because he couldn't handle the ass-whoopin' but because his feelings were hurt. Seeing him cry caused me to shed a few tears too. After all, I did love Booda like a brother.

Corcoran prison was very dangerous, and like no other. From the rigged fights I experienced in the SHU, to the racially unbalanced numbers on the mainline. The gang-truce announced in watts between the Crips and Bloods significantly lowered the number of riots between the two gangs in all of the prisons in California. We even got along well enough to have Crips vs. Bloods football games in Corcoran. Until one day this fat black nigga named Chubs from Hanford 83 Gangsta Crips had an altercation with some tall lanky Blood nigga. They exchanged heated words, but a few of us were telling them to leave it alone until after the game. When Chubs said, "I put that on Crip we gon' get down after the game," the Blood nigga said, "Fuck Crab!" Every Crip on the football field who were headed towards the huddle, turned on their heels and headed towards the lanky Blood nigga; myself included. The homies on the sidelines came onto the field as well, and a melee broke out. I was "puttin' hands" on this one Blood nigga when outta nowhere I was hit in the jaw with what felt like a baseball bat. *Crack!* My body tensed up from the surprising impact and I immediately crawled away from the area on all fours, as fast as I could, to avoid another blow. I was maybe fifteen feet away when I stopped retreating and engaged in combat with the nearest Blood nigga. The melee lasted about two full minutes, but it seemed a lot longer.

"Down on the yard! Down on the yard!" yelled the C.O. in the gun tower. There were no shots fired, but we laid down on our stomachs. To my surprise, Booda was laying right next to me. He told me that he was clear across the field when he saw me get sucker punched in my jaw. So, he fucked up the Blood nigga who punched me. His name was Ice, but I forgot what hood he was from. We all got cuffed-up with plastic ties and escorted to the Program Office. While we were waiting to be interviewed, we all got our stories together. We simply said the Football game got a little out of hand, but it was nothing serious. And we agreed not to play rough anymore.

If it wasn't for this crazy ass Mexican Lieutenant named, F.A. Rodriguez, we would've all ended up in the SHU. A lot of prisoners and C.O.'s didn't particularly like F.A. Rodriguez. He could be an Asshole at times, but I liked his no-nonsense approach.

One day I was talking to him on the yard about a complaint

I had when a C.O. rudely interrupted us. F.A. Rodriguez looked at me and politely said, "Excuse me for a second," then he faced the rude C.O. and shouted at the top of his lungs, "Can't you see I'm talking, you Dumb Fuck!? Show some fuckin' respect!"

He cussed his ass out while everyone on the yard looked on, and until the rude C.O. was "beet red" and hung his head in embarrassment. The C.O.'s back in the early 1990's were really tough and were quick to prove it. I remember being at work in the Chow Hall during roll call, and I was being disruptive. The young Mexican C.O. named Cortez stopped calling names and focused on me. I didn't realize everyone else was focused on me too. Cortez finally had heard enough of my disruptive behavior and told me to stay back after everyone else was dismissed. I hunched my shoulders and mumbled, "so what," under my breath. After all the other prisoners left, Cortez had me follow him into his office where only one Free-Staff was. First he gave me the story about him growing up in the hood just like me, and how he wasn't no punk. He then went on to say all he wanted was his respect, and that he felt disrespected because I had been talking during his roll call. He wasn't a big guy, and he wasn't mean-looking. Actually, he looked like a "Square". He only stood 5'8" tall and weighed maybe 150 lbs. But, the more he talked, the tougher he sounded. Then all of a sudden he took off his police belt and his badge, and put them inside a locker and locked it. He stood across the desk facing me and looked into my eyes.

"Go ahead, take the first punch. Even if I don't kick your ass, you'll know you've been in a fight. Come on, hit me," he challenged me.

I looked deep into his eyes and realized this little mutha-fucka' was serious. However, I had to weigh the situation.... He's a C.O., I'm a prisoner, the Free-staff cook is a witness, and it'll be my word against theirs. The odds didn't look good at all, but another part of me wanted to knock his ass out. I hadn't walked away from a Fight since Squirt punched me in the chest as a kid. With lightening speed, I grabbed Cortez by his shirt collar with both hands and pulled him towards me, nearly pulling him over the desk. He grabbed both of my wrists and tried to free himself, but my grip was way too strong.

"Go ahead!" he said again.

I could've shook him like a Rag-Doll, but I didn't. Looking into his eyes sent me on an emotional roller coaster, and I felt sorry for him. At the same time, I had to give him his respect because no other C.O. had ever challenged me, let alone taken off their badge and police belt. I finally released my hold on him and backed away from the desk.

"You know what man? I gotta give you yo' respect," I said to him.

Then, I apologized to him for disrespecting his roll call. We didn't have anymore conflicts after that.

The riot with the Bloods was two weeks old now, but I was still feeling effects from it. My jaw was hella sore, and I would find myself opening and closing my mouth so that I could work the soreness out. And for months I wanted to whoop on the nigga who cracked me in the jaw, but the homies said I would've been wrong, so I let it go.
    I was getting stronger from lifting weights with D-Bone and Baby Smokey. We all became 300 Club members at the same time. Being able to bench-press 300 lbs. was a major accomplishment for us all.
    The weight pile, basketball courts, handball courts, and tables were split up into specific sections according to "Race" and "Gangs". No race was allowed to walk near the areas of other races. Rules like that were implemented to help prevent surprise attacks by other races.
    One morning while we were lifting weights, a non-english speaking Mexican walked through our work-out area. Baby Smokey immediately approached him and told him that he was

"out of bounds," and advised him not to do it again. A few hours later while we were posted up in the shade on Building 3's wall, two Mexicans approached Baby Smokey. One of the Mexicans was the same non-english speaking one who Baby Smokey had "checked" earlier on the weight-pile. Normally we would've been suspicious of two Mexicans approaching, but these two 4', innocent looking, Mexicans seemed harmless. The Mexican who Baby Smokey "checked" earlier had the other Mexican act as his interpreter. When Baby Smokey leaned down to hear the interpreter better, the non-english speaking Mexican moved with lightening speed and stuck Baby Smokey in the neck with an ice-pick. Before anyone could react, the two Mexicans fled around the track and to the protective huddle of their comrades.

    I showed up on the scene a few minutes later to find Baby Smokey so mad that he was in tears, and most of his homies from Hoover were preparing for war. In prison, Crips and Bloods fight each other, and sometimes Crips attack other Crips. But when a Crip goes to war against another race, other Crips and black men in general will show support. This current situation was no exception. I dug up my knife and posted up with Casper, Beads, and Blue. The two Mexicans responsible for the attack on Baby Smokey were nowhere to be seen, so nobody made a move on the yard against anyone. At yard-recall I said my goodbye's to Blue and Casper, then me and Booda made our way to our building. When I entered the building's sallyport, there was six homies from Hoover inside, along with 8 to 10 Mexicans and a couple of Woods. Then, all hell broke loose inside the small confines of the sallyport. Punches were thrown, people were pushing and shoving, and some were hollering. A couple of more homies from Hoover who were in the sallyport were also stabbin' and stickin' mutha-fuckas too.

    The sallyport gate finally opened and we poured out of there in all different directions before the C.O.'s on the dayroom floor realized what happened. We were placed on Lockdown pending investigation but, those of us who worked in the kitchen were allowed to go to work.

    I had become the Lead Table wiper, and Bob-a-Lou from 92 Hoover worked with me. Our jobs were to wipe the tables in the Chow Hall but, we had more serious duties now that we were at war with the Mexicans. We had to transport weapons from the back of the kitchen into the dining area, and pass them to the homies during chow. Since we were on a modified schedule, the buildings were released to Chow one section at a time.

Me and Bob-a-Lou did our jobs and sent at least fifteen knives out. But the Mexicans were "on us". They were relaying messages to one another and nodding in our directions. They were saying, "The short one" and "The one with the goatee" referring to me and Bob-a-Lou. So we knew they were "on us" but we didn't give a fuck. We were young Bangers looking to earn more stripes.

After being on Lockdown for two weeks, we were all finally allowed to go to the yard. Everyone mingled in their respective groups discussing the events that led up to the Lockdown and talked about who all went to The Hole.

I had a Super Radio II with my walkman hooked up to it, and I was bumpin' Snoop Dogg's, "Nuthin' but a G thang," while me and one of the homies walked a lap around the track. Halfway around the track I could feel and hear a breathtaking buzzing and humming sound. It was tension. I instinctively lowered the volume on my Super Radio II and noticed that I was the only one on the entire prison yard with my radio on. I made a quick survey of the whole yard and realized that I had just walked pass a group of Mexicans in their designated area near the handball courts. I cursed myself for "slippin" like that and hurriedly made my way safely to the bleachers. The homies who were waiting on the bleachers thought me and the homie was walking around the track in an attempt to catch one of the Mexicans slippin' so we could stick him. But the truth is, me and the homie were slippin' in a major way. The homie JoJo From Hoover stood up, walked down the bleachers, and headed towards the buildings.

"Where you goin' JoJo?" I asked.
"I'm goin' to my building," he answered.

His building happened to be the one near the handball

courts and the group of Mexicans. I told JoJo he should wait for some homies to go with him, but he said, "Fuck them Mexicans, I'm goin' in!" as he walked quickly towards his building.

The bleachers were located on the far end of the yard near Building 5. There was six of us sittin' on the bleachers watching JoJo make his way across the yard. When he got to the handball courts, near the group of Mexicans, they swarmed on him like Bees. All I could see was about eight Mexicans in a huddle with JoJo in the middle jumping up and down. They were stickin' the hell outta him. We leaped off the bleachers in a desperate effort to rescue JoJo, but the C.O. in the gun tower had already yelled for everyone to get down on the yard and had fired two shots. The Mexicans all scattered like roaches, tossing their weapons, and getting as far away from JoJo's bloody body as they could. I was mad at JoJo for putting himself in that situation after I had already warned him. It really pissed me off when I had to walk pass the bloodstains JoJo left on the track for two weeks.

When we finally came off Lockdown, a lot of people got hurt that day on both sides, and some were even taken off the yard on stretchers and by ambulance. This time we stayed on Lockdown for two months. During the Lockdown I went to Classification for my Annual Review. My points had dropped, but not enough to change my custody level. However, I asked to be transferred to a Level-III prison closer to Bakersfield, and I was transferred during the Lockdown.

CHAPTER 29

Wasco State Prison is a Reception Center prison located 26 miles From Bakersfield, in a very small town called Wasco, California. This prison didn't exist when I first went to prison, and it had only been open for two and a half years when I got there in 1993.

Unlike the Reception Center in Tehachapi, the C.O's in Wasco did all of the intake and processing of newly arriving prisoners. Every prison has an R&R (Receiving & Release) located on the prison grounds. R&R is the first place you go to upon entering a prison, and the last place you go to upon your release, and Wasco has a huge R&R compared to most prisons throughout California.

A lot of counties (Kern, Los Angeles, Kings, Orange, Fresno, Ventura, San Luis Obispo, and Tulare) send their newly committed prisoners to Wasco State Prison. Facilities B, C, and D were for Reception Center prisoners. And Facilities A and E are General Population yards for prisoners who have already been classified. A-yard was for Level-III prisoners and E-yard was Level-I. Since I was a Level-III prisoner, I got housed in the Orientation Building on A-yard.

I arrived there with a few Mexicans, a couple of Woods, and with this bald-headed nigga named B-Ball from Dodge City Cribs, who ended up in a cell right next to me. The following day, my homie CoCo arrived from Soledad. We had another homie from our hood named Len-Dogg, who was already in a regular building on the yard. After ten days of being on CTQ, we were allowed to go to the yard. There was about fifteen homies on the yard from 805 Mob. There was Gino, C-Dog, Sweet Pea, Sweets, Scooby, Tip, Tex, Kev, Tone, Tiny Toones, Capone, and Blue Beard. The homies who had been there for awhile put me up on everything that had been going on with the homies from 805 Mob. Two of the homies (Big Nose Rob & Mike) were in The Hole for a melee they had with an 83 Gangsta and Grape Street Watts nigga. I was told that it all started because Big Nose Rob refused to pay a debt he owed. Apparently, Big Nose Rob owed money to someone from 83 Gangsta who had transferred to another prison, and had left instructions for Big Nose Rob to pay his homie. When Guz from 83 Gangsta got at Big Nose Rob about the money, Big Nose Rob told him he wasn't gonna pay it. The debt was only $11, but that wasn't the point, it was the principle. Big Nose Rob and Mike were both from the same hood, and they kicked it pretty tough on the yard everyday. They were both big and strong corn-fed niggas. They were approached by the two niggas from 83 Gangsta and Watts, when words were exchanged and the nigga from 83 Gangsta slashed Big Nose Rob on the neck with a piece of metal. But before the cut could bleed, Big Nose Rob had unleashed two devastating blows to the head of his attacker and knocking him out cold. Since Tex was a Spoonie Gee Crip, he often socialized with a lot of niggas from Watts because Spoonie Gee Grips originated From Watts. That's why Mike believed Tex knew "what time it was" regarding the attack. Tex told me he didn't know it was goin' down, and went on to say that even if he would've known, he still wouldn't have said nothing because it wasn't his business. And I had to agree.

    I called a meeting with all the homies from 805 Mob, and discussed the situation regarding Mike and Tex. The meeting didn't go well because Mike said he didn't trust anybody and he walked off. I played the role as the Mediator and tried to get them both to shake hands and call a truce. The three of us sat on the bleachers away from everyone and I sat in the middle of them. Tex agreed to "shake on it", but Mike was stubborn and refused to. Tex then felt insulted and became furious.

    "Fuck that nigga!" Tex said as he stood up.

Mike also stood up and I stood between them as Tex moved towards me in an attempt to get to Mike. I glanced down at Tex's right hand and saw the knife he held close to his side. Mike noticed it too and grabbed my jacket to pull me in front of him as a shield. Tex looked over my shoulder and focused on Mike.

"E-Loc don't let him stick me! Don't let him stick me!" Mike pleaded with me as he continued to pull on me and use me as a shield.

"Tex!" I yelled in an attempt to get his full attention. "You bet not bust on him!" I said in an almost threatening tone.

He looked dangerously hungry to kill. I yelled at him again, "Tex! If you bust on him I'm gon' bust on you!"

Tex then stopped moving towards me and focused in on me to see if he had actually heard what he thought he'd heard me say. Mike used this opportunity to get far away from Tex. He walked towards the weight-pile and I followed close behind him in an attempt to get him to stop and talk to me, but he wouldn't stop. When he reached the weight-pile I could hear him asking different niggas to give him a knife. I was pissed off now because Mike was asking strangers for a weapon to attack an 805 Mob homie. No one gave Mike a knife, and I was finally able to catch up to him. He was visibly shaken, but I didn't give a damn. I was highly upset for a number of reasons. The main one being him asking niggas for a knife to "blast" a homie. So, I screamed on him.

"What the fuck is wrong with you!?" I shot at him.

He was speechless, and I could see the fear and shame in his face, so I toned down my verbal reprimand.

"Damn Cuz, you trippin'," I said in a more comforting tone.

I talked to Mike for nearly an hour, but the conversation seemed useless, so I left it alone. A few days later Big Nose Rob came back to the yard. Tension Filled the air and everyone was on edge.

With Los Angeles County Jail sending their prisoners to Wasco State Prison, I was able to capitalize on their practice of allowing their prisoners to have cash money in their possession. A lot of niggas would rob, steal, and hustle in L.A. County Jail, then show up at Wasco State Prison.

I had gotten a job in the main Laundry Room with my homies CoCo and Len Dogg. Our jobs consisted of us making bed rolls for incoming prisoners and taking the bed rolls to R&R. During our trips to R&R is when we would get our Hustle on. I had it all... Weed, Rocks, Heroin, Meth, and cigarettes. I would accept cash or postage stamps in exchange for my products. My "Square" girlfriend named Stephanie was visiting me every week and would bring my Goods to me. I had first met Stephanie while I was on the run for shooting Big Marv. Actually I was on The Road sellin' dope when Stephanie came through looking for some weed. I hooked her up and exchanged phone numbers with her. She had gotten in touch with me when I first got arrested and stayed in touch with me off & on while I was doing my time in Tehachapi, Soledad, and Wasco. I would counsel her on her relationship with her baby's daddy, and she would go back & forth between me and him. I fell in love with her, but she still ended up marrying her baby's daddy named Kevin, and even had another baby by him. Every time they would break up, she'd come back into my life.

Me and Stephanie ended up fuckin' on our visits a couple of times. One time we snuck into the Mop Room when the C.O. wasn't looking. It didn't go down as expected because we were both too nervous. We even tried to fuck outside on the patio a couple of times, but I couldn't enjoy it.

The best pussy I got while I was locked up in Wasco was from this young, white, C.O., named Karen. She was average built with a lot of earrings in her ears, and wore a Halle Berry haircut. I had changed my job from Main Laundry to Lead Porter.

I worked in my building and the job gave me a lot of privileges and one of those privileges allowed me to go in & out of other buildings whenever I wanted to. Karen worked in my building two days a week and then worked in Building-4, and on the yard on her other days. I would flirt with her on the days she worked in my building, and she loved the attention. Some of my statements were sexual in nature, but I'd be indirect whenever I flirted with her. One day when she was working in Building-4, I paid her a visit. She was sitting alone at the podium with her legs crossed and propped up. While I was talking to her, I hungrily stared at her crotch area and licked my lips. She opened her legs and slowly swung her feet from left to rights giving me an eye full. When I looked into her face, her eyes met mine.

"Did you see that?" she asked teasingly.
"Hell yeah. I want to taste some of that," I softly said.
"We'll see," she replied.

I couldn't believe how easy it was to get some play from this bitch. I walked back to my building and thought long and hard of how I could get in her panties. I laid awake all night until I came up with a cold game plan. The very next day I spotted Karen on the yard and found an opportunity when she was alone to talk to her.

"Hey beautiful," I said as I approached her.
"What's up sexy?" she said to my surprise.
"You know you've been on my mind all night?" I said.
"Really?" she asked as she smiled her picture perfect smile.
"I wish I could talk to you in private," I told her.
"Do you wanna help me pick up the trash?" she asked.
"Yeah." I answered, then grabbed a laundry cart that was next to the wall and I began pushing it around the track with Karen walking along side of me.

There was trash in front of every building, waiting to be picked up. Once we collected all the trash, Karen led me to the breezeway which is a door with a long hallway leading to another section of the prison, where the Main Kitchen and Laundry Room has their trash bins. Once we got inside the breezeway, she locked the door behind us. I pushed the Laundry Cart full of trash to the other end of the breezeway with Karen following behind me. When we got to the end, she walked on the side of the cart and ended up right in my face. She grabbed my face and hungrily kissed me like an animal in heat. She damn near made me gag with her tongue darting in my mouth like a beast. She let go of my face, but she didn't stop kissing. Her horny ass unfastened her pants and helped me unfasten mine. She grabbed my dick and stroked it roughly. I was already "hard", so I turned her around and pressed on her upper back to let her know I wanted her to bend over. She poked her little ass out and placed her palm on the wall with her other hand, she reached between her legs, grabbed my dick, and guided it to her sopping wet pussy. I slid deep inside her, causing her to nearly lose her balance. She then put both palms on the wall and met my every thrust by backing herself into my dick. Just as I shot my load deep into her, she too came. She shook, bucked, and held back her screams, while her hot juices flowed from her honey hole. We both hurriedly pulled our pants up and she unlocked the door. The cool breeze was welcoming as we both tried to catch our breaths.

    I really liked Karen a lot, even though she was very flirtatious and always in everybody's face. But, flirtatious women in prison are big trouble, so, I had to stop fuckin' with her. It's a good thing I did too because not long after I stopped fuckin' with her, I found out that she had two other prisoners wanting to kill each other over her.

    I flirted with other female C.O.'s too. There was this fine ass older black one named Yolonda who worked in my building's gun tower. She was light-skinned, with a southern drawl, a cool shape, and wore sexy prescription glasses. She was hella jazzy to me, and most other prisoners thought she was beautiful too. But, a lot of them either couldn't stand her or was intimidated by her. She had a "mouth" on her, and would cuss out somebody everyday. I was always polite and respectful whenever I spoke to her. I eventually got her to let her guards down and I flirted with her by using my indirect technique. She was old enough to be my mother and was wise enough to see through my bullshit. But, she did flirt back. I guess she did her homework too because one day when I was trying to flirt with her, she mentioned another female C.O.

named Rosanda. I was caught off guard when she brought her name up, but I quickly denied any knowledge of Rosanda havin' a thang for me.

Rosanda was dark-chocolate, with tight eyes, a nice ass, and had a cool personality. She was originally from Los Angeles, but lived in Bakersfield. She was 8 years older than me and had been working for The Dept. Of Corrections for about 7 years at the time. She worked in my building five days a week as a Floor Officer. I was always at the podium flirting with her and questioning her about all the latest trends taking place in the free world. She told me she had a boyfriend and that she'd been living in Bakersfield for the past few years. She named a few people that I knew, and let me know who her boyfriend was. I would look into Rosanda's eyes while at the podium and say things like, "I should grab yo' booty" and "I should kiss you in the mouth." She would get so nervous and say, "Boy! Don't play!"

I had a good rapport with every C.O. that worked in my building on 2nd and 3rd Watch, and I used it to my advantage in operating my drug business.

There were two cool ass white C.O.'s named Smail and Meserol, who worked on 2nd Watch, which was the watch I was assigned to as the Lead Porter. They didn't have any idea that I was selling, nor using drugs. Nor did I ever let them see me collect money from anyone. They allowed me to keep my cell door unlocked during their shift as long as I kept it pulled like it was closed. They would even alert me whenever their superior officers or The Goon Squad was on their way inside our building. I gained an enormous amount of respect and trust from them when I went out of my way to help them. One time a prisoner snuck into our building and stood by the cell door of another prisoner who owed him money for a drug debt. Smail was working in the gun tower while Meserol was pointed at and yelled out the cell numbers to be unlocked. The guy that snuck into our building went inside the cell, placed a t.v. inside of his laundry bag, and walked out of our building with it. The owner of the t.v. filed a 602 complaint against both Smail and Meserol. When I found out what had happened, I located the guy who had taken the t.v. and I bought it from him for $80 worth of weed. The relief on Smail and Meserol's faces were rewarding enough for me. But, they rewarded me more by being more vigilant for me and would even allow me to store some of my excess property in their storage room during raids. They also did other small favors for me like making sure I didn't have to wait in line to get my packages or my food from Commissary. They would make a phone call and I could go straight to the front of the line to get my shit. They never did bring me any drugs though. And I never propositioned them either; however, I did "get at" this young black C.O. from Bakersfield named Jay. He was a square, and was working in my building's gun tower on Smail's off days. I would make small talk with Jay about sports, politics, the economy, and about females. One afternoon he came to work looking like he had a lot on his mind, so I called him to the sliding window of the gun tower and asked him if he was alright. He took a deep breath, exhaled, then began to explain his marital problems and alimony issues. All I said was, "Damn! That's fucked up!" and let him do all the talking. When he finished spilling his guts, I told him that I might be able to help him out, but I needed to sleep on it first. I knew I had his full attention and could get him to do damn near anything I asked of him. The desperation in his voice was a dead giveaway.

  The following day I looked up into the gun tower and waved at him, but I didn't make any eye contact with him. I didn't want him to think I needed him more than he needed me. After maybe an hour of him being on duty, he slid the glass window open in the gun tower and called for me.

  "Hey Money!" he yelled out only loud enough for me to hear. I turned his way and walked right up under him.
  "What's up?" I said, greeting him like he was one of my homies.
  "What's up Money?" he asked.

  He had been calling me Money since the very first time we met. I guess that's how he addressed all men.

  "Have you come up with a way to help me yet?" he asked.
  "Yeah." I said, not wanting to sound too excited. "I got a phone number for you." I told him.
  "Go into the sallyport," he instructed.

So, I went into the sallyport, out of everyone's view. He opened a small door that's in the floor of the gun tower and in the ceiling of the sallyport.

"What's the number?" he asked.

I gave him Stephanie's phone number and told him he had to pick up the product from her.

Since he was not working in my building for another week, I didn't hear from him and neither did Stephanie. I had to bring in the "Clavo" myself, and I was getting tired of having to put stuff in my asshole. But, I didn't get tired of the money or the visits. But "going to the hoop" (putting balloons full of drugs in my ass) was an act I grew to despise. That shit hurts!

My name was "ringing" on the yard and the Goon Squad got on my bumper. They started harassing me by tearing up my cell and searching it every other day. I was put on Potty Watch and forced to shit in a bag so they could search it for drugs. But they were always a little too late to catch me. They even brought K9's in my cell at 2AM. I didn't have anything in my cell, but the scent from rolling up weed on my desk was there, and the K9's went crazy when they smelled it.

I was feeling really uncomfortable and unsafe with the Goon Squad constantly calling me into their office, because it doesn't look good for any prisoner to get called to their office without getting an 115 write up or a D.A. Referral. So, I filed a complaint and the Program Administrator made the Goon Squad get off my bumper.

I didn't let them stop my program and I never told Stephanie how much I was being harassed because I didn't want to "spook" her or discourage her from bringing me my Goods. But, I did give her some survival tactics, just in case the shit hit the fan. I told her if they ever approached her on prison grounds and asked to search her, she was to refuse. I made sure she knew her Rights. I even told her to say she had been raped before and did not feel comfortable being searched by anyone.

A week after I "laced her boots", she was approached by Goon Squad members and asked to submit to a search. She refused and told them the Rape story. They escorted her off prison grounds and restricted her visiting to non-contact visits only. Those restrictions would eventually ruin the once close relationship Stephanie and I shared. With Stephanie unable to bring me my Goods, I worked fast to capture another woman's heart and have her "Run" for me.

Her name was Ruby...I met her through her homeboy named Blue-Beard. He wanted me to bring in an ounce of weed that his homegirl Ruby had for him about a month before Stephanie got her visits restricted. So, I had Stephanie meet up with Ruby and pick up the weed. After Stephanie had gotten the weed from Ruby the first time, Blue-Beard called Ruby on the phone to thank her. When he made the call, I was standing next to Blue-Beard and asked him to let me holla at her. I only talked long enough to get her phone number and address. I wrote Ruby that same night and sent her a couple of pictures of myself. To my surprise, she wrote back with the quickness and sent me pictures too. I couldn't believe how pretty she was and how young she looked for her age. I had heard of her, had known her sisters Traci and Lois, and even knew her younger brother named Lynn. But, I had never met Ruby or her oldest brother Cliff, who was in a Federal Penitentiary at the time.

A lot of niggas from Bakersfield who were in Wasco Prison with me were more excited about me hooking up with Ruby than I was. They were speaking highly of her and telling me how lucky I was to have her in my life. They told me she was the type of woman who would take care of her man and cater to her man. But, they also let me know that she had a reputation for being physically violent and was the type to punch her man in the nose or hit him from the blind-side while he's in the middle of a dice game. I wasn't worried about her doing me like that though because I was sure that she was wise enough to know that a young nigga like me wasn't goin' out like that.

Ruby was aggressive and didn't waste any time getting Stephanie outta the picture. She even went as far as locating Stephanie at a pool party and intimidating her. I was somewhat upset about her pushin' up on Stephanie because I truly loved Steph and didn't want to see her hurt. At the same time, I was a little relieved that I didn't have to be the one to break the news to Stephanie about Ruby being my new Queen.

Since Ruby had served time in prison at Chowchilla, I didn't think she'd be able to get approved to visit me. But she did. Her husband Matt had gotten killed about eight months prior to us hooking up, and I kinda felt like she was using me to get over her loss. But she quickly changed my thoughts of her by smothering me with love, love letters, and by visiting me every Thursday, Friday, Saturday, and Sunday. She got my name tattooed on her chest, and I got her name tattooed on my neck. I had fallen in love with her. We would go outside on the patio regularly and get our fuck on. Yeah, our visits were off the hook. One time she sat down at the table on the patio with her tennis skirt on and no panties on. I played with her pussy for a little while and sipped on the Hennessy that she brought and poured inside my can of Pepsi. I was feeling really good that day, and she took advantage of me too.

Ruby sat with her back to the visiting room windows, while I stood a few feet from her and looked between her spread legs. Her bald pussy turned me on so much that I felt like tackling her right there on the patio. She sensed my horniness, as well as my drunkenness. So, she sat the Pepsi can on the ground beneath her spread legs, and told me to get the can. I reached down to get the can and stuck my head between her legs. I licked her pussy excitedly and flicked my tongue on her large clit. She even grabbed the back of my head to encourage and assist me. When I finally came up for air, I kissed her lips and stuck my tongue in her mouth. Ruby turned me on in every way, especially when it came to making money.

A few 805 Mob homies were getting visits once or twice a week, but none of them could really afford to visit as much as me. It's not that their wives or girlfriends didn't want to come visit, but with gas and food, visits could get to be expensive.

Ruby and Kim (Big Nose Rob's woman) would take turns giving each other rides up to the prison to help save money. Other homies' wives and girlfriends did the same thing. Ruby told me how some women would have Yard Sales just to get enough money to make it to a Visit. Since I was selling weed, me and Ruby didn't have those problems. It was Ruby who came up with the idea to have the women bring the weed to the prison and let their husbands and boyfriends take the weed back to the yard for me. She talked the women into doing their parts and left the convincing of the men up to me. We made it happen. We paid the women $50 a week, but they brought weed in two days a week, and I gave the men $50 worth of weed per week for getting the weed back to the yard for me, which was crumbs compared to the amount of weed I had coming in each week. Not only that, but I also had a homie from Hoover who worked in the visiting room bringing me back two ounces a day.

Now that me and Ruby were operating a successful drug trafficking business through the prison, my taste in things started to change. Instead of wanting a case of noodles, jars of coffee, and cartons of cigarettes, I now had a taste for jewelry, a bank account, and a nice home. I was giving Ruby cash every visiting day, and throughout the week I had people wire her money through Western Union and mail her money orders to our post office box.

Square C.O. named Jay worked in my building's gun tower again and he "got at me" when he saw an opportunity to holla at me by myself.

"What's up Money?" he asked, trying to sound like we were the best of friends.
I acted like I wasn't really interested when I answered, "Same shit, different day."
He looked around nervously before he softly said, "I'm ready to do that for you."

I held in my excitedness, but I did smile a little when I told him to make that call and pick up the Goods from Ruby. I instructed Ruby to buy a can of Bugler cigarette tobacco, empty it's contents, and put 5 oz. of weed inside the can. I also had her place some Rock Cocaine and Black Tar Heroin inside each of the 5 oz. of weed. I told Jay that he was only bringing me 5 oz. of weed though.

The following day Jay came to work and told me to go into the sallyport. He opened the floor/ceiling window and handed me the Bugler tobacco can. I took it to my cell and opened every single ounce to make sure everything was there. It was all there.

My cellie was this cool ass nigga from 83 Hoover named Rolaid. He was locked up for killing his own cousin. We became really close while being cellies. He was like a big brother to me and I grew to love him. We talked about everything and shared everything. When my homie CoCo talked about wanting to move into my cell with me, Rolaid had a fit. He wasn't havin' that.

He had a few homies from Hoover on the yard. There was Demp, Priest, C-Note, Wolfie, Red, two niggas named Slim, and a few more with names I can't remember. But, Rolaid didn't want to be in the cell with nobody but me. We ended up going to The Hole together and was cellies in The Hole too. We were only there pending an investigation because we had been making direct phone calls and the Goon Squad couldn't figure out how we did it. The C.O.'s nicknamed us AT&T.

We got outta The Hole ten days later and moved right back into our same old cell. One day Rolaid was out on the yard playing softball while I was in the cell smoking Chronic. I was so high and paranoid that I didn't want to leave my cell with any weed on me. The homie Scooby from Oxnard, California usually held all of my weed and dope for me. But on this particular day I had three caps of weed on me. A cap of weed is equivalent to one chapstick cap of weed. I put the three caps of weed between four slices of bread that were wrapped in cellophane, then I went to the yard to watch the softball game. When I came back inside the building an hour later, there was a young white C.O. searching my cell. I don't remember his name, but I'll never forget the search. He was sweating so much I could see the dampness on the pits of his shirt. My cell looked like a tornado had been through it. I sat at a table in the dayroom and watched the search closely. I saw the C.O. throw small objects into the toilet that was inside my cell and flushed them. He finally stepped out of my cell drenched in sweat and told me he found some weed. I pretended like he was joking...

"Yeah right!" I said, as of I didn't believe him.
"You'll read about it," he said as he left.

When me and Rolaid cleaned up our cell, I looked for the three caps of weed, but they were nowhere to be found. I knew the C.O. had found the weed and it was only gonna be a matter of days before me and Rolaid would get called to the Program Office to pick up our 115 Rules Violation Reports. They had 15 working days to serve us with the 115's, and we still hadn't heard anything 30 days after the search.

Forty eight days later, we both got served with 115's for Possession of Marijuana. Since they didn't serve us within the set time restraint, the only punishment that could be imposed on us if we were found guilty of the charge, was merely 6 points added to our custody score. But Rolaid decided to take the case all by himself, which made me gain even more love and respect for him.

When you live in a cell with someone, there's hardly ever any time spent alone. Throughout the day I'd usually stay away from my cell so that Rolaid could have some time alone. And he'd give me the same respect and consideration. At night after we'd be locked down for the night, I'd wait until Rolaid was asleep to have some "me time".

I purposely got Rolaid drunk and high so that he'd pass out. Then I'd get all of my hardcore porn magazines and naked pictures, and lay them on my bed. I used vaseline, lotion, or baby-oil to masturbate/jack-off damn near every night. Sometimes I'd make a Fe-Fe Bag and fuck it like it was a real pussy. A Fe-Fe Bag is made up of a plastic bag or latex glove placed inside of a rolled up towel and lubricated with either lotion, vaseline, or baby-oil.

I don't know if it was just a phase I was going through or not, but I was horny everyday and would lust for any woman. The first thing I'd look at on a woman was her crotch area and her ass.

And in that order. There was this cute, chubby, little, white C.O. bitch who worked in my building during 1st Watch/Graveyard shift. I don't remember her name, but I do remember the first of many times she caught me jackin'-off. She didn't ask me to stop or appear to be offended. In fact, she wound shine her flashlight on me and my exposed dick, then shine the light on Rolaid, who was sound asleep, then she'd shine the light back on me and my dick before going to the next cell. She worked five nights a week and she'd pause to look at me jack-off my swollen, greasy, black dick every night. I was only 23 years old, and in my mind I thought I was "turning her on", and she was gonna want to have sex with me. That is, until one night after she finished her count, I heard her and a white male C.O. talking and looking towards my cell. When the white male C.O.'s eyes met mine, he stormed over towards my cell. But, before he reached my cell, I had dived into my bed and pretended to be asleep. I heard my cell door open and the C.O cut on the lights.

"Nichols!" he yelled. I still pretended to be asleep.
"Nichols!" he yelled a little louder.

This time I leaned up on one elbow with one eye still closed, and tried to sound like I'd just been woken up.

"What?" I said, sounding sleepy.
"Get your ass up!" he barked.

I sat up, then swung my feet to the floor and looked for my boots.

"You don't need any shoes. Get your ass out here now!" he instructed.

I stood up with only my boxer underwear and socks on, and exited the cell. He led me to the sallyport where a short white Sergeant stood with a coffee mug in his hand. Once I was inside the sallyport, I was told to place my hands on the wall, and the C.O. put his face within' inches of my face and "screamed on me". He said that I was a sick fuck for exposing myself to the female

C.O. Then he went on to say she was his girlfriend. I kept my hands on the wall, but I defended myself by saying, "I didn't hear her coming, she was holding her keys against her leg while conducting her count." I also let them know that whatever I did in my cell after 9PM was my business. That's when the Sergeant asked me to step outside of the building. Just outside the building I was told to stand next to the entrance of the sallyport. It was about 1:30 AM and I only had on my boxers and socks.

"Let's see this dick you've been showing everybody," the Sergeant said.
"What?" I asked in astonishment.
"You heard me. Drop your drawers," he instructed me.
"Aw man." I mumbled like a child who was upset for being told to do his chores.

I slowly pulled my boxers down and let them fall to my ankles.

"My God!" the Sergeant said in amazement, as he stared at my greasy, swollen, semi-erect dick.

He didn't even notice the grease I still had on my right palm and between each of my fingers.

"Go ahed and pull them back up," he ordered.

As soon as I pulled my boxers up, the Sergeant tried to chastise me by poking me in my chest and threatening me. I placed my hand between my chest and his coffee mug to prevent him from poking me in my chest again, and I let him know he could say whatever he wanted to say and could even write me up, but I wasn't accepting no physical abuse.
He looked at me like I was disgusting and told me to return to my cell. I never did get in trouble for "bustin' her eyes", but I didn't let her catch me jackin'-off again either.

CHAPTER 30

Me and Rolaid continued to hustle even though word had spread that we were doin' "big thangs" and we were "hot". Rolaid took care of every Hoover nigga that came to the yard, and I did the same for every 805 Mob nigga that hit the yard. I made sure they all had a t.v., radio, a watch, tennis shoes, food, cosmetics, and brand new state issued clothes. In return, they showed their loyalty by doing any acts of violence that I needed done.

I knew "Networking" was important, so I aligned myself with those I believed to have information I could use in my life once I left prison.

Big Snipe From P.J. watts was a reputable nigga who was two years older than me. He had spent a lot of years in C.Y.A and was instrumental in helping organize the 'Hands Across Watts' peace treaty with the Crips and Bloods. We were both housed in the same building and we developed a true friendship with each other. His mom Teresa was an advocate in their community too, and was part of a group of women who fought for the rights of young black men.

Big Snipe would get visits and correspond with political leaders in his community, such as Maxine Waters and Jim Brown. Big Snipe was amazingly knowledgeable, and is responsible for awakening my interest in politics. We would do a lot of brainstorming in our efforts to find a solution to uplift our communities.

I met this O.G. from East Coast Crips named Sweet Pea. He was originally from Los Angeles, but he had been living in both Oxnard and Bakersfield since the early 80's. He's the one responsible for introducing the Mid City Dancers and Mid-Night Stroller Boys Dancers to Crippin, and he gave me a lot of information regarding crippin.

The O.G. homie Gino was a Smooth operator. He was only about 4'11", but he had "heart" and "Boss Game". He was from Bakersfield and knew my daddy, my uncles, and my aunties. He was known to operate his drug dealing business in the Projects like an organized Mob. He "laced my boots" and told me that he saw potential in me, and that I had the "gift of gab". I noticed how much power this physically small man possessed, and the amount of respect his mere presence demanded. I became a protege of Snipe, Gino, and Sweet Pea.

I had been so caught up in doin' time, that I hadn't even thought about just how soon my release date was, until my counselor called me to his office to sign my Parole Plans. Usually counselors will call prisoners assigned to their caseload to go over their Parole Plans when the prisoner is six months from his release date. But, with my release date changing so many times due to getting in trouble, my counselor did my Parole Plans when I was four months away from my release date. That's when reality set in. I found myself daydreaming a lot and was distant when conversing with others. I was doing more thinking than talking. I even found myself unable to sleep at night. One night, I sat up looking through the six photo albums I had and reflecting on my life. That night I did something I would later regret. While my cellie Rolaid slept, I bagged up my weed, heroin, and powder cocaine. I usually did all of this earlier in the day, but my nigga Scooby was passed out all day from getting drunk on Pruno, and he was my "Point Man". When I finished baggin' up everything, I rolled up a Chronic blunt. I don't know what possessed me to smear the black tar heroin on the cigar-leaf before I sprinkled the Chronic weed in it. And I can't explain why I also sprinkled some of the powder cocaine in it either, but I did. I smoked the strong stinky-smelling blunt all by myself. I lit an incense and blew baby powder in the air to camouflage the smell. I even placed a towel at the bottom of the cell door to keep the smell from goin' under the crack of the door. The Mexicans who lived in the cell above me yelled through the vent.

"Hey E-Loc, that sure smells good," one said.

I panicked, blew some more baby powder towards the vent, and tossed the rest of the stinky ass blunt into the toilet. I didn't get no sleep that night. I felt really bad too but the next night I did the same thing again. After going through another night of being paranoid and tweakin', I knew I couldn't handle that type of "High", so I stopped fuckin' around like that.

The Square C.O. named Jay continued to do business with me and was even wanting to bring in more than what he'd already been bringing. But I wasn't trying to get in more than I could get rid of. I had made enough money to move Ruby and her three kids into a four bedroom house in a good neighborhood, and put brand new furniture in it. My brother D-Nutt bought me a '75 Regal so I wouldn't have to worry about getting a car.

With two weeks left until my release date I was put on "S"-time. That meant I no longer had to report to my Lead Porter job. I didn't sign-up for the Pre-Release class, but the teacher let me take the written Driver's Test. I passed the test, but I would still have to go to the DMV to take the actual driver's test in a car.

I used my last week to say my goodbyes to all of the homies and other prisoners that I'd come to know and care about. I was both happy and sad. Happy to be finally getting my freedom, but sad to be leaving the comrades I had grown to love.

I flirted with the C.O. named Rosanda my last three days and even crossed the line with her. I had grown to like her a lot and finally flat out told her I wanted to kick it with her once I got out. I asked her how good her memory was, then I said my momma's phone number slowly. I repeated the number several times my last couple of days, and told her to leave a message for me at my momma's. She said she was gonna get at me, but I didn't bet on it.

At 3:30 AM I was awakened by a flashlight tapping on my cell door.

"Nichols!" said the male voice on the other side of the door. I sat up in bed like I'd been woken up from a nightmare.
"Nichols are you ready to go home?" he asked while shining the flashlight in my eyes.
"Yeah." I said, tossing the blankets onto the floor and climbing outta bed.

I had mailed all of my mail to my momma, and only had the mail I had received the past thirty days. I brushed my teeth and sat talking to Rolaid for about twenty minutes. When my cell door opened, I hugged Rolaid, grabbed my bag, and walked out of the building without looking back. There was four more people getting released with me, and we all got escorted to R&R. Once inside R&R, we sat in a large cell and waited for nearly an hour before a C.O. called us out one by one to give us our Parole Clothes. Ruby had sent me a cool short pants outfit and tennis shoes. It felt good to have regular clothes on again. Another hour had passed before we were called out of the cell one by one so the C.O. could count our "Gate Money" in our presence and then place it back inside an envelope. I had two-hundred dollars in cash, plus a check for $2,500. But tho C.O. didn't give us the envelope full of money yet. Finally, we were called out of the cell one by one and asked to identity ourselves by stating our full name and our prison I.D. number. Then we were loaded onto a van and driven to the main gate leading into the prison. It's known as the vehicle sallyport. Once there, we had to exit the van and stand in a line-up so that we could answer more questions.

"Nichols, what's your CDC number?" the C.O. asked.
"E-98-6-0-8", I stated.
"Where did you sleep last night?" he asked.

"I slept in A-3, cell 1-10," I answered.
"What's your mother's maiden name?" he asked.
"Washington." I answered.

I was then told to get back on the van. When all of us were back on the van, we were driven to the front of the prison to a check-point booth near the visitor's parking lot. Me and two more parolees had "Gate Pickups". I spotted Ruby's gold Acura Legend immediately. When I stepped off the van I was handed my envelope full of money and told to get in my car and leave the prison's grounds immediately. I walked over to Ruby's waiting arms and hugged her so tight I almost squeezed the breath outta her. We kissed, hugged some more, then hopped in her car. I laid back in the passenger seat, rolled down my window, and yelled, "Yeah!" as we sped away. I was finally free and closing a chapter in my life. But a new chapter was about to begin.

The End.

Epilogue
LOC TALES

The true story of a California Gangsta'

I tell my story in hopes of sharing my life's experiences to be used as a tool smoothing a path leading to a healthier, safer, and more meaningful life. Not to glorify, condone, nor promote gangs, drugs, or criminal activity. Everyone has his/her own journey, and will mature, grow up, and change for the better at different stages; depending on the life changing events that occur in our lives.

For nearly three decades, I believed that a gang loved, respected, and was loyal to me. I was wrong. Not only did one of my so called homeboys attempt to sleep with my wife while I was in prison, but another attempted to assassinate my character and reputation by exposing my drug use, while several more have cooperated with law enforcement to help get myself and others prosecuted. Believe me when I say there is no true love, honor, nor respect amongst criminals.

I indulged in drugs most of my life in an effort to escape reality and to feel better. But, in all actuality, I was never able to escape. Reality remained a reality. I honestly don't ever remember feeling good or feeling better during or after using drugs. I actually felt dirty, paranoid, worthless, guilty, and ashamed. I felt worse.

As for the prison life? It was and always will be a myth. Sure you can get three free meals each day. But that's about the only thing true about the stories I was told of prison before I experienced the harsh realities myself. There's nothing fun or pleasant about the prison life. In fact, I want those of you who have never been incarcerated, as well as those of you who have been incarcerated but still in denial, to know that when you enter prison you literally lose most of your rights, and you are subjected to all of the things in which you longed to get away from as a kid: curfew, permission to eat, sit, stand, talk, shower, use the telephone, get new clothes, and watch TV. Even worse is the fact that you aren't allowed to see, touch, talk to, visit, or kiss your parents, children, siblings, or spouse whenever you want to.

You don't have to go to prison for murder to end up spending the rest of your life in prison. You could easily go to prison for non-violent crimes like theft, drugs, or evading arrest, and find yourself never getting out at all because of prison politics. Whether you're taking part in disciplining/beating a fellow prisoner who couldn't pay a gambling debt, or a snitch who happened to arrive at the prison you're serving time at.

After giving 30 years of my life to a gang, I retired. And I'm proud to say that I left on my own terms and in good standing: Never snitched, Never turned down a fade, and Never betrayed the trust of my comrades; which is why I'm highly respected by those who are still living that life.

Life is about choices. You can choose to do better, be better, live better, and want better for yourself. If you're directly involved in or thinking about joining a gang, using drugs, or committing crimes, I advise you to take this moment to surrender all your bitterness, loneliness, and low self-esteem to God. Don't allow the bad and disappointing things you've experienced to be a crushing blow of defeat. Instead, see those "not so good things" as a test, and turn your test into a testimony to help others. Trust in God and stay prayed up. Make a commitment to dedicate your life to God, to do His will, and follow His plan and purpose for you.

I did.

~ Eric Nichols

Made in the USA
Coppell, TX
09 December 2020